THE TROUBLE WITH CAPITALISM

'It identifies an impressive array of potential problems.'

THE CHRISTIAN SCIENCE MONITOR

'In this succinct analysis, Shutt argues that investors and governments
have pushed global markets to the edge of an abyss. Dismissing supply-
siders and the notion that technology and global trade create more and
better jobs, his research has found instead increasing structural unemployment, diminishing returns to labor and capital, and diminishing
ability to tax ... Shutt is one of the few to expose capitalism's lies and
imperfections, faults that critically threaten our democratic survival
into the next century.'

PUBLISHERS WEEKLY

'In this thoughtful, if at times overly academic, treatment of the current
economic scene, one feels convinced by the end that the collapse of
Western civilization as we know it is at hand.'

LIBRARY JOURNAL

'Marshals a considerable body of evidence to establish that there is a
"capital glut"– oceans of cash sloshing around the world in search of any
profitable outlet however speculative ... Offers no easy answers, but
suggests "the West is going to have to face the fact that profit-
maximising capitalism has run its course".'

TRIBUNE

'Completed before the outbreak of the financial turmoil in Asia, this
book forewarns of just such a catastrophe and explains the underlying
global economic instability it has laid open.'

FORESTS, TREES AND PEOPLE NEWSLETTER

'This timely book coincides with the onset of deepseated problems
for contemporary capitalism. It is based on wide knowledge, well documented source material and sharp analysis. Everyone who reads it
will learn from it.'

LIBERATION

About the Author

Harry Shutt was educated at Oxford and Warwick Universities. He worked for six years in the Development and Planning Division of the Economist Intelligence Unit (EIU). He then moved to the Research Department of the General and Municipal Workers' Union (1973–76), and subsequently became Chief Economist at the Fund for Research and Investment for the Development of Africa (1977–79). Since then he has been an independent economic consultant. His most recent book is *The Myth of Free Trade: Patterns of Protectionism Since 1945* (Basil Blackwell/The Economist, 1985).

HARRY SHUTT

THE TROUBLE WITH CAPITALISM

AN ENQUIRY INTO THE CAUSES OF

GLOBAL ECONOMIC FAILURE

WHITE LOTUS *Bangkok*

IPSR *Cape Town*

THE UNIVERSITY PRESS LTD *Dhaka*

SYNERGY
BOOKS INTERNATIONAL

SYNERGY BOOKS INTERNATIONAL *Kuala Lumpur*

ZED BOOKS
London & New York

The Trouble with Capitalism
was first published in 1998 by Zed Books Ltd,
7 Cynthia Street, London N1 9JF, UK
and Room 400, 175 Fifth Avenue, New York, NY 10010, USA
ISBN 1 85649 565 5 *hardback*
ISBN 1 85649 566 3 *paperback*

Reprinted 1998

Distributed exclusively in the USA by
St Martin's Press, Inc.
175 Fifth Avenue, New York, NY 10010, USA

Published in South Africa by IPSR Books,
Community House, 41 Salt River Road, Salt River 7925, Cape Town, South Africa
ISBN 0 958 4224 9 4 *paperback*

Published in Burma, Cambodia, Laos and Thailand by White Lotus Company Ltd,
GPO Box 1141, Bangkok 100501, Thailand
ISBN 974 8434 64 8 *paperback*

Published in Malaysia and Singapore by Synergy Books International,
7 Jalan Bangsar Utama Tiga, Off Jalan Bangsar, 59000 Kuala Lumpur, Malaysia
ISBN 983-136-098-2 *paperback*

Published in Bangladesh by The University Press Ltd,
Red Crescent Building, 114 Motijheel C/A, PO Box 2611, Dhaka 1010
ISBN 984 05 1461 0 *paperback*

Copyright © Harry Shutt 1998

Typeset in Garamond by Lucy Morton, London SE12
Cover designed by Andrew Corbett
Printed & bound in Malaysia

A catalogue record for this book is available from the British Library

Library of Congress Cataloging-in-Publication Data

Shutt, Harry
    The trouble with capitalism : an inquiry into the causes of global
economic failure / Harry Shutt.
        p.   cm.
    Includes bibliographical references and index.
    ISBN 1–85649–565–5 (hb). — ISBN 1–85649–566–3 (pb)
    1. Economic history. 2. Economics. 3. OECD countries—Economic
policy. 4. Capitalism—History. 5. Business cycles.
6. Technological innovations—Economic aspects—History. I. Title.
HC51.S495   1998   98–3995
330.9—dc21   CIP

Contents

Acknowledgments

My thanks are due to Garth Armstrong, Gabriele Muzio and Steve Pryle for their various comments on the manuscript, which have prompted numerous improvements to the final product. It should of course be understood that none of them can be presumed to endorse the analysis or opinions expressed, which are the author's own.

A special tribute is due to my editor, Robert Molteno, without whose commitment and encouragement this work might never have been published.

H.S.

Introduction

In the dying years of the twentieth century we live in the shadow of a seemingly irresistible consensus. This is the belief that *laissez-faire* capitalism has so clearly demonstrated its superiority over all imaginable economic systems that any deviation from it is ultimately untenable and unsustainable. Accordingly, it is argued, every country must now dedicate itself to establishing a fully liberalised economic system, in which the state will have only a minimal role; societies which henceforth seek to interfere with the free operation of the market will do so to their detriment.

The rapid advance of this new consensus to near universal acceptance owes much to the recent conspicuous failure of economic models based on extensive state intervention to deliver adequate levels of prosperity or security – most spectacularly in the fallen Soviet empire. Yet despite this apparently compelling logic, anyone endowed with a reasonable capacity for impartial observation of everyday realities – and for treating official propaganda with due scepticism – might recognise that such claims of a triumph for the free market and of its supposedly magical powers are profoundly perverse, for at least three reasons.

First, they ignore the truth that over the two decades since the late 1970s – when official opinion in the industrial market economies started to lose faith in state intervention – any moves towards creating a recognisably free market economy have been largely offset by measures of enhanced state intervention in support of private business interests. Thus, notwithstanding an unprecedented shift away from public ownership in favour of the private sector and extensive deregulation of the financial markets, governments in all the industrialised countries have shown a redoubled tendency to use taxpayers' money to subsidise private enterprise (through tax breaks, grants, loan guarantees and other devices). For this reason, and also because it has proved impossible to hold down the fiscal burden of welfare payments in a climate of chronic economic stagnation, they have been unable to prevent the state's role in the economy – as reflected in the share of national income accounted for by governments – from continuing to rise during the years since 1980.

Second, to the extent that liberalisation has occurred in the world's industrial market economies since the late 1970s, it has not resulted in a general rise in prosperity, but rather has failed to stop the spread of poverty to an ever growing proportion of the population, and the remorseless rise in public deficits and indebtedness. Thus in Britain, which is by no means untypical of industrialised countries in general, 25 per cent of the population are now so financially deprived as to be dependent on various forms of state benefit for their survival (compared with less than 10 per cent in the mid-1970s), while the level of public debt as a proportion of national income has doubled over the same period. Closely related to these developments is the inexorable slide in the rate of economic growth, which in the industrialised countries as a whole has fallen continuously, decade by decade, since the 1960s – so that the average for the first half of the 1990s has been less than half that recorded thirty years earlier. Likewise in the rest of the world (comprising the so-called developing countries and the economies 'in transition' from Communism) the application of strongly liberalising economic policies in the 1980s and 1990s – largely at the behest of aid donors in the industrialised world – has failed to prevent their economic performance and living standards from declining, even relative even to those of the increasingly stagnant industrial market economies.

Finally, any genuine move in the direction of *laissez faire* and the minimalist state would represent a total reversal of the historic trend of the past hundred years or more which favours progressively greater intervention by the state (notably in the form of welfare benefits) to offset what have been perceived as the unacceptable side-effects – economic and social – of the capitalist free market. It would therefore appear to put at risk the social and political stability which, since the late nineteenth century, governments, and indeed most private-sector interest groups, have come to see as indispensable to the development of industrial societies.

This book is an attempt to expose the realities of the contemporary evolution of the global capitalist economy, and thereby to dispel the illusions which lie behind the neo-*laissez-faire* prospectus. By viewing it in the context of the longer-term development of the world economy it also seeks to demonstrate that the reason for the aggressive and irrational dogmatism of the Western political establishment in trying to forge this new consensus is a growing sense of the increasing fragility of capitalism rather than of its enduring strength. Indeed the reader may well conclude that only acute awareness of a genuine threat to the survival of the dominant vested interests could explain such systematic distortion of reality.

In some respects, it may be noted, the analysis presented here of the chronic weakness of profit-maximising capitalism is traditional, in that it emphasises the distorting and destabilising effects of the recurrent excess supply of capital in relation to the demand for it. What is perhaps less familiar is the revelation that technological change is leading to a long-term relative decline in the demand for fixed capital, thereby rendering traditional capitalist structures obsolete – much as the new technology of steam power made inevitable the replacement of feudal structures and cottage industries by capitalist enterprise some two hundred years ago.

As well as placing contemporary developments in their historical context, the book attempts to bring together different fields of economic analysis (such as the impact of technological change, the evolution of financial markets and Third World development) which are all too often considered in isolation from each other. Inevitably the treatment of some issues – each of which may properly be viewed as meriting an entire book rather than a single chapter to do them full justice – may be regarded as unduly foreshortened. On the other hand, the risk of some oversimplification may be thought unavoidable if we are to achieve an integrated understanding of the different manifestations of global economic breakdown and their essential interrelationship – and thus to grasp that they are in need of common remedies that are both radical and international.

It will also be apparent that the book steps beyond the confines of economics to consider the cultural, ethical and geopolitical ramifications of latter-day capitalist development. Many of the value judgements expressed are inevitably subjective and may be considered by some to be out of place in a work of serious economic analysis. However, it is the author's strong conviction that we need constantly to remind ourselves of the impact of the economic system on almost every area of human activity, and that only when these connections are more widely understood will economic issues receive the attention they deserve.

Indeed, as failure to resolve the world's profound economic distortions gives rise to more and more symptoms of social breakdown and civil strife in every continent, the need to focus wider public attention on their causes and effects has never been more pressing. Despite this the increasingly monolithic ruling interest group is striving harder than ever to convince the public that management of the economy is a purely technical question which can be understood only by 'experts' – by, for example, entrusting anti-inflation policy to unelected officials – and thus removed from political debate. If this book can in a small way counteract such organised indifference it will have served a worthwhile purpose.

1

The Origins of Modern Capitalism: A Brief History to World War II

Although capitalism is today generally recognised as the dominant economic system in the world, many people are scarcely aware that it has only attained this position relatively recently in human history. Even in Europe, where capitalism first made its appearance, it can hardly be said to have become the prevalent economic mechanism over much of the continent until around the middle of the nineteenth century. Up to that point economic activity had been regulated, in Europe as elsewhere, primarily by a system of customary rights and obligations within a stratified social order, where access to economic resources was generally determined far more by accident of birth than by commercial enterprise or financial acumen.

This system, loosely identified by the term 'feudalism', had been the more or less settled order of Europe – social, political and economic – since the end of the Dark Ages some thousand years before – as it was, broadly speaking, in most other parts of the world, including Japan and much of what is now known as the Third World. In the latter, indeed, feudal relationships often remain of central importance in the economic sphere to the present day, especially in the rural areas where such a large proportion of the population still lives.

Just as there are still many relics of the feudal system surviving in the late-twentieth-century world, so there were many instances of capitalistic enterprise occurring during the feudal era, particularly from the fifteenth century onwards. Yet prior to the late eighteenth century such activity tended to be confined to commerce – where it developed particularly in response to the demand for risk capital to finance long, costly and risky (but potentially lucrative) trading expeditions to the remoter parts of the world. A significant obstacle to the further development of such devices was posed by continuing restraints on the practice of usury (lending money at interest), which was contrary to the teaching of the Church. Indeed religion – along with strong social traditions based on a mixture of sectional vested interests and certain popular notions of equity – was for a long time a powerful force in resisting the more exploitative and adverse consequences of the untrammelled operation of market forces or the exercise of property rights derived solely from financial wealth.[1]

Whereas the expansion of commerce provided the initial stimulus for the first significant manifestation of capitalist enterprise in late medieval Europe, its further development received enormous impetus from the technical advances in navigation which, starting with the discovery of the Americas at the end of the fifteenth century, rapidly extended commerce to the far ends of the earth. But if this initial advance can thus be attributed to one technological breakthrough, it was a series of far more significant ones in the eighteenth and early nineteenth centuries that finally pushed the feudal economy into a state of terminal obsolescence, at least in the Western world, and ensured the irresistible advance of the forces of capitalism. These comprised the various innovations in the harnessing of energy – through the application of steam power – which made possible the mechanisation of key processes in manufacturing, mining, agriculture and transport.

The increasingly large concentrations of capital needed to permit the application of these new technologies – far greater than those demanded by international commerce – would have been unthinkable without a capitalist structure of enterprise. Yet to make this socially and politically acceptable a profound ideological change was also indispensable. This entailed not only abandoning the medieval restraint on usury but, just as crucially, giving primacy to essentially impersonal property rights, derived from monetary transactions, over the personal, customary obligations of the feudal world. Such a transformation had already begun in the seventeenth century in those regions – notably England and the Netherlands – where the growing power of the emergent bourgeoisie, based mainly on the expansion of commerce, gave rise to an ideological rationalisation of the values associated with moneyed wealth. This new doctrine, particularly associated with the tenets of Calvinist religion and of the philosopher Locke – the arch-prophet of private property rights – was to have still greater resonance in the eighteenth and nineteenth centuries. Thus it at once helped the founding fathers of the United States to reconcile their belief in political freedom with their ownership of slaves and enabled the new industrial magnates of England (as well as those who legally expropriated common land through 'enclosure' acts to take advantage of the technical innovations of the agricultural revolution) to rationalise their own vast wealth amidst the degradation of millions of their countrymen.

Yet whatever the moral ambiguities evident in the rise of capitalism, few of its later chroniclers have doubted its inevitability. Indeed even its most famous detractors, Marx and Engels, insisted on the necessity and desirability of capitalistic production displacing inefficient cottage industries as a step along the road of material and social progress, while yet viewing it as merely a precursor to an equally inevitable proletarian revolution. In contrast its supporters, following Adam Smith, tended to suggest that the morally questionable consequences of permitting market forces to operate free of the restraint of medieval taboos should be regarded as the necessary price to be paid for enhancing the prosperity of society as a whole. Indeed this tendency may be seen as linked to the elevation of political economy in the late eighteenth century as a worthy field of study, with the important and quite novel implication that the 'wealth of nations' was at least as great a matter of public concern as the moral and material well-being of individuals, let alone the material well-being of particular disadvantaged groups.

Such considerations also played a part in prompting important changes to the legal framework governing the world of commerce and business. In order to mobilise capital through investment in joint-stock companies on the increasingly huge scale demanded by the new manufacturing industries, as well as the even larger scale of infrastructural enterprises such as railways, it was found necessary to offer investors some protection against the risk of total ruin which they might easily face in the traditionally uncontrolled financial markets. Hence laws were enacted to strengthen the accountability of companies to their shareholders and, more importantly, establishing the right to create companies where the liability of shareholders was limited to the value of the total equity they had between them subscribed.[2] This privilege of limited liability was fundamental to the subsequent development of capitalism and it is perhaps surprising that the justification for it has never seriously been challenged – even though Adam Smith himself had objected strongly to the idea of separating control of an enterprise from its ownership as required in a joint-stock company.[3] In fact such reservations, as well as doubts as to the propriety of giving shareholders, through their executive boards, the untrammelled right to deploy corporate assets in their own interests, were to raise increasing concern in the late twentieth century as companies grew ever larger and more global in their scope – and thus moved beyond the power of any governments (or even the vast majority of shareholders) to control them.[4]

Naturally resistance to the advance of this self-serving ideology of private property based purely on moneyed wealth was strong – and was not confined to the still disenfranchised masses who suffered its worst consequences. It was further deepened by the appearance of a phenomenon hardly foreseen by Adam Smith – the trade cycle – which precipitated periodic deep recessions in capitalist economies. Such phenomena were not unknown in the pre-capitalist era; yet their effect in terms of lost wealth and livelihoods had been generally less severe under a system based on customary obligation than under one where profit maximisation was paramount, and the remorseless demands of shareholders and banks had to be enforced without sentiment.

After first appearing in Britain, the undisputed pioneer of full-blooded industrial capitalism, the cyclical depressions induced by the new *laissez-faire* climate became progressively more widespread and alarming in their intensity. That which coincided with, and was largely precipitated by the end of, the Napoleonic wars in 1815 induced such intense social misery and unrest in both urban and rural areas of Britain that the government of the day felt constrained to introduce ever more savagely repressive laws to counter the supposed threat of revolution. These events may be said to have prompted the efforts of the great classical economists of that era, Malthus and Ricardo, to analyse the causes of such cyclical disasters. However, their conclusion, which amounted to the view that the recurrence of such calamities must be accepted as more or less inevitable, was simply another facile recourse to the Invisible Hand (the favoured metaphysical device of Adam Smith). As such it satisfied few outside the ranks of the ruling oligarchy and the still unreformed parliament through which it ruled, and did nothing to silence the voices of protest, including most leading intellectuals of the early nineteenth century.[5]

Yet these dissidents tended to follow William Cobbett, the great journalist and pamphleteer, in harking back to some kind of pre-industrial Arcadia instead of looking to ways of taming and harnessing the capitalist monster within an industrial economy. With the advent of recurrent economic depression in the 1830s and 1840s, this time affecting the Continent as well as Britain, more radical ideas began to be voiced. The resulting agitation produced a succession of revolutionary uprisings from the July Revolution in France in 1830 to the insurrections of 1848 in Paris and several other continental capitals. It was by no means a coincidence that Marx and Engels published their *Communist Manifesto* at the same time as the latter upheavals. Although it had no impact on the political convulsions of 1848, this polemic was to be profoundly significant in spreading awareness of the inherent threat to social peace and the political order arising from the spread of industrial capitalism.

Following the defeat of these revolutions, however, the danger of further conflict was lifted by the relative prosperity enjoyed for a generation after 1848, notwithstanding periodic sharp downturns in activity. During this time the Industrial Revolution was consolidated and vastly expanded to cover the whole of Europe and the United States, inevitably bringing with it the essential features of the capitalist system. In fact the main basis of this sustained expansion was the propagation of the technologies which had been first developed and applied in Britain to those parts of the world where they had not yet spread, and where it was seen by the European (mainly British) interests dominating the world's capital markets as both advantageous and feasible to extend them. These did not yet include those vast areas outside Europe which were under European imperial domination (or about to become so), and hence treated as the monopolistic preserve of metropolitan suppliers, with whom local manufacturers were still not allowed to compete. Likewise still excluded were China and Japan, which were effectively closed to investment from outside, but which Western powers were starting to force to trade with them.

This period of relatively sustained boom was brought to an end by the stock-market crash of 1873, which was followed by what was later referred to as the 'Great Depression', lasting over twenty years. Perhaps the most plausible explanation for the collapse of the boom at that moment is that it marked the exhaustion of the growth potential of the technology driving the original Industrial Revolution (based on steam power, textiles, railways and iron and steel).[6] As with previous and subsequent booms, its later phases were marked by frenzied speculation and fraudulent flotation of companies, as investors chased new outlets for the accumulated capital no longer needed for new steelworks and railway construction.

It is striking, however, that the ensuing period of depression did not witness the same degree of social misery as had accompanied earlier depressions in Europe. Indeed many industrial and other workers[7] even experienced rising real wages, if only because the widespread deflation induced by the downturn pushed up the purchasing power of wage rates that were held stable in cash terms. This relatively favourable outcome for the working class may be attributed mainly to the significant political advances it was then making in most of Europe, bringing the progressive extension of voting rights to all adult males and greater recognition of the rights of organised labour (as in Britain's Trade Union Act of 1871). These developments may in turn be ascribed to the onward march of political liberalism and a feeling among the bourgeoisie, perhaps born of the experience of 1848, that simple repression of the industrial proletariat in defence of profit margins was no longer a tenable response to cyclical depression.

A related development of great importance in the closing decades of the nineteenth century was the first appearance of publicly financed social welfare systems going beyond the traditional, and very harsh, measures of poor relief (involving, in Britain, consignment to the workhouses immortalised by Charles Dickens). Now for the first time the state became involved in enforcing social insurance, to which employers were obliged to contribute, so as to afford the working masses at least some protection against the destitution or pauperisation which had hitherto been the all too frequent accompaniment of unemployment or old age. The pacesetter here was Bismarckian Germany, where perhaps the teachings of Karl Marx were best understood – and doubtless provided a compelling spur to action in the light of the post-1873 depression.

It may be that the less unbalanced distribution of income resulting from these developments was instrumental in precipitating the next secular upswing in the world economy which began in the mid-1890s. Certainly a noticeable feature of the recovery was the signs of a broadening mass consumer market – based on such products as bicycles, the first domestic consumer durables (notably gas cookers) as well as the emergence of the first mass-circulation news-papers – which also reflected the growth of state-funded universal education and the consequent spread of literacy to virtually the whole population. However, as with all such periods of boom it is hard to find a definitive explanation of why it began precisely when it did. It may indeed be largely attributable to a purely cyclical response to the decline in the market rate of profit (the opportunity cost of capital) to levels at which investment again became attractive – as simple market theory would suggest – particularly as continuing innovation and competitive pressures meant that re-equipment was by then increasingly unavoidable.

The emergence of new technologies certainly provided a constant stimulus to investment and output during this period, with the development of electricity, petroleum, chemicals and the internal combustion engine. Yet not only can these innovations not be clearly linked to the timing of a renewed economic boom, as implied by the theories of the eminent Austrian economist J.A. Schumpeter;[8] they may also perhaps be counted as to some extent a negative influence on growth. For although these technologies gave rise to new indus-tries providing outlets for capital and labour, they also tended to displace some of the old ones, particularly as petroleum-powered motor vehicles and ships began to eat into the market for both coal and railways. Indeed these competitive pressures, threatening invest-ments in the great industries which had been at the heart of the original Industrial Revolution, help to explain why the years immedi-ately before 1914 were marked by increasing labour and social unrest in many parts of Europe, despite the general rise in prosperity.

The consequent secular reduction in the profitability of the older industrial sectors had wider consequences for the economy. For it demonstrated that their proper management was too vital a matter of public concern for this to be left entirely at the discretion of their private owners. Following the outbreak of war in 1914 this consider-ation forced an instinctively very *laissez-faire* British government to assume control of both the coal industry and the railways for the duration of the war. Even before this, moreover, public (including municipal) ownership of vital industries and utilities had become quite common, particularly where (as, for example, in the case of water supply or telecommunications) they were seen to constitute a natural monopoly. At the same time the role of the public sector in providing social and other services (notably education) had been greatly increased, with the result that the share of state expenditure in the economy and the numbers of public servants also expanded rapidly.

Clearly such state involvement in the 'microeconomy' (i.e. in a quasi-entrepreneurial role as well as that of provider of public services) occurred as a largely ad hoc, pragmatic response to the evolving requirements of the economy and society rather than from consideration of fundamental ideological principles. Indeed it would have been absurd to suspect the administrations of Disraeli or Lord Salisbury – still less Bismarck – of harbouring any socialist vision. In Japan, it is true, the involvement of the state in nurturing the giant conglomerate enterprises or *zaibatsu* (Mitsui, Mitsubishi and Sumitomo) in the early phase of its industrialisation following the Meiji Restoration (1868) – before making a virtual gift of them to a few selected private companies – was consistent with a quite traditional feudal world-view in which groups were seen as requiring protection in return for the benefits they confer on the collective. To some extent this attitude, which has largely persisted to the present day, was and is mirrored in the French approach, which was based on a 'corporatist' tradition going back to the era of Colbert in the seventeenth century.[9]

World War I – the first major European war for a century – arguably served to crystallise these tendencies in that it compelled the ruling political elites to recognise more explicitly than before the vital public interest in the way key sectors of the economy were managed, and that this interest could no longer be held to be necessarily identical with that of big business – the classic *laissez-faire* equation. From this it was a relatively short step to accepting the need for a national economic policy – even in peace time – entailing the pursuit of optimum targets not only for monetary and fiscal indicators but, as later became unavoidable, for such intrinsically related factors as the level of output and employment.

The full implications of this change for public policy were by no means fully perceived in the immediate aftermath of the war, although they were already starting to be recognised in Britain, where the post-war Lloyd George government calculated that its new scheme for unemployment insurance was only affordable on the assumption of a maximum unemployment rate of around 4 per cent.[10]

Yet in Britain as elsewhere there was still little idea as to whether or how governments should intervene to try and sustain economic activity at a level compatible with adequate growth, profitability and employment over the long term, and thus avoid the familiar disasters associated with boom and bust. Rather it was still generally believed that the principal, if not sole, contribution of government to ensuring economic prosperity was the maintenance of 'sound money' (stable prices and low interest rates). Few were prepared, or perhaps able, to recognise that such limited priorities – essentially those of the investor and speculator rather than the producer or merchant – could not in fact be expected to prevent, or even moderate, the vicissitudes of the business cycle any more than they had done in the past.

This deficiency was more starkly exposed then ever when, following a boom in most of the industrialised world starting in 1925, the Wall Street crash of October 1929 precipitated a global collapse in asset values and financial institutions, and the Depression of the 1930s. The consequent contraction of output – by as much as 30 per cent in some countries between 1929 and 1933, with a concomitant rise in unemployment ratios to 15 per cent or more – was far greater and more socially devastating than that which followed the 1873 market crash, and its political consequences were correspondingly more profound. The scale of costs implied by the notional commitment of European governments[11] to provide welfare benefits to the unemployed was clearly unaffordable within the prevailing norms of financial orthodoxy – a reality which played an important part in precipitating the financial and political crises that were soon to unfold across the continent. Another crucial element in these upheavals was the collapse of the delicately balanced chain of international loans that had been put in place to sustain the payment of reparations and war debt incurred to pay the enormous costs of World War I. These loans the United States (the main creditor country) now felt compelled to call in, with disastrous consequences for Germany and France in particular.

Another widespread response to the crisis, which only served to exacerbate it, was the resort to trade protectionism. In fact restrictions on trade between the industrialised countries had remained considerable ever since 1918, with France and Germany being particularly constrained by their post-war external debts, while Italy (severely affected by slump immediately after the war) adopted an avowed policy of autarky following Mussolini's assumption of power in 1922. In the wake of the Wall Street crash, however, first the United States and then Britain introduced substantial protective tariffs, something which both were able to do without needing to fear the danger of retaliation, since both were relatively little dependent on trade with areas outside their large domestic or colonial markets.[12]

These developments undoubtedly gave a significant boost to the rise of Fascism – already established in Italy partly because of the effects of the immediate post-war slump – in Europe and Japan. In Germany, a country particularly vulnerable to the effects of the Depression because of its lack of captive markets abroad, they at once brought enormous social distress (with unemployment rising threefold to 6 million between 1929 and 1933) and revived the sense of national grievance over the harshness of the terms of the Versailles Treaty. This explosive political situation made possible the rapid rise to power, by due democratic process, of Hitler and the Nazis, a party seemingly headed for oblivion in the 1920s following its failure to seize power undemocratically in 1923 and the subsequent imprisonment of its leader. At the same time Japan, which was experiencing the effects of global depression for the first time, understandably developed a sense of its own marginalisation in the developing international trade wars. This inclined its rulers to seek relief in military expansionism, with a view to acquiring captive colonial markets and raw material sources comparable to those of its Western rivals. Similar pressures led to the Italian occupation of Ethiopia and also contributed to the emergence of Fascist or quasi-Fascist regimes in Spain and many of the states newly created by the Versailles Treaty.

If Hitler's attainment of power owed much to the failure of traditional *laissez-faire* capitalism and financial orthodoxy, his political success once in power was also attributable in large part to his ability, or rather that of his brilliant economics minister Hjalmar Schacht, to restore growth and sharply reduce unemployment through a programme of public works and rearmament facilitated by running budget deficits in defiance of the dictates of orthodoxy. This approach, based on the principle of using subsidised state investment as a countervailing force to compensate for the withdrawal of private investment, thereby stimulating a more general revival of activity, had already been applied with considerable success by Mussolini.

Indeed such ideas were also beginning to catch on in the Western democracies as a reaction to the palpable failure of orthodoxy. Moreover, an additional spur to action was provided by the unprecedented presence on the fringes of the Western capitalist world of a Communist state, the Soviet Union, apparently demonstrating the effectiveness of a 'socialist' alternative model. As the Depression deepened in the West the evident success of the Soviet Union in raising production at unmatched speed (by an average of over 15 per cent a year between 1927 and 1937) seemed to many Western observers to point to the existence of a better alternative, although few then had an inkling of the appalling human cost of this achievement. The fear which this seeming success engendered among Western business leaders readily explains the support of many of them for the equally illiberal Fascist dictatorships, combining as they did considerable success in checking unemployment and the related social discontent with support for big business and unremitting hostility to Communism.

Hence when US President Roosevelt assumed office for the first time in 1933 he was committed to a programme of vigorous intervention by the federal government to stimulate and underpin a recovery in the US economy – the New Deal – based on broadly similar principles to those applied by the Fascist regimes in Italy and Germany. However, partly because of the limits to the power of the presidency and the strength of opposition from sections of big business and the Supreme Court, it was never possible to implement such far-reaching intervention as that applied by Mussolini and Hitler. Consequently the New Deal did not have the same dramatic impact in restoring growth and cutting unemployment as state intervention had in the Fascist dictatorships.

It is significant that one area where the Roosevelt administration's proposals for state intervention in the economy met with little opposition was support for the financial sector. Nothing had been more fatal to attempts to restore confidence in the United States following the Wall Street crash than the catastrophic collapse in the banking sector, with no fewer than two thousand banks failing in 1930 alone. This prompted the new administration to introduce, as one of its earliest measures, legislation requiring all banks to insure their deposits (up to a maximum level for each one) through a government agency, the Federal Deposit Insurance Corporation, thus guaranteeing small savers against total ruin.[13] This measure, which had its counterpart in measures by European governments to assume responsibility for the liabilities of insolvent banks (or take them into public ownership) foreshadowed what was to become, after World War II, an implicit commitment by the state to act as 'lender of last resort' to the banking industry – in other words, to come to the rescue of any institution whose failure could be considered a threat to the stability of the financial system as a whole, regardless of how reckless its lending policy may have been. Yet as with so many other moves tending to advance the role of the state in sustaining the capitalist system, this far-reaching commitment was made as a purely pragmatic response to otherwise ruinous market trends. It is scarcely a matter of wonder that those responsible, who were also closely linked to the main beneficiaries, were not inclined to emphasise its ideological implications.

The concept of selectively deploying both the state's fiscal resources and monetary policy so as to mitigate and reverse the negative movements of the business cycle was subsequently to be identified all over the world with the name of the British economist J.M. Keynes, who elaborated the theoretical justification for it in his *General Theory of Employment, Interest and Money* (1936) – even though the pioneers in applying this principle had begun to do so without the benefit of his advice, or indeed of any theoretical formulation. Ironically, however, these ideas were slow to find acceptance in Keynes's own country, although already in the 1920s he had been a key influence in persuading Lloyd George's Liberal party (by then a dwindling political force) to favour public works as a means of countering unemployment.

Yet if the British political and business establishment remained throughout the 1930s reluctant converts to what later became known as Keynesianism – as indeed were many of their counterparts in the United States – events were soon to compel them to adopt it willy-nilly. For the growing inevitability of war with Germany and the latter's rapid build-up of its military capability (after effectively repudiating the Versailles Treaty by sending its troops into the Rhineland in 1936) forced the British government to embark on a belated programme of rearmament, with the defence budget trebling between 1936 and 1939. But if this was not sufficient economic stimulus to have any measurable impact on the level of unemployment (which actually began to rise again in 1936–37), the actual outbreak of war led rapidly to full employment in the early 1940s – as it did in the

United States, which had also continued to be plagued by high levels of joblessness throughout the 1930s. Hence preparation for war and then war itself forced both countries to adopt what may be termed military Keynesianism, achieving full employment through involuntary deficit financing. By converting the United States into the 'arsenal of democracy' this laid the foundations for its post-war economic as well as military supremacy. Yet for Britain the enormous public debt created (it rose over threefold to more than £20 billion between 1938 and 1945) left it economically crippled after the war despite the achievement of full employment.

The great significance of the inter-war period in the history of capitalism is that, in sharp contrast to the prevailing view of the pre-1914 era, it witnessed the effective institutionalisation of direct government involvement in guiding key sectors of the economy as well as in the provision of a minimum degree of welfare services needed to maintain social harmony. Indeed when historians wrote, as many were to do during the generation after World War II, that even by the late 1930s the world had passed beyond the point of no return to *laissez faire*,[14] this scarcely seemed a controversial claim. We shall see in the next chapter how in that period 'mixed-economy' capitalism based on still more pervasive state intervention became progressively more entrenched in the industrialised world and why for so long it seemed to offer the ultimate remedy to the problem of capitalism's inherent instability.

Notes

1. See R.H. Tawney, *Religion and the Rise of Capitalism*, Penguin Books Harmondsworth, 1961; F. Braudel, *Civilisation and Capitalism 1400–1800*, Collins, London 1981.

2. The pattern was set by Britain's Companies Act of 1855.

3. *The Wealth of Nations*, Book V.

4. See A.A. Berle and G.C. Means, *The Modern Corporation and Private Property*, Macmillan, New York 1932.

5. Notably Coleridge, Southey and Carlyle. See Raymond Williams, *Culture and Society 1780–1950*, Chatto & Windus, London 1958.

6. E.J. Hobsbawm, *The Age of Capital 1848–1875*, Abacus, London 1977.

7. But not those in agriculture, where the depression hit both prices and incomes most severely.

8. J.A. Schumpeter, *Business Cycles*, McGraw-Hill, New York, 1939.

9. A. Shonfield, *Modern Capitalism*, Oxford University Press, Oxford 1965.

10. A.J.P. Taylor, *English History 1914–45*, Oxford University Press, Oxford 1965.

11. Up to that time it was still non-existent in the United States.

12. Britain was able to fall back on her captive markets in the Empire – including the self-governing dominions of Canada, Australia, etc. This model of 'Empire Free Trade' – which had been a long-cherished dream of Tory imperialists – undoubtedly assisted Britain to recover more quickly than most other European countries from the effects of the Depression.

13. In reality the use of an insurance scheme was cosmetic, since the level of premiums paid by banks never corresponded to the actuarial cost of providing the necessary cover and it has been understood ever since that the federal government will provide whatever support is necessary to avert the collapse of any bank which might entail 'systemic risk'.

14. See Taylor, *English History 1914–45*.

2

The Post-1945 Economic Dispensation in the West

The monumental suffering brought on so many nations by World War II induced an avowed determination on the part of world leaders, backed by strong popular sentiment, to build a post-war world order in which such a disaster could not occur again. There was thus an undoubted political will to learn the lessons so half-heartedly grasped after World War I. Above all this meant a recognition of two central principles:

- The inescapable responsibility of the state for the maintenance of minimum economic security for all citizens;
- The need for institutionalised international cooperation in place of the destructiveness of nationalism.

The political impetus in favour of these precepts was reinforced by the growing appeal to many in the West of the economic and social model adopted by the Soviet Union – based on collective ownership and centralised planning. The attraction exerted by this model was understandable – even though, as already noted, it was largely based on a somewhat idealised perception derived from propaganda and prejudice rather than first-hand knowledge of the Soviet system. For in the 1940s there was unquestionably a widespread feeling throughout the Western world (including even the United States) that the traditional orthodoxies of capitalist economics had been shown by the events of the 1930s to be severely wanting and that, by contrast, the adoption during the war of a collectivist, quasi-socialist approach to economic and social policy had not only been vital to achieving victory but indicated its efficacy in addressing the problems of peacetime. In this context the Soviet example was seen as further compelling evidence, since whatever reservations there might have been about its totalitarian methods there could be no denying it had demonstrated that a state-run system could be the basis for achieving high levels of economic growth and the rapid transformation of a previously backward country with a largely rural economy into a major world power.

Theoretically there was a possibility in 1945 that the victorious allies of East and West could have come together in a joint effort of global post-war reconstruction. Whether or not it could ever have become a reality, given the political will, is a matter for speculation in areas going well beyond the scope of the present work – although it is appropriate to note that there were undoubtedly strong vested interests against such an accommodation on both sides. In the event victory over Fascism was quickly followed by the onset of the Cold War between East and West in which most people soon learnt to see the world in terms of two opposing ideologies and economic systems each conspiring to bring about the downfall of the other.

It is against the background of this emerging ideological contest, as well as that of the immense popular yearning for a better life, that the post-war economic order established in the West must be considered.

The Proactive State

As noted in the previous chapter, even before the war the balance of informed opinion in the Western democracies had tilted decisively away from *laissez-faire* orthodoxy as the basis for managing the economy. Indeed the role of the state as an economic agent – rather than simply a regulator or guarantor of law and order and minimum public services – had come to be accepted as essential to the maintenance of both economic and social equilibrium. In this capacity, moreover, it by now not only provided an ever-widening range of services (in such vital areas as education, social welfare, public health, housing, public transport and utilities); it was also increasingly becoming involved in the ownership – whether as a minority or majority (even up to 100 per cent) shareholder – in commercial enterprises deemed to be of 'strategic' importance. Such investments

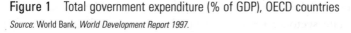

Figure 1   Total government expenditure (% of GDP), OECD countries
Source: World Bank, World Development Report 1997.

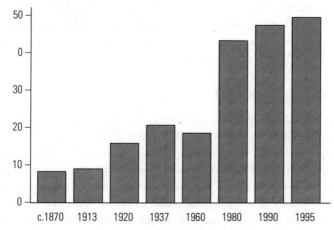

had long come to be regarded as the natural concomitant of the corporatist tradition of many continental countries, the most conspicuous exponent of which between the wars had been Italy, with its extensive state participation in enterprise through the holding company Istituto per la Ricostruzione dell'Industria (IRI).[1] This tendency, moreover, received an involuntary boost all over the Continent during the 1930s as widespread failures in the banking sector forced governments to nationalise many of the major banks.

Yet clearly this spreading of the state's tentacles across the economy had happened almost by default, if not exactly by stealth, rather than as a result of any fundamental ideological transformation. This can perhaps best be illustrated by the case of Britain, which had a long tradition of tenaciously clinging to liberal orthodoxy. Despite this the British government's percentage share in national expenditure roughly doubled over the inter-war period (to an average of over 10 per cent in the 1930s) as compared with the pre-1914 period. By 1947–48, however (even after a substantial reduction in the state budget thanks to reduced defence spending after the end of the war), it had still increased to almost 30 per cent of gross domestic product, and despite a further decline during the subsequent economic boom it was never again to fall even close to the pre-war level. It should be stressed, moreover, that these figures reflect only budgetary expenditure by central and local government and take no account of the state's expanding role as shareholder/owner in the corporate sector. Such comparable data as are readily available for other countries (see Figure 1) indicate that the trend in the rest of the industrialised world was broadly similar, although if anything the state's role in most countries had achieved greater prominence before World War II than in Britain.

The goal of full employment

If the role of government in the economy had grown in a rather ad hoc manner before and during World War II, in the post-war world its importance was much more explicitly enshrined in official policy and openly justified by contemporary political pronouncements. This stance was adopted out of a commitment to a central policy objective whose primacy was then universally accepted: the need to secure and maintain full employment. This new doctrine was unequivocally stated in a famous white paper of the British wartime coalition government, which declared that 'the government accept as one of their prime aims and responsibilities the maintenance of a high and stable level of employment after the war'.[2] It was likewise enshrined in the US Employment Act of 1946, and in the constitution of the French Fourth Republic drawn up in the same year.

Equally, acceptance of such a responsibility went hand-in-hand with one to provide minimum levels of social benefit for those unable to find gainful employment – on the implicit and quite logical presumption that their inability to do so was the result, at least in part, of inadequate management of the economy. Such a commitment was obviously based on a premiss which was quite revolutionary in terms of the early capitalist ideology of a hundred years earlier, namely that the goal of official economic policy was at least as much social as it was that of promoting the 'wealth of nations'. It was also made in the belief that the judicious application of macroeconomic policy instruments could indeed assure a level of economic activity compatible with full employment more or less indefinitely. Numerous official documents of the time spelt out the consensus that

- the traditional market remedy for unemployment – allowing prices and wages to fall in response to a market depression until they reached a level at which demand would recover – was at best unacceptably slow and distressful 'under modern conditions';[3] and

- in order to maintain full employment governments could and should 'adopt a compensatory fiscal policy to offset the irreducible fluctuations in the private sector of the market'.[4]

In thus sanctifying Keynesian doctrine, Western governments gave a significant hostage to fortune. For, in what amounted to an act of faith, they based their policy on the assumption that it would be possible, by using the tools of demand management (monetary as well as fiscal policy) to manipulate the level of economic activity so as to keep unemployment below the level at which the fiscal costs of the welfare and social-security budgets would become too burdensome. This danger had already been recognised in Britain, as noted in the last chapter, when the much more modest scheme of the Lloyd George administration had been introduced in 1921. In fact the Beveridge Report (1942), which provided the blueprint for the post-war scheme of social insurance in Britain (and which also had considerable influence on policy in other countries) explicitly recognised that any such scheme would be unaffordable in the event of significant long-term unemployment. That such far-reaching pledges could be given notwithstanding this obvious risk is perhaps a measure of the immense political pressure in the Western democracies to provide the masses with a genuine and lasting 'new deal' in place of the privations and insecurity of the 1930s.

Investment promotion

Besides undertaking to apply the weapons of macroeconomic management to influence the level of output and employment, governments resorted to other forms of intervention to help sustain activity. Most conspicuously, they became significant promoters of investment, whether through state subsidies or incentives to private investment, or else through direct state equity participation in enterprise. The proliferation of such mechanisms – including grants, tax concessions, loan guarantees and subsidies to research and development – was for many countries (notably those of continental Europe as well as Japan) simply an extension of their traditional approach to economic development. Yet its rapid growth throughout the Western market economies (including the United States) in the post-war period meant that 'corporatism' had become a universally accepted element in the post-war capitalist system. What was scarcely perceived at the time – and is still not widely accepted even in the supposedly more *laissez-faire* 1990s – is that such uncontrolled use of state support for enterprise (whether in the private or public sectors) was bound to result in serious distortion of competition and international trade patterns.[5]

International Collaboration

The potentially disastrous consequences of nationalism, especially in view of the increasingly destructive power of war machines in the industrial era, had been the major lesson learnt from World War I. Hence, in an attempt to ensure that that conflict would indeed prove to be 'the war to end war', the major powers had created the League of Nations in 1920 with a view to providing a means of settling international disputes without war and of achieving collective security. The League was also given a mandate to address the problems of international economic relations – which had been recognised as a significant factor leading to the growth of mutual hostility – and to seek a greater degree of harmonisation in this field. From the out-set, however, it had lacked either sufficiently robust structures or adequate commitment from key members to be any more effective in achieving world economic cooperation than it was in the sphere of peacekeeping – not least because the United States Congress refused to sanction US membership of the League, even though its principal architect was President Woodrow Wilson.

The consequent failure of the League of Nations and its gradual disintegration in the build-up to renewed world war during the 1930s provided important lessons for world leaders seeking to fashion new institutions of international cooperation at the end of World War II. Among these was the need to create bodies with a responsibility for administering internationally agreed guidelines for the conduct of trade and monetary relations, with the authority – at least notionally – to enforce compliance by member states. At the same time, mirroring the broader move towards state intervention in national economies, it was felt essential to establish mechanisms to support the development of more economically deprived countries and regions rather than simply leaving them at the mercy of uncontrolled market forces.

The result was the creation of the International Monetary Fund (IMF) and the World Bank in 1946 and subsequently of the General Agreement on Tariffs and Trade (GATT). Besides seeking to promote closer consultation and cooperation among member states in matters of economic management, these institutions established rules for (a) the management of national currencies intended to ensure the maintenance of relatively stable ('fixed but adjustable') exchange parities and to avoid unnecessarily disruptive devaluations, and (b) for the conduct of trade based on the principles of minimum protection and non-discrimination. At the same time the newly formed United Nations (which replaced the League in 1945) established a group of agencies under the aegis of its Economic and Social Council concerned with different areas of economic development – to which was added the International Labour Office, an organisation originally set up under the League of Nations to promote the wider observance of adequate standards in the treatment of labour.

Yet the most notable expression of the new spirit of international economic cooperation in the immediate post-war period was an initiative not of the new international institutions but of the United States government. This was the Marshall Plan, whereby between 1947 and 1952 some $13 billion of US aid (the equivalent of around $100 billion in mid-1990s prices) was poured into the reconstruction of the war-shattered and bankrupt economies of Western Europe, all in the form of grants or soft loans. The rationale for this programme was no doubt partly a reaction to another of the mistakes of the post-1918 period, when reparations and the rigid enforcement of war-debt obligations had had a seriously negative impact on subsequent economic and political developments. Consequently it was now easier to argue a case for seeking to assist the economic recovery of the vanquished (as well as the other belligerents) rather than punishing them – in contrast to the spirit of the Versailles Treaty. Yet it was also consistent with the emerging US foreign policy, known as the Truman Doctrine, centred on the principle of containment of the Soviet Union – even though the latter was also offered (and declined) the chance to receive aid under the Plan.

Whatever the precise motivation behind the Marshall Plan, it was indisputably a supreme example of enlightened self-interest. For few doubted, then or since, its importance in unleashing the forces which resulted in an era of sustained economic expansion and prosperity throughout the Western world over the succeeding twenty-five years – an outcome which also, of course, served the political objective of limiting the appeal of Communist ideology and hence the threat of Soviet expansion.

The Marshall Plan may thus be seen as combining the two principles identified at the start of this chapter as the dominant themes of economic strategy in the Western industrialised world after 1945: state intervention to sustain minimum economic security for all, and international cooperation. Indeed it can be regarded as an application at international level of the Keynesian policies which were also being followed by national governments within their own frontiers. Given that this was the first time the use of state fiscal resources to stimulate activity had been undertaken in such a concerted way and given also the scale of the boom which ensued, it is hardly surprising that most observers concluded that the two developments were cause and effect and that Keynesianism was indeed the remedy for the inherent instability of capitalist economies.

For the duration and scale of the growth which occurred in the succeeding prolonged boom was without precedent, at least in relation to the relatively short period of economic history for which reliable and comparable data are available. Between 1950 and 1973 average real income per head of population in the combined member states of the Organisation for Economic Cooperation and Development (OECD)[6] – which correspond quite closely to the industrialised market economies – rose by around 160 per cent (over 4 per cent a year), which was at least double the rate of growth achieved over any period of comparable length since the Industrial Revolution and contrasted dramatically with the virtual stagnation of the inter-war years.

Yet while it is wholly understandable that exponents of Keynesianism should at the time have felt justified in claiming that this extraordinary phase of sustained expansion was attributable to their policies, the inability of these policies to prevent the subsequent lapse of OECD economies into prolonged relative stagnation and recurrent recession from the mid-1970s (to be analysed in the next chapter) must now cast doubt on their ultimate significance. This is not to suggest that such an unprecedented boom would have occurred if Keynesian interventionism had been spurned after 1945 in favour of traditional orthodoxy. On the contrary, there can be little doubt that in the absence of governments' explicit commitment to sustaining growth, together with the expansion of the welfare state, the actual rate of growth would have been lower and less sustained. This was principally because:

- The confidence of both consumers and private companies was greatly bolstered by the perception that governments were anxious to utilise the resources of the state to maximise expansion, which consequently increased the willingness of the former to borrow, consume and invest beyond what it might otherwise have been.
- The more even distribution of income, resulting mainly from the redistributive effects of the welfare state, increased effective demand among those – namely the lower income groups – with a tendency to devote a greater proportion of their additional income to consumption rather than saving (or what economists call their marginal propensity to consume).

What now seems clear, however, is that the more essential ingredients for the boom were the coincidence of vast unsatisfied demand, especially for consumer durables, and the availability of technology providing the capability to supply these at increasingly affordable prices. In terms of standard Keynesian analysis, the conditions of 'latent' demand were already in place and all that policies of demand management and market intervention could achieve was to help convert this into 'effective' demand. What they could not do, as certain of the more naive Keynesians and most non-economists appear to have assumed (and in some cases still do to this day), was to generate demand which was not there in the first place. In short, the question of the origins of growth – and how, if at all, it could be artificially induced – remained unsolved, as the more hard-headed of Keynes's followers recognised even at the height of the boom.[7]

Not surprisingly such reservations went unheeded as long as the boom lasted. Indeed the phenomenal success of the industrial market economies in sustaining high growth rates in the 1950s and 1960s led many to assume that the problem of growth had been permanently solved. This was certainly an assumption that politicians found it convenient to make. For growth soon came to be regarded as the panacea for virtually all perceived ills, social as well as economic. Demands from organised labour for higher pay and benefits – which became frequent against a background of full employment – could with some plausibility be countered with the argument that pay restraint, by enhancing competitiveness and holding down inflation, would contribute to achieving high real growth, to the benefit of workers and employers alike. This was seen as particularly important in fending off demands for greater equality of rewards, on the

principle that as long as workers perceived their own living standards to be rising they would be less preoccupied with questions of
equity of distribution. Hence variants on the slogan 'A rising tide
lifts all boats' became part of the stock in trade of government
leaders everywhere.

The impact of trade liberalisation

A more bizarre explanation for the post-war boom offered by some
commentators was that it was the result of the liberalisation of international trade. It is true that, in accordance with the conscious rejection by world leaders of the protectionism of the 1930s in favour
of a commitment to international cooperation, the GATT had been
created in 1948 with a view to establishing a more open international
trading system based on common rules and the principle of non-
discrimination. It is also true that it succeeded in implementing
successive rounds of tariff cuts over the following decades which
resulted in the progressive and quite drastic reduction in this form
of protection. Yet since at the same time, as noted above, all OECD
governments had adopted policies of selective intervention and subsidy in support of particular sectors, enterprises or regions within
their own domestic economy, this served largely to offset the impact
of tariff cuts and left them substantially just as able as before to
protect what they saw as politically sensitive or 'strategic' parts of
their economy. Moreover, this form of protectionism had the advantage that it was not only more flexible but also less conspicuous and
thus less likely to attract the attention of foreign competitors or the
GATT. In some cases, such as textiles, it was clearly too costly, or
politically untenable, to use such means to prevent the decline of
major industries in the industrialised West. Yet even then it was
possible to devise mechanisms – in the shape of the Multi-Fibre
Agreement introduced in the 1960s – which made it possible to
slow down the process of decline.

It is thus utterly implausible to suggest that the lowering of tariffs
under the GATT acted as a significant stimulus to the rapid economic growth that occurred in the OECD countries between 1950
and 1973 – or even as the main explanation for the fourfold rise in
the volume of world trade which occurred during that period. If
there were any doubt about this it was surely dispelled by the failure
of successive rounds of tariff reduction to prevent the end of the

boom and the onset of stagnation in the 1970s. It can, however, be concluded with more accuracy that the working of the GATT *facili-tated* the expansion of trade, and thus indirectly the high rate of output growth, so that it was higher than it would otherwise have been. In this sense it was complementary to the policies of official intervention and macroeconomic management in support of growth, but provides no more of an explanation than the latter for why that growth occurred on the huge scale it did in the 1950s and 1960s.

Emerging Contradictions

The evident success of the post-war capitalist order in promoting global economic expansion resulted, not unnaturally, in a tendency to view it rather uncritically and ignore many of the anomalies inherent in its structures and relationships. Inevitably, however, the dynamics of explosive growth began to disturb this climate of euphoria so that it gradually became harder to ignore such weaknesses. At their heart was the contradiction between the increasingly interventionist stance of national governments in seeking to promote their domestic objectives of growth and employment and, on the other hand, a structure of international economic relations that was based on a pattern of exchange which was less controlled and coordinated than it had ever been – albeit extremely distorted (often by the very measures of intervention that national governments had been induced to implement) in relation to anything resembling a 'free' market.

This anomaly arose despite the existence of a far more structured framework of institutions and regulations governing international economic relations than had ever previously existed. For these institutions lacked the status, individually or collectively, of an effective supranational authority with the power to enforce compliance by member countries, which retained full sovereignty and hence a large measure of de facto discretion over the extent of their adherence to nominal commitments or regulations. Consequently national governments inevitably began to challenge, circumvent or simply ignore rules or structures which they perceived to have been designed for the benefit of others and to be contrary to their own best interests.

The resulting tendency towards international economic anarchy was accentuated by two other quite novel features of the post-war world economy.

A profusion of new nations

The dissolution of the (mainly European) colonial empires which had been an important factor determining the pattern of world economic development since before the Industrial Revolution became inevitable after 1945. While the reasons for their demise are too complex to warrant full analysis here, they may be summarised as a combination of (a) political pressures for decolonisation in a world where the principles of democracy and equal rights were becoming more and more firmly established (at least rhetorically) and (b) the inability of the colonial powers to sustain the financial cost of continued occupation in the face of both rising local resistance and the increasing need to be seen to promote the well-being of the subject peoples (in line with principles laid down in the United Nations Charter – as in the Covenant of the League of Nations before it).

An important consequence of the decolonisation process was a rapid proliferation of new nominally sovereign and independent states, so that the membership of the United Nations rose from 50 countries at its foundation in 1945 to 137 by 1974. This apparent triumph of the hallowed principle of 'self-determination' distracted attention from the truth that many of them were largely artificial creations without any kind of homogeneous national identity or with far too small an economic base to be capable of attaining meaningful independence. Certainly such realities were not to be allowed to stand in the way of the political imperative of formally transferring power.

Indeed virtually all these new states, as well as many pre-existing ones in Latin America and elsewhere, were relatively poor and 'underdeveloped' and had economic structures dominated by a combination of

- subsistence agriculture and other 'informal' activities largely outside the cash economy, and
- heavy dependence on markets in the industrialised countries for certain export commodities (the heritage of the orientation imposed on them by colonial rule).

More considered analysis of the problems of the less developed countries (LDCs) – also known as the Third World – is reserved for a later chapter. For the moment, however, it is important to note that the very creation of so many new and relatively poor states raised serious questions over the long-term manageability of the post-war world economic order – although it was then still easy for the authorities in the industrialised world (and even in many of the new states themselves) to ignore the potential problems.

For the very existence of so many countries – each having a sovereign government with autonomous powers of taxation and public spending, and also having the same right as other countries to engage in trade and financial transactions with the rest of the world – created almost limitless scope for distortion and disruption of international patterns of investment, production and trade. This arose, in particular, from the great dependency of most LDC governments on the inflow of resources from abroad, whether provided by other governments, international aid donors (such as the World Bank), private companies or financial institutions. This meant there was a strong propensity for these governments to act in ways tending to favour particular commercial, economic or indeed political objectives of external organisations or interest groups in return for provision of financial benefits to their country – or, as was more often the case, to a few highly placed individuals with the power of decision.

Such suborning of governments by external interests was, of course, nothing new. What was new, however, was the vastly increased number of governments exposed to this kind of manipulation (many of them with less developed structures of democratic accountability than existed in the industrialised world) and the much greater potential for distortion made possible by the freer flow of goods and capital between countries instituted under the post-war international economic regime. Thus the potential was created for disrupting the markets and profitability of major enterprises or industries in particular countries or regions, by the granting of subsidies or tax concessions to their competitors making new investments elsewhere. The translation of this potential into a real source of market instability was hastened by the emergence of a second more or less new phenomenon.

Transnational corporations

The same tendencies that made it increasingly possible to manipulate sovereign governments also naturally made it more attractive for major corporations to try and do so. Another crucial factor was the accelerating speed of international communication, thanks to the development of jet air travel and ever faster telecommunications, as a result of which corporate managements could monitor and control their subsidiary companies around the globe much more closely and effectively than ever before. At the same time the prolonged boom and the restrictions imposed (by anti-monopoly laws) on companies based in OECD countries expanding in their home markets effectively compelled them to look overseas for growth opportunities. The result was the emergence of what came to be known as multi-national or transnational corporations (TNCs), operating in many different countries and increasingly having no particular loyalty to any of them – and of course none which had priority over the interests of their shareholders.

For some time it was widely believed that these corporations either had become or would soon become all-powerful bodies controlling the course of the world economy. This view – which was based on consideration of TNCs' size (many had sales volumes larger than the national income of the majority of individual countries) and their supposed effective control over markets, capital and technology – was particularly widespread in the late 1960s and early 1970s.[8] It was, however, to be largely undermined by the collapse of the prolonged boom in the 1970s, which demonstrated that the world economy was not really under the control of anyone, either governments or corporations.

Such was the basis of what was later to become known as the 'global economy'. Perhaps surprisingly, it has been widely acclaimed in the 1990s as the very model of a dynamic, free-market economic system in which the inability of either governments or private corporations to control the pattern of development is treated as a positive virtue. However, as suggested in this chapter, it is really the legacy of a post-war attempt to organise the world economy along the lines of international cooperation rather than uncontrolled competition – in a climate of opinion which had, indeed, come to reject *laissez faire* as an intolerably unstable basis for economic management. The fact that it proved a recipe for anarchy based on rampant market distortion was the result of misplaced commitment to the idea of the sovereign nation-state, combined with a lack of political will to curb the power of transnational corporations.

We shall see in subsequent chapters how the collapse of this post-war, Keynesian dispensation induced a gradual retreat, ostensibly at least, from most of the interventionist assumptions behind it. But it will also become apparent that it is a legacy latter-day capitalism has been unable to shake off and that, for all the revival in ultra-liberal ideology, its dependency on the state has inexorably increased.

Notes

1. Even in a traditionally *laissez-faire* country such as Britain state share-holdings had been taken in purely commercial companies even before World War I, notably in the Anglo-Iranian Oil Company, later to become British Petroleum (1914).

2. Employment Policy Cmnd 6527, HMSO 1944.

3. Ibid.

4. *Action Against Unemployment*, International Labour Office, Geneva 1950.

5. See H. Shutt, *The Myth of Free Trade*, Basil Blackwell/The Economist, Oxford 1985.

6. As with all other OECD statistical data used in this book, the figures relate to those twenty-four countries which have been members of the organisation since 1975 or earlier, namely Austria, Belgium, Denmark, Finland, France, Federal Republic of Germany (excluding East Germany), Great Britain, Greece, Iceland, Ireland, Italy, Luxemburg, Netherlands, Norway, Portugal, Spain, Sweden, Switzerland, Turkey, Canada, USA, Japan, Australia and New Zealand. Excluded are those member countries (Czech Republic, Hungary, Poland, Mexico and South Korea) which have been admitted since 1994.

7. See R.F. Harrod, *Economic Dynamics*, Macmillan, London 1973.

8. See J.K. Galbraith, *The New Industrial State*, Hamish Hamilton, London 1967.

3

The End of the Boom
and the Neo-classical Reaction

By the middle of the 1960s, in the wake of the phenomenal apparent success of Keynesian economic strategies, belief in the possibility of more or less perpetual growth based on judicious state intervention in the market had become the virtually universal creed of Western economists. Yet almost as soon as this idea had attained the status of unchallengeable orthodoxy it was shaken, in the early 1970s, by a return of sharp cyclical fluctuations in the global economy such as had not been seen since before World War II.

At the time the onset of recession in 1974 was almost unanimously blamed in the West on the oil 'shock' – whereby the world price of crude petroleum was suddenly increased fourfold at the end of 1973 by decree of the producer countries' cartel, the Organisation of Petroleum Exporting Countries (OPEC). This interpretation was convenient to economists seeking to explain the crisis as an aberration resulting from irrational behaviour by a particular group aiming to disrupt the world economy for essentially non-economic reasons – and also to political leaders in the industrialised countries only too glad to find a Third World scapegoat for their predicament. It was, moreover, a highly plausible explanation in that the oil price jump clearly was the immediate cause of the collapse of the sharp surge in growth which had arisen in 1972–73, and hence of the onset of recession, and was in part politically motivated.[1]

In fact this development can now be seen to have been more of a symptom of the gathering world economic malaise than its cause. For the rise in crude oil prices, which had up to then been stable at around $2 a barrel since the early 1960s, could certainly be explained as a logical response by OPEC – if a rather extreme one – to the mounting global inflation which had resulted from a combination of the collapse of the Bretton Woods system of more or less fixed exchange rates in 1971[2] and the rapid overheating of OECD economies in the speculative boom of 1972–73. These events must likewise be seen as the culmination of a process of progressive deterioration in the medium-/long-term prospects for economic growth. This in turn stemmed from two related factors: the increasing saturation of consumer markets in the OECD countries and the growing relative scarcity of new outlets for fixed investment (so essential to the health of any capitalist economic structure).

Yet, as in the case of the Oil Shock, the official explanations for this collapse of the post-war international monetary order did not focus on such fundamental weaknesses, concentrating instead on analysis of technical monetary factors and on the relative deterioration of US economic performance vis-à-vis that of much of Western Europe.

Market Saturation

The increasing maturity of most consumer markets in the industrialised countries was becoming a noticeable constraint to economic growth in the industrialised world by the end of the 1960s. This meant that in addition to static demand for non-durable goods (food, drink and clothing) the markets for most durable products (automobiles, television sets etc.) tended more and more to be governed mainly by replacement demand rather than by the continuous opening up of new groups of first-time buyers, which had been possible throughout the 1950s and early 1960s. Hence demand for goods generally began to grow more in line with population – which was in any case increasing more slowly than in the immediate post-war period – rather than at the rapid rates recorded up to the mid-1960s.

The result was that companies serving these markets were obliged to diversify into new products or services in their unavoidable quest for further expansion, especially as they were barred by anti-monopoly restrictions from taking over their competitors, at least within their national frontiers. One consequence of this was the emergence, particularly in the USA, of 'conglomerate' groups or companies with diversified activities ranging from telephone equipment manufacture to hotel chains.

These efforts at diversification naturally mirrored the evolving pattern of consumer demand, which increasingly encompassed services as well as goods. The most obvious example of this was international tourism, which had traditionally been a form of consumption open only to the relatively well-to-do – i.e. those with sufficient leisure and money to undertake relatively time-consuming and expensive foreign holidays. From the early 1960s, however, the advent of cheap air travel gave even those of relatively modest means in all West European countries the opportunity to spend their annual fortnight's holiday on the Mediterranean, thus rapidly converting tourism into a mass-market industry.

Yet gradually, as may now be recognised with the benefit of hindsight, the development of such new consumer markets proved insufficient to offset the impact of the saturation of existing ones. That this was only dimly perceived by most economists at the time is largely ascribable to their familiar tendency to adopt rather rigid assumptions as to the way economies develop, and in particular to suppose that the long term will always more or less resemble the immediate past. Thus for many it was an article of faith that every economy was subject to a normal or 'underlying' growth rate or trend, from which it might be expected to deviate only under abnormal circumstances and, implicitly, for relatively short periods. Likewise, as already noted, many of the cruder apostles of Keynes had convinced themselves that 'demand management' could actually permit the stimulation of increased consumption simply by injecting more money into the economy, and that consequently excess productive capacity need never be a problem again. Thus they, along with most OECD governments, failed to appreciate that, once the short-term limits of purchasing power have been reached, the only consequence of artificially trying to extend them further is bound to be inflation.[3]

This danger was one governments began to discover from around 1970, as they resorted to stronger than ever doses of fiscal and monetary stimulus to sustain growth. This was reflected both in higher state budget deficits (reaching the equivalent of 1.1 per cent of GDP in the OECD area in 1970, compared with a surplus equal to 0.7 per cent of GDP ten years earlier) and sharply accelerated expansion of bank lending (see Chapter 4). Moreover, to the extent that such artificial boosting of demand was achieved by making consumer credit more readily available, it was simply serving to make future recession even deeper. This is because, by increasing the level of consumer debt relative to current income, it was making it more inevitable that a greater proportion of future income would have to be devoted to debt repayment in later years – to the obvious detriment of the level of consumption.

The maturing of established consumer product markets helps to explain the intensifying effort to open up new areas of consumption and the consequently growing pressure on governments and legislators to relax restraints on the range of goods and services that could be respectably offered to consumers. In the United States this was manifested notably in the abolition of legal restrictions on pornography in 1973 and in more explicit depictions of violence in television and motion pictures, even including such critically acclaimed films as *The Godfather* (1972). Likewise in Britain this tendency was reflected in moves to relax restrictions on gambling and pornography – a symptom of the 'permissive sixties' which many current detractors of that era continue to profit from.

Naturally an important consequence of the slowing growth of consumer demand was that competition for market share intensified, leading to a drive to cut costs and hence in turn to a squeeze on staffing levels and higher rates of unemployment in most OECD countries in the late 1960s and early 1970s – that is, even before the end of the boom. Yet predictably this process, by squeezing purchasing power, did nothing to reverse the decline in the marginal propensity to consume of the population as a whole.

More Limited Investment Opportunities

The inevitable result of twenty-five years of sustained profitability in the corporate sector up to the early 1970s, without any check from a major recession, was a more or less continuous expansion in the volume of investible funds. This was true notwithstanding a progressive reduction during this period in both the rate of return on capital achieved by the corporate sector and the share of corporate profits in total value added (national income). Coupled with apparently unshakeable confidence in the durability of economic growth (itself the product of the prolonged boom), this fuelled an explosion of bank lending from the mid-1960s. This was reflected in a rise in

Table 1   OECD: variations in rate of change in output, private consumption, fixed investment and consumer prices (annual average % change)

	1953–60	'60–65	'65–73	'73–79	'79–85	'85–89	'89–95	'50–73	'73–95
Gross domestic product	2.9	5.3	5.0	2.7	2.1	3.4	1.8	4.3	2.4
Private consumption	2.9	5.1	5.1	3.0	2.1	3.5	2.0	4.3	2.6
Fixed capital formation	4.4	7.1	5.9	1.2	1.1	5.3	1.8	5.7	2.1
Consumer prices	2.5	2.6	4.8	10.3	7.5	3.5	3.4	3.4	6.4

Sources: OECD National Accounts Statistics; IMF International Financial Statistics.

the level of banks' outstanding loans to the private sector – expressed as a proportion of GDP – by 40–50 per cent between 1965 and 1973 (on average in the major OECD countries).

Yet it is striking that this surge in lending was not matched by a corresponding growth of fixed investment during the same period. On the contrary, from the late 1960s the average growth rate of fixed investment actually started to decelerate relative to that of total output (GDP) in the OECD countries as a whole. This is reflected in the fact that, although fixed investment continued to register bigger annual percentage increases than GDP as a whole, the difference in the rate of increase narrowed as compared with the 1950s and earlier 1960s (see Table 1). This decline in fixed investment growth proportionate to that of GDP – coming on top of the absolute decline in the latter (from an average of 5.3 per cent annually in 1960–65 to one of 5.0 per cent in 1965–73) – clearly suggests that the intensifying competition caused by the relative stagnation of final demand was leading to a squeeze on the marginal propensity to invest in fixed assets. Aside from fixed capital, moreover, the demand for funds to be employed as working capital also began to diminish (relative to the gross value of output) from the 1970s – thanks to such factors as the spread of 'just-in-time' techniques of stock control pioneered in Japan – although the full impact of this tendency was not to be felt until later.

This evident rise in the marginal productivity of capital may also have been facilitated by technological change, although the impact of this factor during this period in reducing the growth of fixed-asset creation was not as great as it was to become later on (see

Chapter 7). This does not mean, of course, that there was not substantial unmet demand for capital in the economy as a whole; but such demands were largely confined to those areas such as public infrastructure (both physical and social) where private investment was for the most part deemed not to be appropriate – primarily because it could only generate a rate of return far below that demanded by the capital markets.

Inevitably this coincidence of a continuing steady growth in investible funds with slowing demand for both fixed investment and working capital meant that a significant proportion of such funds were channelled into speculation – that is, into assets which held out greater prospect of gain from capital appreciation than from earnings yield. This tendency was encouraged by the general, and quite accurate, perception that governments remained committed to expansionary fiscal and monetary policy, even if this meant an increased risk of inflation. In such a climate it was entirely rational to suppose that the value of assets such as real estate would be unlikely to fall for any sustained period. Indeed it may even be inferred that, at a time when there was still a general lack of concern about inflation, the investor community was giving tacit support to inflationary official policies in the expectation that this would boost the value of the assets on which they were betting.[4] This problem was undoubtedly accentuated by the belief that governments could and would intervene to support financial markets and thus protect investors from risk of serious disaster, thereby contributing to the intensity and recklessness of much of this speculative investment (notably in real estate and commodities). Yet this use of the official life support machine to prop up sagging asset values could not avert the collapse of the boom and the onset of a downturn – both in output and in financial markets – much greater than anyone expected.

The initial response of economic policy-makers in the OECD countries to the onset of recession at the end of 1973 was essentially that dictated by the Keynesian doctrines which were then still prevalent. This meant seeking to soften the blow of falling output by increasing government borrowing rather than by the orthodox approach of bringing reduced state revenues into line with expenditure – through either big tax increases or corresponding cuts in public spending, which would only have intensified the downward spiral. This approach was based on the concept of automatic 'stabilisers', whereby the tendency of public spending to rise during a recession (because of higher aggregate welfare spending) is supposed to act as a countervailing influence against recessionary tendencies.

Such a reaction, it must be stressed, was scarcely controversial at the time, being wholly in line with the post-1945 consensus. Hence it was largely endorsed by all major economic interest groups and the related political constituencies. For not only would the application of more traditional orthodoxy – involving drastic measures to curb public-sector deficits – have been viewed as unacceptable by the mass of voters; it would have been regarded as equally intolerable by most of the financial and investor community, who would otherwise have been faced with potential ruin through the unravelling of vast chains of unfundable debt. The dangers posed by the latter problem were graphically demonstrated by banking crises in a number of Western countries in 1974 – mainly associated with bad loans in the real-estate and shipping sectors – which were only prevented from precipitating more widespread financial collapse by timely government bail-outs of the failing institutions concerned.

Implicitly of course this counter-cyclical approach was seen as justified on the grounds that the downturn would be temporary and that, following a relatively brief period of retrenchment, the industrialised economies would resume their 'normal' growth trend, permitting tax revenues to rise and state spending to fall, in real terms, and thus bringing public finances back to something like balance. Hence the resulting rise in the ratio of public debt to national income was generally seen as perfectly manageable and compatible with long-term economic health. What was scarcely foreseen, despite the indications of an emerging long-term shift to both lower demand growth and higher unemployment, was that 1973–74 would be a watershed marking the end of the prolonged post-war boom.[5]

Obviously such optimism was also conditioned by political necessity. Electorates had been led in the 1950s and 1960s to believe that full employment and rising living standards could be more or less indefinitely maintained, and that in any temporary recession they would be protected against serious deprivation by the welfare state. In the light of this 'revolution of rising expectations' – fostered most notably by President Johnson's vision of the Great Society in the United States in the mid-1960s – it was scarcely conceivable that any Western government would readily call for sustained austerity, even if it had recognised the potential need for it.

Yet almost immediately such hopes were dashed. In particular the high rates of inflation which had appeared in the speculative boom of 1972–73 proved resistant to the traditional remedy of a mild fiscal and monetary squeeze. Indeed inflation remained a problem throughout the 1970s, inhibiting business confidence and contributing to the half-hearted nature of the recovery. Coming on top of the relative stagnation of consumer markets, the result was that real GDP growth in the OECD countries averaged under 3 per cent a year in the 1973–79 period – little more than half the level recorded between 1965 and 1973 – and was then followed by a further bout of recession from 1979 (see Table 1). At the same time inflation rates in the industrialised world soared to an average of over 10 per cent between 1973 and 1979, compared with one of under 5 per cent in the 1965–73 period.

The emergence of this phenomenon of 'stagflation' – which according to conventional economic theory should have been virtually an impossibility – seemed to vindicate the so-called monetarist critics of Keynesianism and those political tendencies on the right that had long sought to identify it with 'socialism'. Certainly the inability of governments – widely demonstrated in the early 1970s – to hold down inflation (other than for very short periods) by such means as direct controls on prices and incomes, combined with the reluctance of the preponderant school of economic opinion to concede the importance of monetary influences in generating inflation, was a major factor leading to the dethronement of the Keynesian model during this period. Yet the model's equally conspicuous failure to sustain real growth and employment – as market forces refused to respond any more to the levers of demand management – was clearly at least as crucial a factor, and one which (as already noted) was itself a principal cause of the rise in inflation.

Ambivalence on Inflation

Indeed it is noteworthy that there was a continuing widespread tendency in the 1970s not to regard inflation as a serious problem. This was to a large extent understandable in that it had been prevalent, albeit at modest levels (2–3 per cent a year) throughout most of the post-war period and had not prevented the fastest rise in living standards in the history of the Western industrialised world – in contrast to earlier periods when for the most part price stability had prevailed but only at the cost of low average growth and exposure to recurrent recession and high unemployment. Hence it is in no way surprising that the initial reaction of most people to the acceleration of OECD inflation rates from the late 1960s (see Table 1) was that it was an acceptable price to pay for the maintenance of growth and full employment.

The most concrete manifestation of this attitude was the abandonment of the fixed exchange rate system enshrined in the Bretton Woods agreements which had formed the basis of the international monetary system since World War II. This was precipitated by the US administration's removal of the dollar from the gold standard in 1971, following which all currency parities were effectively 'floating' even though most governments continued (as they still do) to try and influence the market valuation of their national currencies (mainly through the manipulation of interest rates) in the interests of domestic economic stability.

While it was obvious to all that the removal of any fixed anchor for the world's currencies created a danger of increased inflation, it was still widely believed that this could be compatible with a return to sustained growth. Some even suggested that much higher rates of inflation (over 10 per cent a year) could be viewed as a necessary and quite acceptable concomitant of high economic growth. This hypothesis was held by its advocates to be validated by the experience of countries such as Brazil, which at that time had enjoyed several years of rapid growth while experiencing continued hyperinflation and rapid depreciation of its currency. Undoubtedly this facile line of argument found ready acceptance in the early 1970s among those groups in the industrialised world who had confidence in their ability to protect themselves from the effects of inflation, if not positively to benefit from it. These included

- owners of relatively scarce income-generating assets, such as real estate;
- organised labour groups with apparently entrenched bargaining strength;
- governments and other borrowers who thought it might be possible indefinitely to finance their activities by repaying debt in devalued currency.

Inevitably the consequences of soaring inflation in the first half of the 1970s – including the oil crisis itself – undermined these delusions in the industrialised world and paved the way for a policy shift back in the direction of financial orthodoxy. In doing so, however, they served to revive another traditional fallacy, namely that inflation was itself a principal cause of recession – rather than a symptom of the failure of Keynesian policies to prevent recession – and that therefore ending it would suffice to promote a revival of growth. Moreover, as the decade advanced and growth failed to revive, it became more obvious that public-sector deficits and borrowing could not continue to be allowed to grow indefinitely in the forlorn hope that the supposed automatic stabiliser of increased welfare spending would eventually induce a return of rapid growth. With the average ratio of gross public debt to GDP in the OECD countries already by 1980 rising rapidly above 40 per cent, compared with 35 per cent in 1974, it was understandably felt necessary to try a different approach.

Hence by the late 1970s economic policy everywhere began to shift back – ostensibly at least – towards the principles of classical orthodoxy, based on strict monetary control combined with minimal state intervention in other aspects of the economy. Yet, in view of the overwhelming historical evidence that such an approach could not deliver sustained recovery, it is hardly surprising that the then economics establishment – as represented particularly by the academic world – strove vigorously to resist this turning back of the clock. The most conspicuous example of this in Britain was the famous letter to *The Times* from no fewer than 364 economists (mainly academic) protesting at the austerity of the Conservative government's 1981 budget.

What is on the face of it much more surprising is that a significant body of opinion, which rapidly became dominant, was apparently convinced that there was 'no alternative' to a form of economic management which was, at least in theory, closely akin to one that had brought disaster to the Western world on more than one previous occasion, most notably in the slump of the early 1930s. It is hard to tell to what extent the different protagonists of this 'neo-classical' school adopted this position out of a genuine, if perverse, conviction that it could actually deliver sustained growth, or rather from desperation, in the Malthusian belief that widespread economic hardship was necessary to ensure the survival of the system and the retention of ultimate power by the controlling interest groups.

Clearly, to the extent that the latter was the guiding belief, it was not politically expedient to admit this. Indeed since the genie of rising expectations could not be returned to the bottle – or only, as may have been hoped, in the long term – it needed to be humoured. Consequently the proposed return to pre-war economic orthodoxy had to be presented to the public – or at least to a large enough proportion of the electorate to ensure support for it – as a more effective recipe for general economic prosperity than that of the Keynesians, even if it required the imposition of much greater austerity initially. In fact it was not too difficult to gain quite wide political acceptance for such an approach, given the atavistic tendency of most societies to accept the idea that collective misfortune may be the result of collective wrongdoing or excessive indulgence, and that therefore a degree of sacrifice (human or otherwise) may be required to atone for it and thereby restore general well-being.

At the same time the necessity for restoring financial rigour had as far as possible to be managed in such a way as not to damage the interests of financial and industrial capital, still desperately in need of new investment outlets. Thus it was vital to sustain the perception, on the part of investors and ordinary voters alike, that the pain induced by the necessary cure for inflation would ultimately (indeed quite rapidly) make possible renewed growth. As subsequent events were to reveal, however, this stance was more the product of confusion and self-deception on the part of the policy-makers than a single-minded intention to conceal the harsh realities from the public. For there was a seeming failure on the part of the newly ascendant forces of the right to grasp that a reversion to genuine financial orthodoxy (with 'sound' money and balanced budgets) would be inimical to sustained recovery – and thus ultimately as damaging to their own constituency (the private corporate sector) as to that of the mass of ordinary people menaced by unemployment and cuts in welfare benefits. The consequences of trying to balance these inherently conflicting objectives were to become apparent as the 1980s unfolded.

Notes

1. Since it was clearly linked to the desire of the dominant Arab members of OPEC, as well as Iran, to put pressure on the West and Israel in wake of the Yom Kippur War of October 1973.

2. Following the enforced devaluation of the US dollar and abandonment of the gold standard by the Nixon administration.

3. Even now it is quite common to find economists who reject any notion of limits to demand growth, usually on the grounds that it is based on the 'lump of labour fallacy' – that is, the suggestion that there is a fixed amount of output (and hence labour) required to meet demand (cf. S. Brittan, *Capitalism with a Human Face*, Fontana, London 1996). The obvious perversity of this argument is based on a refusal to bring the time factor into the equation, since it is not a question of suggesting that demand is finite in any absolute sense but only over a given time period. Yet since rates of return on capital are reckoned in relation to periods of time it should not be necessary to point out that it is the short- or medium-term limitation which is crucial in defining whether there is a ceiling on demand growth.

4. This reflects a very different 'inflation psychology' from that which was to emerge later, once markets began to lose faith in the revival of growth and in the idea that inflation could likewise be sustained for long enough periods to permit the devaluation of most debts.

5. Although the pressures tending to undermine the post-war boom and to result in long-term fiscal imbalance were identified by some – see J. O'Connor, *The Fiscal Crisis of the State*, St Martin's Press, New York 1973.

4

The Illusion of Orthodoxy

In theory the neo-orthodox strategies which came to be widely
adopted in the 1980s were based on the twin objectives of price
stability and balanced budgets. Not that these were regarded as
immediately attainable goals in the absolute sense; but they were
none the less clearly identified as the central guiding principles of
policy. Events were to prove, however, that official commitment to
them – particularly balanced budgets – was very tenuous beyond the
rhetorical smokescreen. This point may perhaps best be illustrated
by reference to the record of the Conservative administration in
Britain under Margaret Thatcher, particularly since, of all the governments of major industrialised countries, it was during the 1980s
the most consistently vocal and enthusiastic advocate of the radical
orthodox agenda.

'Monetarism'

Initially protagonists of 'neo-classical' economic policies purported
to base their approach on the principle of strictly controlling growth
in the money supply. This policy, closely identified with the ideas of
the Nobel Prize-winning Professor Milton Friedman, was held by
this school of thought to be the one sufficient and essential condition for the control of inflation. In this its proponents differed
sharply from those who, clinging to Keynesian doctrine, advocated
the administrative control of prices and wages as the most appropriate means of controlling inflation – an approach which had been

widely practised in OECD countries during the 1960s and 1970s, but with a uniform lack of success.[1]

Yet quite quickly this new doctrine of monetarism, as it became popularly known, was revealed as totally unworkable. This was not because it was ineffective in bringing down inflation, but because it could only do so by means of strangling the 'real' (i.e. productive) economy, and then could not prevent a recurrence of inflation in the event of a sustained revival of growth. The reasons for this comprehensive failure were essentially twofold.

The fantasy of monetary targeting

The essence of monetarist doctrine was the notion that governments should seek to control expansion of the money supply in line with what was deemed to be the 'natural' rate of economic growth, thereby preventing any inflationary excess. In fact it was never clear how this control was to be achieved other than by announcing official targets for growth of the money supply – as measured by various indicators – and exhorting the financial sector to observe them.

Whether such an approach could ever have succeeded in restraining profit-oriented banks, particularly when their solvency remained largely underwritten by the state, seems very doubtful. In a climate where the financial system was simultaneously being deregulated – so that private banks were, in effect, increasingly free to print money – it seems hard to credit that it was ever thought feasible. In fact one of the first acts of the Thatcher administration – the removal of exchange controls (in place for over thirty years) in 1979 – could be said to have guaranteed that monetary targeting would be impossible. For this freed financial institutions from the restraint hitherto imposed by the government's capacity to apply quantitative restrictions on credit creation by enabling them to borrow abroad.

Hence the Friedmanite model of monetary control was rapidly revealed to be no more practicable under free market capitalism than Keynesian wage and price controls had proved to be. Instead it was discovered that the only way to prevent inflation arising from excessive expansion of domestic credit was by choking off the demand for it through the blunt instrument of high interest rates. This did not, of course, preclude the possibility of borrowing from abroad at lower interest rates. Yet because the relatively high domestic interest rates had the effect of pushing up the sterling exchange rate (to a level which might well appear unsustainable beyond the short term) there was a strong foreign exchange risk deterring banks and other borrowers from raising loans in foreign currency.

It is a remarkable feature of the debate over monetarism and monetary policy during this period that virtually all the protagonists seemed to confuse the idea of financial orthodoxy with that of market liberalisation, without recognising that one should properly be viewed as a negation of the other. In Britain it sometimes seemed that the Tory government's public relations machine was devoted to fostering this misconception, as when it encouraged (or permitted) Mrs Thatcher to give simplistic lectures on the virtues of thrift and never spending beyond one's income – when all the while her administration was busy creating the conditions for an unprecedented upsurge in financial profligacy. What is especially surprising is that this contradiction was consistently missed by both the Labour opposition and the more recalcitrant Keynesian economists, who mindlessly demonised the very word 'monetarism' without bothering to ask themselves whether the Tories' supposedly monetarist policies could actually keep inflation under control – which many on the left in any case tended to deny was a serious problem.

Damage to the real economy

Thus very soon all that was left of monetarism was a crude reliance on high interest rates to contain inflation. Moreover, because of the lack of any other means of restraining monetary growth, interest rates had to be kept higher than would have been necessary had it still been possible to impose quantitative restraints as well, thus adding to the costs of non-financial enterprises and of the government's own already considerable burden of debt. The difficulty this posed in balancing the need to restrain inflation with other economic objectives was all the greater because of the absence – after the demise of the Bretton Woods international exchange rate system in 1971 – of any fixed exchange standard for currencies such as that previously provided by the US dollar at a fixed parity with gold, so that currencies were thereafter deemed to be 'floating'. This was both because (a) in the absence of any other barrier to speculation against the pound – such as that previously provided by a fixed parity for sterling which all the world's major central banks were committed to defend – an additional interest premium had to be offered to induce people to hold the currency; and (b) any rise in interest rates – or even the expectation of one – tended to be quickly translated into a stronger exchange rate and hence a loss of competitiveness by domestic suppliers of tradable goods and services.

Consequently the net effect of Thatcherite monetary restraint in the early 1980s was that Britain suffered a sharper fall in output than any other OECD country during the 1980–82 recession, 20 per cent of all factories were forced to close, substantial segments of manufacturing industry were wiped out completely, and unemployment quadrupled as compared with 1979. Remarkably this did not prevent the Tories winning a landslide victory in the 1983 general election.[2] Nevertheless, the pretence of monetary targeting was soon to be quietly abandoned, even though lip-service was naturally still paid to the goal of price stability.

In fact for all the pain inflicted on the productive sectors of the economy the results in terms of lowered inflation were far from impressive. In the 1980s as a whole British inflation fell below the average for OECD countries in only two years (1983 and 1984) and for the decade as a whole averaged 7.5 per cent annually compared with an OECD average of 5.9 per cent. It is true that the British economy recovered from the 1980–82 recession more strongly than the rest of the industrialised world, recording a higher than average growth in GDP during the rest of the decade. Yet arguably all this demonstrates is that the side-effects of the 'monetarist' medicine were intolerably strong even for the government's own closest supporters.

The Pursuit of Fiscal Rectitude

The commitment of the Thatcher administration, if only rhetorically, to the idea of balancing the state budget was at least more durable than its adherence to monetary orthodoxy – and superficially it appeared more genuine. Thus it not only called for tax cuts on the grounds that the role of the state in the economy had grown too large, and insisted that these must be balanced by cuts in public expenditure; it can be said to have been true to its rhetoric in so far as it did introduce significant spending cuts in some areas – even though these were more than offset by increases in others, particularly the welfare budget. Hence the British government succeeded in maintaining a proportionately much lower fiscal deficit than most other industrialised countries – even achieving a budget surplus towards the end of the brief boom of the mid-1980s (unlike all the other members of the Group of Seven major industrialised countries except Japan).

Yet in the final analysis this commitment was no more real than that to monetary rigour, notwithstanding the leader's primitive Micawberesque diatribes on the virtues of thrift and living within one's means. Arguably indeed her government was only able to maintain any claim to fiscal virtue thanks to the windfall of North Sea oil revenue – which grew rapidly from a very low level during the early 1980s – and to a much lesser extent the one-off gains from privatising state assets. Once the receipts from these sources had stabilised or tailed off, and as recession returned at the end of the 1980s, the hollowness of Thatcherite claims to fiscal discipline was fully exposed.

Privatisation

In fact privatisation is perhaps the best illustration of the essential fraudulence of the government's supposed commitment to strict financial stewardship. Its main argument in support of the policy was that it removed the burden of loss-making enterprises from the taxpayer and that, by enabling them to make profits under private ownership (while allegedly providing customers with cheaper and more efficient services), it would actually result in their making a positive contribution to the public purse through the tax system. Yet such claims ignore some rather obvious counter-arguments, which received surprisingly little mention from the official opposition or the largely uncritical media; namely,

- In respect of the most valuable assets sold (telecommunications, gas, electricity and water utilities) all the businesses concerned were in fact profitable and fully self-financing under state ownership. Consequently there was a decline in the government's annual dividend receipts from state enterprises of some £3.5 billion (in 1993 prices) between 1982 and 1992. (This annual loss was offset by once-and-for-all net receipts from the sale of public assets over this period amounting to a mere £60 billion.)
- The undoubted increase in profitability achieved by many utility companies following privatisation (and hence in the revenues they

generated) was achieved largely at the cost of a massive shake-out of labour. In a climate of already high unemployment this has simply had the effect of increasing the social security budget, with obvious negative consequences for the overall fiscal balance.

These little publicised facts cast doubt on whether there has been or could be any net long-term fiscal gain from such privatisations, not to mention the obvious risk to consumer interests of entrusting such monopolistic enterprises to profit-oriented private-sector companies.[3] What is remarkable is that virtually nobody raised the question of why it had never before been recognised as so obviously of public benefit to privatise such utilities, many of which had originally been established under predominantly state or municipal ownership in the Victorian era, often by Conservative administrations. Had anyone bothered to do so they would have discovered that it was precisely because they were recognised to be natural monopolies which most contemporary business interests did not wish to fall under the influence of hostile competitors.[4] In fact, as will be argued more fully in a later chapter, the central reason for the trend to privatisation (in Britain and other countries) was the need to find outlets for the ever swelling volume of private investible funds in a world where profitable opportunities for such investment were fast drying up.

In the United States, even under the ultra-conservative Reagan presidency (1981–89), there was really no serious question of a reversion to traditional financial orthodoxy – for all the virtually unanimous political rhetoric in favour of a balanced federal budget. One reason for this was that, unlike the Thatcher government in Britain, it could not look to either a windfall comparable to North Sea oil or the possibility of selling substantial state assets in order to finance tax cuts or other electoral bribes. Instead the administration relied almost entirely on the assumption put forward by the so-called supply-side school of economists that cuts in direct taxes would stimulate increased investment and output to such an extent as to more than offset the impact of falling tax rates on government revenues. The fact that this theory – which had been lampooned by George Bush as 'voodoo economics' during his campaign against Ronald Reagan for the Republican nomination in 1980 (before he became the latter's vice-presidential running mate) – was taken seriously by the US establishment is a measure of the growing national mood of escapism in face of the intractable fiscal problem. Arguably the willingness and ability of both the administration and Congress to indulge this tendency was reinforced by the constitutional peculiarities of the USA, which encouraged politicians to identify themselves with such apparently popular causes as that of balancing the budget in the knowledge that the checks and balances of the system would almost certainly ensure it could never be implemented.

Perhaps because the United States had long had financial markets completely open to the rest of the world, there was no possibility of it even purporting to adopt an orthodox monetarist stance such as the Thatcher government had done in Britain. Indeed earlier attempts to impose quantitative restrictions on credit expansion, such as that of the Johnson administration in 1968, had already demonstrated the futility of this approach in an open world financial market.[5] In any event the Reagan administration proved to be more concerned with trying to stimulate the investment boom in the financial markets which was to become such a feature of the 1980s. This entailed not only an increase in the budget deficit (as tax reductions failed to be matched by cuts in public spending) but also a more or less explicit relaxation of anti-trust enforcement – the latter having the effect of fuelling the takeover boom which was arguably the major catalyst of the rise in equity markets in the 1980s. But most significant of all was the increasingly permissive attitude to regulation of the financial sector – such that (for example) some banks and savings and loan institutions (familiarly, and perhaps ironically, known as thrifts) were allowed to continue operating even when they were clearly insolvent – in the full knowledge that the government would largely bail them out through the Federal Deposit Insurance scheme and other publicly financed facilities.

Thus the supposed US reversion to fiscal orthodoxy under Presidents Reagan and Bush was, if anything, even more bogus than the Thatcher experiment in Britain. Indeed it has been argued by many that, thanks to the failure to achieve public spending cuts on anything like the scale of its cuts in taxation, the outcome was really more in line with the already discredited Keynesian device of trying to stimulate the economy through deficit financing.[6] The resulting surge in US net public indebtedness, from 25 per cent of GDP in 1984 to over 40 per cent in the early 1990s, was thus perhaps the most conspicuous symptom of the inability of the industrialised nations to shake off the profligate habits induced by the prosperity of the 1950s and 1960s.

The fashion for neo-classical economic ideas became increasingly widespread during the 1980s, particularly in the Anglo-Saxon countries. Indeed it is ironic that probably the two most committed exponents of the doctrine were the nominally socialist governments of Australia and New Zealand. The latter in particular embarked on a systematic programme of deregulation, including the unilateral reduction of tariffs and removal of controls on imports as well as on the financial sector, while also proclaiming its support for fiscal and monetary discipline. However, although these experiments were much lauded at the time by establishment economists throughout the world, they have not so far enabled either country to escape from the trap of low growth and chronic budget deficits affecting all OECD countries.[7]

Such was the momentum in this direction that even Japan, hitherto the industrialised country most subject to official control and intervention in different aspects of the economy, was induced to expose itself to international market forces to an unprecedented degree. In particular, responding to strong pressure from the USA – which had long resented the large implicit subsidy to the cost of capital enjoyed by Japanese manufacturers thanks to the restriction on export of capital from Japan and the low interest rates imposed on financial institutions – it largely freed capital movements in and out of the country. In fact this shift in Japanese policy, perhaps more than any other single measure implemented in the 1980s, served to boost the trend towards the much trumpeted 'global economy', since it led to a more than fivefold increase in the value of Japanese direct investment overseas in the 1980s as compared with the 1970s.

Likewise in continental Europe there were significant moves to deregulate financial markets and free the export of capital, notably in France and Italy – where restrictions had previously been almost as great as in Japan – and in the Nordic countries, where liberalisation was accompanied by a laxity of banking supervision even greater than in the USA (and with even more disastrous consequences). The result was to give added impetus to the so-called globalisation process as the non-Anglo-Saxon countries – of which only the Netherlands had previously been substantially geared to investing overseas – joined the trend to expanding the world-wide presence of their major corporations.

In all these OECD countries it is evident, if only with the benefit of hindsight, that the emphasis in the economic 'reform' process was much more on liberalisation and deregulation than on fiscal orthodoxy and restraint. This is not to say there were no attempts to curtail public expenditure; there were even many cases of tax increases, albeit invariably of a regressive kind and often disguised as cuts in subsidies or welfare payments. In no country, however, were these sufficient to offset the effect of tax cuts or the increases in expenditure occasioned by persistent economic stagnation.

In fact the initial impact of this switch to liberalisation was made to appear quite positive. This was because the conditions for an upsurge in growth in the mid-1980s had been created by the response to the renewed bout of recession which occurred in 1980–82, involving a severe monetary squeeze in most OECD countries. This led to a sufficient build-up of excess capacity, reflected in record post-war rates of unemployment in the early 1980s, for there to be obvious scope for at least a short-run recovery based on meeting the demand pent up during the recession. The fact that it was possible to accomplish this while yet permitting a fall in inflation rates – which had returned to high levels in 1980–81 but were then brought down quite rapidly under the impact of monetary tightening and the associated high unemployment – seems to have encouraged the belief that non-inflationary growth might be sustained indefinitely and thus imparted a powerful stimulus to the newly liberalised financial markets.

The extent of this enthusiasm was reflected in a rise in fixed capital formation in the OECD countries (particularly in plant and machinery as opposed to construction) between 1985 and 1989 at a rate half as fast again as that of GDP overall – in marked contrast to the pattern during the whole period since the end of the post-war boom (1973–95), when the average rate of growth of fixed investment was significantly less than that of GDP (see Table 1 and Figure 2). Remarkably this brief revival of real investment – which reached such intensity in some quarters (particularly in the Anglo-Saxon world) as to generate talk of a new 'economic miracle' – occurred despite the continuing overhang of excess capacity and the restraint on overall growth resulting from still subdued expansion of consumer demand.

This apparent anomaly is to be explained partly by the irrational confidence initially induced by the general switch to 'monetarist' policies, instinctively favoured by the financial markets. Yet it also reflected a recognition that, even in a climate of relatively depressed consumer markets, profitable fixed investment in both manufacturing and service sectors was possible based on the application of cost-cutting new technology (involving increased automation), since this could achieve high returns even without the benefit of demand growth. There is little evidence that governments noticed that such a shift in the pattern of fixed investment was occurring. Still less do they seem to have appreciated that it was bound to mean an ever greater shake-out of labour and long-term decline in the growth of consumer purchasing power (as aggregate personal income was concentrated among a shrinking proportion of the population). Such wilful igno-rance was symptomatic of the new emphasis on micro- rather than macro-economics as the key to sustained prosperity (that is, the health of the individual enterprise rather than that of the economy as a whole). Put more bluntly, it was a measure of how far by that time Keynesian ideas were at a discount and the post-war commitment to maintaining full employment had been effectively abandoned.

On the other hand a significant proportion of the growth in fixed investment during the 1980s' upswing was accounted for by more or less speculative construction activity – an inevitable concomitant of the real-estate price bubble which affected all OECD countries during this period. This tendency to increased speculation was mirrored in the general steep rise in real asset prices – even faster relative to the growth of the economy as a whole than in the boom of the early 1970s.[8] Not surprisingly this trend was reflected in a steep rise in the ratio of aggregate private debt to GDP, which reached a peak around 1990 of over 30 per cent higher[9] than that attained in the early 1970s' boom. The ease with which consumers were thus per-suaded to mortgage their future income on a grossly exaggerated promise of sustained rapid growth is another measure of the fragile basis of the 1980s' upswing.

This fragility was dramatically exposed by the sharp fall in world stock markets in October 1987 – an event which had been widely anticipated in the financial community for many months beforehand in the light of the increasingly obvious overvaluation of shares relative to corporate earnings. Yet such was the political momentum and conditioned optimism behind the liberalising approach that this sell-off was soon brushed aside. Rather, an official consensus developed that it need not be regarded as heralding any serious economic slowdown, particularly as it was thought that inflation rates were still low enough to justify a relaxation of fiscal and monetary policy in the interests of countering deflationary pressures arising from the crash. Remarkably this response was virtually identical to the one which had been elicited by the similar market downturn heralding the onset of recession in 1974 – demonstrating that, notwithstanding the neo-classical counter-revolution, the ghost of Keynes still haunted the finance ministries of the West.

Thus the weight of mainstream economic analysis in the two years immediately following the 1987 'crash' was devoted to demonstrating that, so far from its portending another major recession, there was every prospect of the world economy achieving a 'soft landing' (i.e. a mild slowdown) before resuming an upward growth path comparable to that of the 1984–88 period (even though the latter was quite modest relative to the growth rates recorded before 1973 – or even to those of the late 1970s' recovery). Duly fortified by such optimism, investors were readily induced to regard the 1987 sell-off as a buying opportunity and within two years had driven equity markets to new historic peaks.

By 1989–90, however, such escapist illusions had dissolved as the speculative build-up of private-sector debt and the return of inflationary pressures combined to undermine confidence. Since the threat of inflation precluded any resort to countervailing fiscal and monetary measures, there was no way of preventing the major economies from slipping into recession again. The result was a 30–40 per cent fall in overblown real-estate prices in nearly all OECD countries in 1990–92 – although, remarkably, stock markets remained largely unscathed[10] – and the consequent outbreak of banking crises, requiring the usual government intervention to avert total disaster, particularly in the United States, Japan and Scandinavia. The fallout for the 'real' economy has been that average OECD growth rates so far in the 1990s (1990–95) have been much slower even than the inadequate levels recorded in the 1980s (see Figure 2).

Not only had the supposed reversion to classical orthodoxy thus failed to deliver the sustained recovery its advocates had promised. It had not achieved any measurable success in 'rolling back the frontiers of the state' within the industrial market economies as a whole. On the contrary the share of GDP accounted for by government expenditure in the OECD countries continued to rise between 1980 and 1990, from 42 to 45 per cent (see Figure 1).

Figure 2   OECD: the pattern of production and fixed investment growth since the 1950s (average annual % growth)   *Source:* OECD National Accounts Statistics.

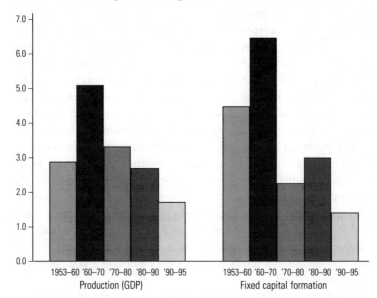

A Policy of Desperation

Even though the impact of the purported revival of financial ortho-doxy in the 1980s is still unfolding in the 1990s, it is already possible to try and view it in historical perspective. The main conclusions to emerge are that

- The 'revolution' was more a desperate ad hoc response to the failure of Keynesianism than a genuine, reasoned attempt to address the problems arising from the reappearance of the business cycle.
- The experiment lacked credibility from the outset, since it was never possible to impose the economic austerity which a more genuine orthodoxy would have dictated without both undermining the fragile financial markets and creating a politically quite un-acceptable level of social deprivation.

For these reasons the commitment of governments to the new ortho-doxy – even those ostensibly most in tune with ideology of the 'New Right', such as the Reagan administration – was always more rhetorical than real. Thus it was politically convenient for such right-wing governments to pay lip-service to the virtues of lower taxation while actually using patronage and taxpayers' money to protect and subsidise favoured corporations or interest groups – including, naturally, key categories of voters. In the USA this most conspicuously included the defence industry – a major contributor of both campaign finance and personnel to the Reagan administration – which benefited from a massive increase in military spending in the early 1980s at a time when taxes were being just as massively cut. Likewise in Britain the electoral strategy of the Thatcher government in the 1980s hinged on targeting financial benefits to socio-economic groups seen as holding the balance of political power (such as the better paid manual workers still in full-time employment). This was done through such measures as giving the tenants of municipal housing the right to buy their homes at low prices and with subsidised loans, public offers of discounted shares in privatised utilities to those having the quite modest amount of money needed to make the initial investment (equivalent to cash hand-outs), and successive cuts in income tax.

Indeed the tendency of those who insist on the virtues of the free market as a general principle to find reasons why they themselves need special protection – a phenomenon familiar from the writings of Adam Smith – has been even more noticeable in the post-Keynesian world after a generation when selective state intervention had become all-pervading and indeed indispensable for much of the private sector. Hence when it came to applying *laissez-faire* principles to specific areas of state intervention and expenditure, it was often felt to be impossible to do so in practice. This was demonstrated not only by the massive interventions by the Reagan and Bush administrations in support of failing financial institutions (from the de facto nationalisation of the Continental Illinois Bank in 1984 to the mass bail-out of Savings and Loan institutions in 1990) but also by the Thatcher government's numerous schemes to subsidise private investment (see Chapter 8) and even the use of the social-security budget to pay the mortgage interest of previously wealthy individuals who found themselves in difficulties following the collapse of the real-estate market in 1988 and the subsequent recession (rather than exposing them to market forces and so requiring them to sell their often very expensive properties in a depressed market).[11]

Governments would certainly have been forgiven their shameless application of double standards if only they had achieved the sustained revival of growth which Keynesian policies had proved no longer capable of delivering in the 1970s, but which financial markets had by the mid-1980s convinced themselves could result from liberalisation. Yet the reality is (as demonstrated in Figure 2) that in each decade since the 1960s aggregate GDP in the OECD countries has grown more slowly – on an annual average basis – than in the previous one, with growth in the 1990s so far averaging only one-third of the 1960s' level. The consequences have been disastrous not only in terms of the continuing shortage of outlets for productive investment but, above all, because of the impact on public finances. For in the absence of renewed growth, and in view of rates of unemployment even higher than those prevailing in the 1970s, the so-called stabiliser of increased social-security payments rapidly turned into a millstone weighing down state budgets and enforcing persistent deficits. The scale of the latter has, of course, been all the greater on account of the ascendant view that tax cuts were likely to stimulate growth and that tax increases would consequently stifle it – a prejudice which remains politically potent even now that the supply-side myth has been exploded.

Ironically the one relative success of neo-orthodox policies – the reduction of inflation to below the high levels experienced in the 1970s (though still well above the 1960s' average) – only served to exacerbate the problem of low growth; all the more so because, as noted in our discussion of the British experience, reliance on the blunt instrument of interest rates – imposed by deregulation of the financial markets – precluded any selective application of credit tightening. Yet even if it had been possible to curb inflation through a more targeted approach to credit restraint it could scarcely have been compatible with a sustained recovery of growth. For perhaps the most fundamental delusion propagated by the advocates of neo-orthodoxy was the assumption that price stability was a pre-condition for a return to sustained high growth rates. They thus chose to ignore the ample historical evidence that at least a moderate degree of inflation was an almost inevitable concomitant of rapid growth, and that therefore any attempt to restore pre-Keynesian price stability was likely to entail accepting pre-Keynesian rates of growth (i.e. very low ones). Predictably, therefore, attempts to eliminate inflation 'permanently' by imposing the kind of squeeze deliberately engineered by the Thatcher government at the beginning of the 1980s – and then again at the end of the decade – were bound to damage long-term economic health by increasing the public debt burden to levels that would be difficult to reduce during subsequent periods of recovery (which could not be sustained in any case).

As we have suggested, the most likely explanation for the adoption of such an evidently irrational strategy is that it represents a frantic clutching at straws by governments desperate to stave off disaster in the short run and unable take account of the adverse effects in the longer term. Yet in view of the obvious damage caused to the public patrimony by the effective looting of state assets and the running down of public finances (to be described at greater length in later chapters) it is legitimate to wonder whether more sinister forces were not at work. Thus there is no doubt that the huge rise in unemployment induced by the British government's savage economic squeeze of the early 1980s was politically convenient to the extent that it seriously weakened the power of organised labour in advance of moves drastically to curb trade-union rights. A related theory with some plausibility is that there has been a concerted effort so to weaken the resources and power of the state – through tax cutting and privatisation – as to preclude the possibility of a revival of

Figure 3   OECD: gross public debt, 1970–97 (% of GDP)

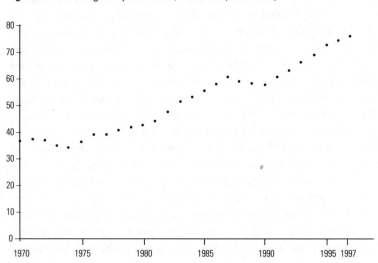

more collectivist approaches to economic management. Such a 'scorched earth' hypothesis is by no means inconsistent with another; namely, that years of state subsidisation of unaccountable private business combined with the expanding influence of organised crime (see Chapter 11) had induced a climate of such irresponsibility that progressively fewer of the effective decision-makers made any attempt to take account of the long-term sustainability of their policies.

At all events the result of the purported return to orthodoxy was that the gross public debt of OECD countries, having already increased from 35 per cent to 42 per cent of GDP between 1974 and 1980, rose at an accelerating pace in the early 1980s and again, after a pause in 1986–89, up to 1997, when it stood at 77 per cent of GDP – more than double the 1974 ratio. The problem has been made still worse by the steep rise in real interest rates since the 1960s and 1970s – the direct consequence of both the alleged return to financial orthodoxy and the accompanying market liberalisation – so that public debt-service costs as a proportion of national income of the OECD countries have actually trebled since 1974 (to over 3 per cent). Hence the whole industrialised world is now caught in a vicious circle of increasingly unaffordable public debt-service costs and remorselessly rising structural deficits.

The dilemma this now poses, as the leaders of the capitalist establishment try to reconcile their need to cut state spending with their inability to survive without ever larger doses of it, is examined in the next chapter.

Notes

1. It was found that, while it was possible to suppress inflation to a limited extent and for short periods by applying such controls, it was not possible to sustain these in face of the dynamics of the marketplace and the resistance of those (mainly workers in the public sector) who could not circumvent them and thus, not unreasonably, felt themselves to be victims of discrimination.

2. Thanks more, perhaps, to the national euphoria following the Falklands War in 1982 than to any consideration of the economic factors.

3. The system of state regulators designed to protect consumer interests has not prevented significant rises in user charges since privatisation (at least in respect of water) and a measurable rise in the level of consumer complaints at the quality of service of different utilities.

4. R.C.K. Ensor, *England 1870–1914*, The Oxford History of England, Oxford University Press, Oxford 1936.

5. P. Einzig, *Parallel Money Markets. Volume I: The New Markets in London*, Macmillan, London 1971.

6. See J.K. Galbraith, *The World Economy since the Wars: A Personal View*, Mandarin, London 1995.

7. Although New Zealand did manage to raise its GDP growth rate in the 1980s compared with the 1970s – unlike virtually every other OECD country – it has seen it fall back to the earlier (very low) level in the 1990s.

8. For eleven OECD countries (USA, Japan, Federal Republic of Germany, France, UK, Canada, Australia, Denmark, Finland, Norway and Sweden) real aggregate asset prices grew by a weighted average of 2.13 times as fast as GDP – even faster than the 1.72 times by which they outstripped GDP growth in the boom of the early 1970s – a differential which is still more impressive if one bears in mind that the 1980s' boom lasted on average over twice as long as that of the early 1970s (source: Bank for International Settlements, Annual Report 1993).

9. On average for those OECD countries for which figures are available.

10. With the striking exception of Japan, where the stock-market index fell steeply in the early 1990s and has never recovered to much more than 50 per cent of its 1989 peak level since. Elsewhere, while equity markets have shown remarkable vigour in face of persistent economic stagnation since 1990, real-estate values everywhere have scarcely recovered any of the 30–40 per cent losses in real terms that they suffered in 1990–92.

11. Numerous other examples could be cited of selective market-distorting intervention, subsidy and tax breaks applied to the private sector by the Thatcher and Reagan administrations and their counterparts in other OECD countries. For a detailed exposition, see the author's *The Myth of Free Trade*, Blackwell/The Economist, Oxford 1985 (Chapter 5).

5

Incurable Addiction
to State Support

It remains the central economic policy tenet of all mainstream political parties in the industrialised countries that a sustained revival of rapid growth is both desirable and possible – even though the rival Keynesian and neo-classical prescriptions have both proved incapable of delivering it in over twenty years since the early 1970s. As this prospect has become ever more elusive in the 1990s, governments have been given to proclaiming that even quite modest annual growth rates of 2.5 to 3 per cent (barely half the average achieved by the OECD countries in the 1960s) can actually be viewed as 'strong', even though it is obvious they are not enough on their own to prevent budget deficits from rising even further, and are in any event proving hard to sustain even at these levels.

In the continued absence of a more genuine recovery, however, it has become impossible to avoid confronting the need for more drastic and painful remedies, involving either tax increases or public spending cuts on a significant scale. In either case, however, the political and economic difficulties entailed are daunting.

The problems associated with raising taxes are essentially two-fold. First, it is generally recognised by economists that in a climate of weak demand and consequently low economic growth any major tax increases across the board are almost bound to depress effective demand and hence economic activity even further, thereby offsetting any revenue gains resulting from higher tax rates and perhaps even leading to a net increase in the deficit. On the other hand it is arguable that a more selective approach – targeting those who have benefited from the redistribution of income in favour of wealthier individuals since around 1980, as well as the profits of the corporate sector which have substantially increased in the same period – would not have this negative effect. This is because the low 'marginal propensity to consume' of rich people means that they are unlikely to reduce their purchases of goods and services (as opposed to their savings) if their net post-tax income is reduced, while private companies in a strong financial position are also unlikely to respond to tax increases by cutting their levels of consumption or investment in an already stagnant economic climate.

However, any proposal to raise taxes on these groups would fall foul of the second major obstacle: it runs counter to the political interests of the dominant social and economic groups – and to the ideological wind prevailing since the late 1970s – favouring tax-cutting, deregulation and the minimalist state. More importantly, this narrow 'class' interest is linked to the attempt to resolve the central conundrum of latter-day capitalism – how to sustain and increase the asset values of the corporate sector in face of stagnating economic growth and declining demand for capital. For any reduction in the net disposable income of the investor community – comprising both financial institutions and wealthy individuals – would inevitably depress both the flow of funds into the financial markets and the net returns to their investments – and hence the market value of traded assets and securities. (By the same token it may be inferred that the political pressure for tax cuts since the early 1980s has been based less on the bogus theories of supply-side economists – that lower taxes on the wealthy stimulate them to expand productive investment and output, and conversely – than on a concern to maintain the flow of funds propping up asset values.) Likewise any increase in rates of corporate taxation would obviously have the effect of reducing net profits and thus tend to depress the market rating of company shares, so important to maintaining what Keynes called the 'animal spirits' of investors.

These considerations have not prevented right-wing governments from raising taxes substantially when there seemed no alternative in the face of a spiralling budget deficit, as the British government did in 1993. Yet in the latter case the increases were mainly in the form of regressive indirect taxes – even though these were bound to have the most immediate negative impact on consumption – because of the Conservative Party's long-standing political commitment only to change direct tax rates in a downward direction. That this bias of right-wing governments has remained unshaken, despite the manifest destruction in the 1980s and 1990s of the supply-side myth, is hardly remarkable. Perhaps more surprising is that political parties supposedly on the left have totally failed to exploit this propaganda gift by arguing for the reversal of earlier tax concessions to higher-income groups.

The political consensus against raising taxes on income or profits has, it is true, been reinforced by the extensive moves towards liberalisation of international economic relations which have occurred since 1980, particularly affecting capital flows. These changes have gone a long way towards creating a 'global' economy in which it is difficult for national governments to raise taxes on business or wealthy individuals without adversely affecting the level of private investment in their domestic economies. The fact that the same British government that used this argument against higher personal and corporate tax rates was an enthusiastic leader of the movement to create this deregulated world economic order through the dismantling of controls is conveniently ignored. Rather, the restraints imposed on national state action by the global economy are presented as irresistible forces beyond the control of governments.

If the options for attacking public-sector deficits through increased taxes appear either self-defeating or politically unacceptable, those for doing so by cutting expenditure are hardly less so – and for much the same reasons. For if tax increases curtailing the purchasing power of the mass of consumers tend to have negative consequences for effective demand levels and hence the rate of economic growth, the same applies to many cuts in public spending. Indeed it is an elementary principle of economics that a subsidy reduction is the equivalent of a tax increase (and conversely), although this point tends to be overlooked by those political parties proposing to make cuts in spending in order to create space for tax reductions favouring key segments of the electorate. Increasingly, however, it is understood by taxpayers, who see – as, for example, in Britain – reductions in their income-tax bill offset by rises in the cost of their children's university education and of the residential care of their elderly relations (among many other items of hitherto state-supported assistance).

Thus although the weight of official opinion – heavily backed by big business and the financial markets – invariably prefers spending cuts to tax increases as a means of redressing imbalances in public-sector budgets, there is a growing if tacit recognition in political circles that both routes pose equally unpalatable choices. Still more significantly, as stagnation persists and the fiscal crisis deepens, it is becoming ever harder for *laissez-faire* ideologues and their big-business supporters to avoid recognising that their advocacy of drastically reduced public expenditure ultimately strikes at the heart of their own interests and indeed at the very foundations of the modern capitalist economy.

This is not simply because cutting state spending through the reduction of subsidies and protection for individuals and companies tends to exacerbate the problem of chronic economic stagnation. Rather, what would be threatened, in the event of a systematic effort to remove all state support and protection for markets, is the essential underpinning of corporate and consumer confidence, without which it is difficult to envisage a minimally acceptable degree of economic stability, let alone sustained growth.

The Interventionist Tradition

In fact, despite a long ideological tradition of opposition in principle to government interference in the working of the free market, it is beyond dispute that the development of capitalist enterprise has always been crucially dependent on significant state intervention. Of the myriad examples which could be cited one of the earliest and most conspicuous was that of successive British governments in deploying naval and military power to extend and defend the Empire and guarantee the exclusive rights of British companies (including statutory monopolies such as the East India Company) to trade with its dependencies. As noted by numerous economic historians, such state promotion of national economic development – commonly referred to as mercantilism – has scarcely ever ceased to be the essential basis of official policy of both Britain and all its competitors among the nation-states of the Western world.[1] Historians have also generally agreed that the only serious attempt to pursue a genuine policy of *laissez faire* was that undertaken by Britain after 1860 (at a time when it was still clearly the dominant world economic power)[2] and that it was rapidly undermined by a combination of the onset of world-wide economic depression from 1873 and the country's loss of competitiveness vis-à-vis less liberal nations (notably Germany and the USA).

Yet even this short-lived experiment (which was effectively ended by World War I, although not finally buried until the formal re-introduction of trade protection in 1932) can only be defined as *laissez faire* if that term is equated with free trade and nothing else. For this was a period when the role of government in the British economy was being greatly extended, principally at local or municipal level, so as to provide facilities and services which the private sector could not or would not – such as universal primary education, water supply and other public utilities. In fact, as the then governments of Germany and other continental countries were quicker to recognise, such state-funded investment and welfare programmes were actually in the interests of big business. For they not only helped to assure social stability but provided improved physical infrastructure and a healthier and better-educated labour force – such as the private sector would scarcely have found it practical or cost-effective to pay for itself.

In the present century no country has come close to adopting an economic system free of government intervention. Indeed, as we have seen, from the 1930s to the 1970s – and especially in the twenty-five years immediately following World War II – scarcely anyone even pretended to believe that it was a desirable goal.

After World War II there was ingrained in the capitalist tradition, over a period of some thirty years, a much more pervasive dependence of the private corporate sector on public spending and state intervention. This was, of course, based on the general acceptance of the revolutionary Keynesian doctrine that such intervention was actually desirable, if not essential, if growth was to be sustained and economies to be kept relatively stable rather than left to the mercy of the traditional cycle of boom and bust. Subsequently this expanding public sector of the economy came to provide an important and relatively stable market for the private sector through state investment and procurement programmes. In the United States, where the public-service and corporate sectors were relatively small, the principal market (expanding rapidly as the country assumed the role of leading world power after 1941) was defence – giving rise to the famed 'military–industrial complex'. At the same time private businesses in all industrialised countries became accustomed to receiving direct subsidies to investment and production, whether systematically or on a selective, ad hoc basis.

Along with the revival of *laissez-faire* ideology since the early 1980s there has been an increasingly vocal commitment on the part of Western governments to curb if not eliminate such market-distorting subsidies. The pressures to do so have perhaps been strongest in the European Union, where their existence has tended to make a nonsense of the attempt to create a 'single market' in the 1990s. However, as will be demonstrated in later chapters, the intensifying pressures to co-opt the taxpayer to support shareholder value mean there is less chance than ever that 'corporate welfare' can be dispensed with.

Lenders of Last Resort

Moreover, in the one area where state support is most crucial to protecting the interests of the private corporate sector in general and of the financial sector in particular there has clearly never been any serious intention that it should be scaled back – or even prevented from increasing to whatever extent might be dictated by the need to avert a collapse of the financial markets. This is the de facto under-writing of the financial system by governments (usually through the agency of their respective central banks) acting as 'lenders of last resort'.

The origins of this practice, at least in the Anglo-Saxon world, can be traced to the 1930s,[3] when the high incidence of bank failures – and perhaps even more the fear of such failures – was a major cause of financial instability and lack of confidence in the economy. This was particularly true in the United States, where no fewer than 2,000 banks failed in 1930 alone in the panic following the Wall Street crash of 1929. This eventually led to the enactment in 1933 of legislation requiring all banks to insure their deposits (up to a maximum level for each one)[4] through a government agency, the Federal Deposit Insurance Corporation, thus guaranteeing small savers against total ruin. At the same time a similar banking débâcle in Germany and Central Europe led the US Federal Reserve and the Bank of England to assume responsibility for acceptance credits and other instruments held by their own banks on insolvent continental institutions.

Ever since that time it has been generally understood, although never explicitly laid down, that official intervention would be used to avert the collapse of any financial institution or group of institu-tions where this was deemed to threaten systemic breakdown (i.e. a chain reaction of bad debts leading to mass insolvency). This does not mean that no bank is now allowed to fail and go into liquidation, but that where its losses are deemed large enough potentially to undermine a significant number of other institutions to which it owes money (often a highly subjective judgement, leaving ample scope for abuse) the authorities will provide sufficient liquidity to prevent this happening.

Since 1945 the presence of this safety net has come to be taken for granted by the entire financial community, many of whose members have been encouraged to regard it as an essential public service whose validity no reasonable person would question – any more than they would the benefits of police or fire services. This view has, moreover, been sanctified by the most authoritative sources, including the following unequivocal pronouncement from the OECD itself: 'A continuous supervisory role for the state in the area of commercial banking occurs because banks and their liabilities are seen as special. They are special because they have the attributes of public goods. Money is the means of payment in a capitalist economy … and in order to preserve systemic stability confidence in the institutions that hold these liabilities is a public policy necessity.'[5]

Until the 1970s the potential danger implied by such a state guarantee of the banking system was hardly an issue, such was the sustained stability of the banking system in an era of seemingly endless growth. Moreover, such complacency at the implicit under-writing of the banking system by the taxpayer was reinforced by the widespread practice, most conspicuously and successfully applied under the Marshall Plan, of using state guarantees or subsidies to loans to give selective support to investments deemed too risky or unprofitable to attract straight commercial finance.

This view of the government's role in supporting the financial system perhaps came most naturally to the countries of continental Europe, where a high proportion of banks were in any case owned by the state – largely a legacy of the banking disasters of the 1930s – while in Japan such corporatism was an even stronger tradition, dating from the earliest years of the country's economic modernisation in the late nineteenth century. Yet scarcely a critical voice was raised anywhere – even in the United States – and least of all from big business itself, the major beneficiary of this new wonder tranquillising drug.

Strikingly the metaphor of addiction in relation to state support is the one most commonly used by the political agents of big business to disparage the negative economic and social consequences alleged to flow from the creation of the welfare state. Yet what they are, naturally enough, unable to come to terms with is the reality that this 'dependency culture' not only pervades the whole of the modern capitalist world economy, but that it is at once both indispensable to its survival and ultimately unaffordable.

As with the guarantee to provide social security to all citizens, the acceptance by governments of this liability to support the financial system was made on the implicit assumption that the costs involved in periodically bailing it out would never be so great that they could not be recouped from future tax revenues. In other words it was really viewed as another 'stabiliser' in terms of the Keynesian model of economic management, in that it would help to limit the severity of recessions and sustain long-term high economic growth, thereby effectively paying for itself. Yet just as in the case of the social-security commitment, no allowance was ever made for the possibility that this ability to assure virtually everlasting growth might prove an illusion. Thus it was (and largely remains) implicit in such thinking that the capacity of the state to run up debts by way of underwriting the improvidence of the financial sector was more or less limitless. Indeed this assumption that the solvency of governments may be taken for granted is still enshrined in the international Basle Accord on the solvency criteria for commercial banks, under which 'sovereign debt' (i.e. lending to governments) need not be counted in calculating the limit on banks' overall capacity to lend.

Likewise in this period of 'the economics of euphoria' little consideration was given to an inherent problem associated with such official guarantees to bank finances – that of 'moral hazard'. This was the technical term used to denote the danger that financial institutions would be willing and able to lend money for highly risky and speculative investments in the knowledge that, if successful, they stood to make large profits, but that in the event of failure the taxpayer could probably be made to bear the equally spectacular losses. Worse still, such a guarantee was bound to attract the interest of deliberate fraudsters and ultimately of organised crime.

As long as the prolonged post-war boom continued, such concerns could reasonably be viewed as minor, since it was still relatively easy for banks and investors to make satisfactory profits without either incurring undue risk or resorting to fraud. Consequently any losses resulting from failure to apply proper prudential standards could generally be absorbed by banks without the need for an official bail-out. Yet as the good times drew to an end in the early 1970s the orgy of speculative investment in real estate, shipping and commodities might have suggested that such unconcern was no longer justified. Certainly the subsequent secondary banking crises of 1974 in Europe, requiring significant central bank intervention to prevent them engulfing larger institutions, should have left no one in any doubt of the long-term threat to the industrialised world's economic health posed by the commitment of governments to underwrite the balance sheets of unaccountable financial institutions.

A handful of commentators did indeed draw attention to this danger even in the 1970s.[6] Yet it is hardly surprising that their cries of alarm made little impact at a time when there was still an understandable inability in official circles to contemplate the possibility that the rapid growth of the 1950s and 1960s might be a thing of the past. More telling still, perhaps, was the realisation that any remedial action would have required either subjecting the banking sector to much tighter official control and supervision (which was unacceptable to the leaders of the politically powerful financial community) or else to leave it exposed to the potentially ruinous currents of the untrammelled marketplace (which was unacceptable to just about everybody).

What is more remarkable is that, so far from seeking to impose greater restraints on bankers in this more volatile economic climate, governments were subsequently (in the 1980s) induced to remove many of the existing ones. A detailed account of how and why this happened, and of its wider consequences for the world economy, is reserved for the next chapter. But its significance in relation to the ever rising burden to taxpayers of their involuntary commitment to indemnify the banks against their own greed is now obvious, if only with hindsight.

The most notorious of the numerous state-financed rescues of bankrupt financial institutions in the OECD countries since the beginning of the 1980s was that of the US Savings and Loan corporations. Officially the cost to the US taxpayer of bailing out depositors caught up in this fiasco was around $100 billion. However, it would undoubtedly be a much higher figure if one included the covert subsidies provided by the government (with the assistance of the central bank) to the whole financial sector in the early 1990s, when it issued government debt to banks and other institutions at an effective discount to its market worth, thus enabling the institutions to make abnormally high margins on the deposits received from the public. Similar methods were used by the British authorities to help restore bank balance sheets damaged by plummeting asset values during this period.

In contrast to the Savings and Loan affair in the USA, the use of public money in Norway, Sweden and Finland to save a number of major banks in 1991–92 – amounting to de facto nationalisation – was much less politically controversial (even though the cost was proportionately much higher), probably thanks to the more corporatist tradition of the Scandinavian countries. More surprising, perhaps, is the fierce political resistance to similar bail-outs in Japan – a country with as strong a corporatist tendency as any – in response to the crippling bad debts afflicting most parts of the financial sector in the wake of speculative excesses in the late 1980s. It is noteworthy, however, that this opposition appears to be more a symptom of revulsion at the manifest corruption and criminality involved in inducing such mass insolvency than one of concern at the high cost, although this may ultimately prove even greater than that of the Savings and Loan rescue in the USA.

As this series of state-supported bail-outs unfolded, few remarked on the irony of this outcome to an experiment which had been proclaimed as a means of liberating the financial sector from the deadening consequences of state intervention. It did not, however, escape the notice of the supreme regulatory authority of the international banking system, the Bank for International Settlements, which drily observed that 'the experience of those countries in which a financial crisis has erupted indicates that ... deregulation may paradoxically lead to more, rather than less, government involvement.'[7]

The precise scale of the budgetary burden generated by these salvage operations – not to mention the contingent liabilities arising from the strong likelihood of even greater banking disasters in future – is almost impossible to estimate. Yet it is undoubtedly very large and hence should be a matter of major political concern in all industrialised countries. In most of them, however, the growing cost of the state underwriting the financial system, and thus ultimately the financial health of the corporate sector as a whole, is hardly allowed to be mentioned or quantified in contemporary public debate, let alone called seriously into question – in stark contrast to the official attitude to the swelling social welfare budget, and many other areas

of public spending which have also come to be regarded by beneficiaries as their established right. This omission, it might be thought,
is all the more culpable in that the problem is both bound to get
worse and yet is ultimately more preventable than the alleged one of
excess population (comprising both elderly and young unemployed)
which is identified as the main bugbear by most mainstream analysts.

Yet if maintaining the value of financial assets through bank bail-
outs is now increasingly burdensome to taxpayers, the long-term
consequences of doing so are scarcely more satisfactory for the
immediate beneficiaries, the members of the investor community
itself. This is because the continued high market value of stocks and
bonds resulting from this process requires the businesses which
support them to sustain a high rate of return in order to keep the
investment funds flowing in. In other words the refusal to allow the
value of assets to fall imposes an intensifying need to make them
'sweat' even in the face of chronic economic stagnation.

The result is never-ending pressure not merely to squeeze costs
and boost competitiveness within enterprises but to push up the share
of value added going to capital within the economy as a whole – or
in the last resort simply to fabricate higher profits through false
accounting. In the past, as Marxist analysis would remind us, the
business cycle would periodically have removed the necessity to do
this by forcing a crash in the financial markets and the eventual return
to more sustainable rates of return once asset values had stabilised
at a much lower level. The delusion of the post-1945 era has been
to suppose that the need to submit to such medicine can be avoided
by maintaining high growth rates more or less in perpetuity.

The Fiscal Crisis: Threat and Opportunity

The intensifying financial crises facing both the state and the private
corporate sector in the industrialised world are thus revealed to be
profoundly interrelated. In the absence of sufficient growth to meet
the escalating needs of the profit-hungry private sector the public
purse is being called on to fill the gap – whether through direct
subsidies to the profits of companies, making good the losses of
financial institutions which would otherwise fail, transfer payments
to the rising numbers of unemployed or underpaid members marginalised by the merciless cost squeeze, or otherwise offsetting the
collateral damage arising from the ever more desperate search for

shareholder value. Yet the same growth deficiency means the capacity of the state to meet these extra demands is rapidly dwindling, as the tax base stagnates or shrinks and it struggles to meet the demands made on it in relation to its more established functions (such as maintaining law and order or essential public infrastructure). Hence its ability to continue to meet the corporate sector's demands will depend on how far it can make the mass of the public (whether as taxpayers or users of public services) pay an increasing share of the rising cost burden. Obviously, however, it must be assumed there is a limit, both physical and political, to what can be tolerated, as informed opinion is starting to recognise.[8]

It thus seems inevitable that continued economic stagnation will sooner or later precipitate the effective bankruptcy of the state, leading rapidly to a financial crisis engulfing the private sector as well. In the short run, however, there is seen to be considerable scope for the private sector to turn the fiscal crisis of the state to its advantage. This it can do, paradoxically, by diverting its excess profits (i.e. the increasing proportion of total profit which cannot find a profitable investment outlet in the private sector) to meeting the shortfall in the state's own finances – even though this is ultimately almost bound to put the public finances in an even worse state as the taxpayer is obliged to meet the private investor's demand for return on capital. This is achieved through the private sector not only meeting governments' soaring borrowing requirements but providing infrastructure and services, which the state can no longer afford to do (the emerging pattern of this privatisation of the state is described in more detail in Chapter 8).

Obviously such an Alice-in-Wonderland arrangement cannot endure indefinitely. From a long-term capitalist perspective it could make sense to the extent that it reduces the net outgoings of the state in the short term – for example, through the sale and lease back of government offices – on the assumption that this will permit it to stave off bankruptcy pending the early revival of rapid economic growth. In practice, however, it is not to be expected that private companies whose overriding preoccupation is the short-term maximisation of shareholder value will show much restraint in extracting profits from the taxpayer in the interests of securing the long-term survival of the state.

In any event, however, there will be no escape from ultimate financial 'meltdown' – when, as frequently happens in Third World countries, governments are no longer able to borrow and people resort to barter rather than accept the official currency – unless there is some quite unforeseeable turnaround in the present dismal growth performance in the OECD countries. Given what now seems the receding prospect of such salvation (see Chapter 12), the behaviour of corporations and governments alike in face of this danger can at best be described as reckless.

To the extent that major political parties are aware of the real nature of the fundamental obstacles to the creation of sustainable economic security, as outlined in this chapter, it may be wondered why they have not developed more realistic strategies for overcoming them. Yet once it is appreciated that any such approach would entail a combination of greatly enhanced public accountability of the financial sector and massive redistribution of income and wealth, it becomes clear why the ruling vested interests prefer fantasy to reality. Hence we can expect that mainstream politicians and the institutions of organised capital which increasingly represent the former's main source of finance will continue to disregard these dangers unless and until disaster overwhelms them.

In evading the issue, however, these ruling interest groups have found it necessary – both psychologically and politically – to adopt often contradictory positions which combine wishful thinking with a bizarre rewriting of history. Thus on the one hand they maintain the belief, at least in their public pronouncements, that growth will eventually revive – not in spite but because of the counter-inflationary policies which they have promoted – and thus simultaneously resolve the problems of low returns on assets and the budgetary burden of the welfare state. Yet at the same time there is a propensity to suggest that the real culprit is the political self-indulgence of the post-war generation in convincing the public that perpetual growth and continually rising living standards could be guaranteed for virtually everyone. Meanwhile, of course, the one central reality that these same groups can never face is the inescapable dependency of big business on the state.

Such massive self-deception is a further illustration of the fundamental fraud at the heart of the neo-orthodox prospectus. The same tendency to double-think may perhaps explain the shrill insistence on ever more sweeping measures of liberalisation – in the apparent belief that by being thus forced to tighten their belts and become more competitive the vast majority of people will ultimately be made more prosperous. The consequences of applying, or purporting to apply, this theory to the real world of the 1980s and 1990s are examined in the next chapter.

Notes

1. E.J. Hobsbawm, *Industry and Empire*, volume 3 of *The Pelican Economic History of Britain*, Penguin, Harmondsworth 1969; A. Shonfield, *Modern Capitalism*, Oxford University Press, Oxford 1965.

2. Hobsbawm, *Industry and Empire*; W.M. Scammel, *The International Economy since 1945*, Macmillan, London 1980.

3. Or earlier if one includes the isolated case of the Baring's crisis in 1890, resolved by a Bank of England bail-out.

4. This upper limit has been set at $100,000 since 1984.

5. OECD, *Regulatory Reform in the Financial Services Industry. Where Have We Been? Where Are We Going?* Financial Market Trends No. 67, June 1997.

6. See M. Mayer, *The Bankers*, George Allen & Unwin, London 1976.

7. Bank for International Settlements, Annual Report 1993.

8. George Monbiot, 'Scroungers', *Guardian*, 21 January 1998.

6

Globalisation
and the Power Vacuum

As already noted, the principal reason for the inability of governments to put their own neo-orthodox rhetoric into practice in the 1980s was the danger of precipitating a collapse of the securities markets, leading to a catastrophic financial crisis. Indeed this problem, combined with that of the inexorable flow of new investment funds looking for an outlet, induced the authorities to liberalise the financial markets to such an extent that the application of genuine financial orthodoxy (which would have required the full exposure of failed banks to market forces) was rendered more inconceivable than ever. On the contrary, given that the virtual guarantee of state underwriting of the financial system was still in place, the stage was set for a global outbreak of imprudent lending by banking institutions.

Under the influence of the Thatcher government in Britain and the Reagan administration in the USA, there was progressively in the 1980s a general acceptance of the rhetoric of liberalisation and deregulation, even though the extent of real commitment to it – as reflected in actual policy changes – varied considerably from country to country. Yet in all cases not only were restrictions on the movement of capital across national borders substantially eased or removed through the relaxation of foreign exchange controls; at the same time, and largely as a consequence of the increased need for national capital markets to compete for and retain footloose investment funds because of the ending of exchange controls, previously tight restrictions on the activities of banks were generally relaxed.

Banking Deregulation

Indeed one inevitable consequence of the removal of exchange controls was the end of quantitative restrictions on bank lending by national governments, since borrowers could now simply borrow from abroad if any limits were placed on lending by domestic banks. It is true that banks were in theory required to limit their lending to a given ratio of their capital. However, in response to international competitive pressures this restraint also was effectively relaxed by central banks' agreeing – under the aegis of their collective organisation, the Bank for International Settlements – to more flexible definitions of a bank's capital (for example, by including certain assets such as equity investments in the total).

At the same time the ability of banks in many countries to engage in different areas of business with the minimum of supervision was greatly enhanced. In particular, deposit-taking institutions were allowed much greater freedom to put their funds into securities – from which they had previously been largely barred, at least in Britain and the United States – and other potentially more risky forms of investment than the secured loans for enterprises and individuals which had traditionally been their main activity. The pressure for them to be allowed to do this stemmed from a combination of the intensifying competitive forces in the industrialised economies since the late 1960s and the growing sophistication of financial markets. These factors led larger corporations with relatively strong balance sheets to seek to reduce their borrowing costs by raising loan capital through the issue of bonds and other forms of commercial paper rather than the more traditional but also more expensive method of borrowing from banks. This process of 'disintermediation' tended to hit commercial banks by taking away much of their most profitable business and leaving them only the less secure and hence less profitable clients.

It was thus natural that the major commercial banks should demand to be allowed to engage in other areas of investment where the risks might be greater but the rewards higher. These included not only dealing in all kinds of financial assets and instruments (including some newly developed and highly leveraged[1] ones such as options and other derivatives, which some of their senior executives seem barely to have understood),[2] but the lucrative business of corporate mergers and takeovers which had traditionally been the preserve of merchant or investment banks. As a result of the Financial Services Act enacted by the British government in 1986 the barriers to combining these activities in the same organisation were removed in the UK, although in theory potential conflicts of interest which might arise in fulfilling the different roles were precluded by the establishment of 'Chinese walls' (invisible barriers) between, for example, their investment and deposit-taking arms.

Thus it was tacitly accepted – forgetting both the disasters of the unregulated banking industry in the 1930s and the continuing commitment of the state to underwrite the financial system as a 'public good' – that banks could after all be treated as profit-maximising enterprises just like any other corporation. Hence, for all the supposed safeguards and the authorities' promises of continuing strict supervision, banks were able to put their depositors' funds at risk to a far greater degree than before while still enjoying the same implicit guarantees of state support in the event of threatened insolvency. Moreover, the degree of moral hazard involved was intensified by the incentive given to banking executives – in the shape of profit-related bonuses – to present the most positive view of their accounts by deliberately underproviding against potential bad loans.

Nowhere was the corrupting effect of these pressures more disastrously manifested than in the United States in the 1980s. The most notable example of this was that of the Savings and Loan institutions – organisations originally created, like Britain's building societies, to provide loan finance for housing. In the permissive financial climate of the Reagan era, however, they were deregulated and thereby enabled to embark on much more speculative investments with little restraint from the responsible regulators.[3] Such was the unrealism and irresponsibility of the latter that they even allowed a number of these 'thrifts' to continue taking and investing deposits after they had become technically insolvent in the downturn of 1990–92, ostensibly in the hope that their non-performing assets would miraculously regain their face value. Given that it was obvious by then that a significant proportion of the lending involved was less the result of profligacy than of deliberate fraud, and that some of the institutions had even been infiltrated by organised crime, such insouciance seems astounding. It none the less epitomised the problem of moral hazard and a financial system which was aptly summed up by the statement of one contemporary US banker that 'in this country the best way to rob a bank is to own one'.

Speculative Excesses

The increasing pressure on financial institutions and investors to find outlets for their funds in speculative assets, combined with the growing laxity in the supervision of banking and securities markets, had other equally damaging consequences. Most notable among these in the 1980s was the practice on the part of certain major investors – often with the backing of one or more large banking institutions – of buying a large block of shares in a major quoted company with the ostensible intention of mounting a takeover bid. Such moves, typically accompanied by a public-relations campaign denigrating the competence of the company's management and suggesting that a takeover could lead to significant enhancement of shareholder value, often resulted in a marked increase in the share price of the company 'in play'. However, in many such cases the putative bidders would then indicate to the directors of the target company their willingness to withdraw their bid on condition that the company would agree to buy back their (the bidders') shareholding at the newly inflated price.

It should be noted that an indispensable element of such deals was the ability of companies to buy back their own shares, something which had been greatly facilitated by regulatory changes in the early 1980s, in both the United States and Britain, easing restrictions on what had previously been effectively outlawed as a manipulative practice. Furthermore the process was typically aided by the offer of a loan (from one of the institutions backing the bidder) to finance the repurchase. Since the besieged directors had a natural inclination to avoid such a takeover – which could well be expected to cost them their well-paid and powerful positions – they were usually disposed to succumb to such 'greenmail', even if to do so might not obviously have been in the interests of their shareholders or the long-term health of the company. Moreover, in certain cases where there was serious resistance by the company to the idea of accepting the offer of a loan to buy back the shares, it was not unknown for the banks involved to threaten to lend the money instead to other potential predators. Such extortion is notably said to have occurred in the case of the assault by greenmailers on United Airlines in 1989.[4]

For some time in the 1980s public opinion, influenced by a largely complaisant financial press, was prepared to accept the self-image of these 'corporate raiders' as defenders of the interests of shareholders (and indeed of the public at large) against ineffective company managements.[5] Yet it has become progressively harder to defend such deals as serving the long-term interests of the companies concerned or of the economy as a whole. In the vast majority of such cases, indeed, it can scarcely be claimed that they amount to more than either (a) the manipulation of asset values with a view to short-term speculative profit or (b) a stratagem whereby financial institutions compel non-financial companies to give them back a share of their value added – thus reversing the effect of disintermediation.

In any event the long-term viability of companies is often threatened by the resulting big increase in their total borrowings, particularly where this reflects a substantial overvaluation of the assets relative to their underlying capacity for generating earnings. This is because the increased proportion of debt on the balance sheet intensifies the pressure to squeeze yet higher margins from the existing assets in order to service the increased debt. Even if this does not jeopardise necessary long-term fixed investment, it is almost invariably at the expense of the employees, who increasingly lack the bargaining power to resist the parallel downward pressure both on their wages and on the size of the workforce. (Moreover, as Keynesians would correctly observe, it tends to damage the 'macro-economy' by intensifying the squeeze on the purchasing power of consumers at the lower end of the income scale.)

Another factor which undoubtedly lent impetus to the growth of speculative investment was the advance of technology in the field of telecommunications. This made possible the instantaneous buying and selling of securities by traders dealing with their counterparts anywhere in the world, and the equally rapid international movement of money by means of Electronic Funds Transfer. In the newly deregulated financial markets this meant that huge fortunes could be won and lost in the space of a few minutes. Naturally this attracted the attention both of profit-hungry investors and companies and of the most highly qualified members of the labour force, who could expect very large remuneration as successful market traders. Their perception that the gains were likely to far exceed the losses was bolstered by the brief coincidence in the 1984–88 period of low inflation and rapid growth in the major Western economies, which lent plausibility to the claims of the ascendant political ideologues that *laissez-faire* economic policies could and would deliver a sustained economic boom. Such over-optimism only served to fuel the flames of speculative excess and thereby generate the huge burden of bad debts which was to cripple the global economy in the 1990s.

It may be noted that a significant consequence of these often damaging tendencies in the 1980s was to call in question the right of a handful of speculators and corporate directors to determine the fate of enterprises on which the livelihoods of many thousands, if not millions, may depend – often without even the shareholders being able to hold them to account. This was later to give rise to a wider debate, not only in the United States, over the whole question of 'corporate governance', as the public became increasingly conscious of the enormous power and negligible accountability of the chief executives and boards of directors of giant corporations.

Anarchy in the Foreign Exchange Markets

The clamorous pursuit of opportunities for profitable speculation has led investors into other fields where their activities have inflicted damage on the real economy. Undoubtedly the fastest growing of these has been the foreign exchange market, where the liberalisation of cross-border capital movements had a particularly significant impact. Hence the global volume of business rose over tenfold in constant value terms between the early 1980s and the mid-1990s – to a level estimated at no less than $1,500 billion *a day* by 1995.[6] Its attractions for investing institutions – particularly commercial banks – are obvious, since it involves dealing in the most liquid of all assets (cash), of which they are bound in any case to hold large quantities and which can be placed in interest-bearing deposits for very short periods.

Yet the sheer scale of the funds involved now dwarfs the volume of reserves at the disposal of governments and central banks seeking to intervene in the market in order to stabilise currency values. This means individual states are increasingly powerless to resist any concerted move by speculators (or even an isolated initiative by one of the larger ones) to push down the value of their currencies. The negative consequences of this situation for the economy as a whole stem from the rigid commitment to low inflation and the consequently tight monetary policy (based on relatively high official interest rates) which are needed to induce speculators to hold a particular national currency and thus maintain the market's confidence in the sustainability of its exchange rate.

Clearly the greater a country's acceptance of financial liberalisation and its consequent exposure to the whims of the foreign exchange markets the more vulnerable it will be to such pressures. No government has more cause to be aware of this than that of Britain, which since the mid-1980s has been continually torn between its aim of achieving greater price stability at home and the need at the same time to maintain the international competitiveness of its suppliers of goods and services. Yet, as it found in 1989 and again in 1997, the relatively high interest rates often required to achieve the former tend to undermine the attempt to secure the latter, leading first to an overvaluation of sterling and then to its collapse once the foreign exchange markets have recognised that the high parity was unsustainable – the end result being a very sharp credit squeeze imposed by the even higher interest rates needed to protect the currency.

Such negative side-effects of the attempt to combine tight control of inflation with monetary and financial deregulation have often appeared to take the authorities in Britain and other affected countries by surprise. If this is so it is perhaps because they have failed to appreciate the extent to which foreign exchange speculation has been transformed into a huge investment business, with major market players able to make big profits very quickly and thus achieve astronomic rates of return. In fact the scale of the funds invested in the foreign exchange markets is reflected in the immense importance this business now has for many financial institutions. Thus the profits from currency dealing now make a substantial contribution to the profits of banks and have greatly assisted the recovery of a number of them following their huge losses on bad loans at the start of the 1990s. This trend has led to another growing point of conflict, particularly in Europe, between the interests of the financial sector and those of the wider business community supplying goods and non-financial services. For increasingly the former has become identified with the political tendency opposing moves towards Economic and Monetary Union, set to culminate in the introduction of a single currency for the European Union in 1999 under the terms of the Maastricht Treaty. Undoubtedly an important reason for this – although naturally not one of those openly cited by opponents of EMU – is that the disappearance of national currencies in Europe would also mean the elimination of the present scope for profitable 'arbitrage' (the polite term for speculation) in this segment of the foreign exchange market, thus hitting banks' profits. By the same token, of course, it would be beneficial to the rest of the corporate sector, which presently has to pay the substantial costs of hedging the currency risks on intra-European trade – costs which obviously have to be passed on to the public at large.

Offshore Financial Centres

Yet perhaps the most telling demonstration of the growing impotence of nation-states in the new 'global economy' of the electronic age since the late 1970s has been the mushrooming of 'offshore' financial centres, better known as tax havens. A relatively small number of these (including Liechtenstein, the Channel Islands, Bermuda and Luxembourg) had existed for many years, providing an opportunity for wealthy individuals to escape high levels of taxation in their country of residence while providing a basis for economic activity in small states where there was otherwise little scope for it. As such they had no major distorting impact either on international capital flows or on the revenues of other national governments, particularly in an era when there were still quite severe constraints on international capital movements, and the speed with which funds could be transferred was also slow.

From the late 1960s, however, demand for and supply of such facilities began to grow at an accelerating pace. This was a function of many different factors, the most important of which initially was the huge increase in international flows of corporate funds stemming from the growth of transnational corporations. At the same time there was a big rise in the number of nominally sovereign states, stemming from the wholesale granting of independence to European colonies in Asia, Africa and elsewhere during the 1960s and 1970s. Many of these new 'nations' were either not economically strong enough to resist pressure from foreign-owned companies to allow them to move capital in and out at will or else were subject to lax and corrupt administration. Other such states – notably in the Caribbean and the South Pacific – were so small that they found it convenient to convert themselves into tax havens as one of the few means of generating economic activity open to them. Likewise in a number of territories which have remained under colonial rule (such as the Cayman Islands and the Netherlands Antilles), the authorities saw it as a useful way of creating a source of revenue to support the local administration at a time when financial support from the metropolitan power was becoming harder to obtain.

A still bigger boost to this phenomenon was provided by the liberalising tendency of the 1980s, which was also accompanied by an intensification in the search for new sources of income by smaller nations, many of which (e.g. Cyprus) set up small offshore financial enclaves within their boundaries – often as an adjunct to tax-free zones aimed at attracting manufacturing investment or warehousing operations geared to export. The result was a doubling in the number of such tax havens since the early 1970s to 128 in 1997.[7] Combined with provisions of banking secrecy, they attracted not only companies and individuals seeking to evade tax but every other kind of fraudster and the proceeds of organised crime.

The Triumph of Short-termism

Whether by promoting or simply acquiescing in these successive moves to deregulation and loss of control over big business, governments effectively connived at their own emasculation. It is striking, moreover, that in doing so they contrived to inflict additional wounds on a real economy already bleeding from the consequences of declining growth rates and rising public indebtedness which had appeared in the 1970s. For the increased freedom of capital to move anywhere in the world in pursuit of the highest return inevitably added still further to the pressures on the corporate sector generally to extract more and more profit from their investments, thus making it all the more difficult to justify putting funds into projects which would create jobs rather than destroy them.

Indeed a survey of British corporate attitudes in the early 1990s revealed a striking response to these trends. This was that boards of directors were unwilling to sanction any new investment which did not indicate a potential return of at least 20 per cent a year – far higher than the levels considered acceptable in the early 1970s, when inflation was on average also much higher (so that the difference in real terms was greater still). This discovery evidently came as a shock to some ministers in the Conservative government, prompting them to urge companies to adopt a more flexible attitude in the interests of securing a higher national growth rate. This in turn brought an understandable retort from one of their leading supporters among the fraternity of corporate dealmakers, Lord Hanson, to the effect that the government had better remember its *laissez-faire* principles and not try to influence the market-determined investment decisions of big business.

Such attitudes are symptomatic of a growing, and much criticised, tendency to 'short-termism' on the part of the corporate sector, particularly in the Anglo-Saxon countries, leading enterprises to concentrate on obtaining a high rate of return on capital in the short run even at the expense of their long-term profitability and security. Yet this tendency is all too understandable in a climate where corporate predators and speculators stand ready to take advantage of any development or management decision which may create an opportunity for short-term arbitrage (or a 'quick killing', as it is called in the vernacular). Since any sizeable fixed capital investment, such as the building of a new factory, is liable to depress corporate earnings in the early years of the project – thus potentially leading to a reduced stock-market rating – it is not surprising that many company boards shy away from thus exposing themselves to the threat of a hostile takeover.

A striking expression of the way this perspective has permeated the whole investor community is the increasing tendency for good news about the real economy – such as a rise in output or a fall in unemployment – to provoke a negative reaction on the stock and bond markets, and conversely. This is because a depressed level of activity is viewed as portending low or falling interest rates, and hence a general rise in the price of stocks – even though it must imply worse financial results in due course for the businesses underlying those stocks. Nothing could better illustrate the growing obsession – especially in the United States and Britain – with short-term speculative gain at the expense of longer-term viability.

While any attempt by governments to persuade the corporate sector to resist market forces and moderate its tendency to short-term profit maximisation typically evokes a chorus of outrage from captains of industry and finance, few such rebukes have met the frequent decisions of Western governments to use the state's scarce fiscal resources to subsidise investments by TNCs so as to bring the returns up to levels the latter are prepared to accept. Such deviations from market logic are always justified on the basis that otherwise the investment would be made in another country, to the detriment of domestic employment and the balance of payments. Not infrequently, moreover, insult is added to injury by a refusal – on the grounds of 'commercial confidentiality' – to inform the taxpayers how much of their money has been spent for this purpose (as, for instance, in the case of a number of investments by Far Eastern electronics companies in Britain in the 1990s).

The strength of the pressure on national governments to humour big business is likewise reflected in a tendency to push down rates of corporate taxation in an effort to attract or retain employment-generating investment – a trend which is also mirrored in a general 'race to the bottom' in terms of lowered standards of company and financial regulation. Despite some expressions of concern at the self-defeating nature of this 'tax competition', it is scarcely surprising that there have been no serious steps towards international harmonisation of tax rates – even within the European Union as it supposedly moves to create a single market.

In fact the weight of official opinion is still clearly convinced that the primary duty of government in the global economy is to prop up corporate profits at all costs despite the demonstrable reality of a surplus supply of capital. The perception of the banking community that this is still the case is reflected in their willingness to lend money to the corporate sector on finer terms (i.e. narrower margins) than ever, notwithstanding their huge loan losses at the end of the 1980s. The clear implication is that they are as confident as ever of being rescued by a state bail-out in the event of another major threat to their solvency – or that in any event senior executives of financial institutions are so mesmerised by the huge potential bonuses they stand to gain from successful speculation that there is little incentive for them to exercise caution. Yet despite the authorities' continuing commitment to the principle of thus publicly underwriting the ever higher profit demands of the corporate sector, there are clear signs of nervousness. Thus early in 1995 both the Bank of England and the US Comptroller of the Currency felt constrained to warn banks against lending to large companies at dangerously thin margins.

The feebleness of such exhortations in face of the monster created by the combination of deregulation and guarantees from the public lender of last resort are mirrored in the ever more conspicuous impotence of intergovernmental bodies. Perhaps the most glaring example of this weakness is provided by the Group of Seven (G7) industrialised countries, whose leaders have now been meeting annually ever since 1975 to discuss ways of coping with their common economic problems. Seen in a historical perspective the inaugural date is significant, as it marks the point at which the leadership of the industrialised West clearly acknowledged that the postwar economic certainties were at an end. Yet it also surely reflects the residual existence in the 1970s of a Keynesian belief in the efficacy of action by national governments, concerted or otherwise, to avert recession and otherwise influence the course of economic development – a perception which now seems positively quaint after twenty years of global liberalisation.

In fact almost their only concerted actions over the years have been precisely those designed to dismantle the few instruments of control previously available to them (such as those over cross-border capital movements). On the occasions when they are moved to express concern about the damaging consequences of the growth in money laundering, corruption and organised crime, nobody ever points out that the G7 have the collective power to close down the offshore finance centres which play such a large part in facilitating these activities. Instead their meetings have been reduced to nothing but exercises in platitudinous exhortation based on spurious economics – such as urging the need to hold down wages, reduce public spending and thereby curb inflation as the essential prerequisites to reviving economic growth.

Given the manifest futility of these conclaves, it is perhaps surprising that they have not been abandoned as damaging demonstrations of the incapacity of governments, both collectively and severally, to take effective remedial action against chronic economic failure. However, the fact that this has not happened may reflect a view that actually to terminate the ritual would be an even bigger public-relations disaster, signifying in most people's eyes not only a confession of helplessness but an abdication of responsibility.

Superficially the European Union has made more positive progress towards the goal of effective supranational action in economic policy. However, as the member states have all since the early 1980s been induced to fall in line with the prevailing ideology favouring reduced state power and global liberalisation, they have effectively negated the potential benefits of pooled national sovereignty. A good example of this is the approach to achieving Economic and Monetary Union (EMU), referred to above. Since it has been agreed that members can only adhere to EMU, involving adoption of the Single Currency, if they reduce their budget deficits to a level deemed compatible with low inflation – and hence currency stability – and since that level (as noted above) is now determined by the all-powerful currency speculators, the commitment to EMU has willy-nilly locked the whole Community into a downward spiral of deflation and low growth.

The failure of OECD governments not only to act cohesively in seeking to strengthen their collective capacity to deal with their deepening common economic problem but to resist a weakening of their existing power to act even at national level calls for some explanation. In fact, it may be concluded that the chronic stagnation and resulting fiscal weakness which set in during the 1970s confronted all of them with a stark choice by the early 1980s. This was either to adopt a far more interventionist strategy than previously – involving a combination of more direct state involvement in the productive sectors of the economy and much higher taxes – or else to reduce the role of the state, stabilise or reduce taxes, and trust in the private sector's capacity to deliver recovery. Given the balance of political forces, and particularly the continuing disproportionate influence of big business over all governments, it was inevitable that the former option would find little favour.

On the other hand, as already noted, bearing in mind the rising expectations of the mass of voters engendered by the post-war boom and the increased dependence of the business community on state support, it was not to be expected that a radical rolling back of the frontiers of the state could be undertaken without running serious risks, both political and economic. Hence for the most part the switch to reduced state involvement in the economy has occurred on a piecemeal basis – by way of sudden, unplanned reactions to new fiscal or monetary crises – rather than being driven by any vision of an ideal *laissez-faire* state. Indeed it is probably true that most of the governments responsible for implementing these changes (even those of the centre-right such as that led by the CDU in Germany) have been reluctant to do so and that they have continued to hope that any really radical change could be avoided.

It is likewise possible to construe most of the measures taken to liberalise markets – while yet continuing to protect and subsidise major banks and other large corporations – purely as a succession of ad hoc responses to the desperate need to sustain the profits of the corporate sector at all costs, especially in view of the potentially catastrophic consequences for the world financial system of failing to do so. On the other hand, it must have become obvious – at least by around 1990 – to all but the most bigoted adherents of *laissez-faire* ideology that liberalisation offered no better prospect of reviving growth in the industrialised world than the exhausted theories of Keynes. It is thus perhaps not fanciful to suppose that a more politically drastic, longer-term strategy has begun to evolve designed to reconcile the voting public with the prospect of a much bleaker future.

This possibility is indicated by the widespread tendency in public discourse to suggest that the deregulated global economy is a fact of life – if not a God-given phenomenon – the influence of which no country or group of countries can ultimately escape.[8] From this it would perhaps be but a short step to reviving Adam Smith's notion of the Invisible Hand guiding the economic destiny of nations beyond any human power of control. The successful dissemination of such a perception would clearly be highly valuable to political leaders seeking to lower expectations among the public, which to date remains obstinately attached to the idea of the welfare state and a social 'safety net' ensuring tolerable minimum living standards for all.

If such is really the aim of Western leaders and their corporate paymasters, it may be doubted if they could ever succeed in so drastically reshaping public perceptions – at least under anything resembling democracy. For to do so they will need to explain to the mass of voters why the promises of perpetually rising living standards – which were honoured so consistently for a generation up to the mid-1970s, and which were also part of the prospectus on which Thatcherism, Reaganomics and kindred liberalising doctrines were sold to the public – have ultimately proved empty. This task will be made all the harder by the ever more conspicuous contrast between the stagnating or falling living standards of a growing proportion of the population and the fabulously high (and lightly taxed) incomes of the tiny minority who constitute the core of the dominant economic interest group. In such circumstances exhortations to the mass of the population to accept a steady decline in real income levels towards those of, say, Thailand (involving real cuts in earnings of 70–80 per cent) seem unlikely to be accepted by Western electorates.

Indeed the question now facing the governments of the industrialised countries is, rather, how long they can maintain public belief in the ability of the capitalist system eventually to restore acceptable economic conditions and dispel the climate of spreading insecurity and deprivation. Yet a realistic attempt to address this issue, shorn of the hysterical rhetoric of post-Cold War triumphalism, would also have to confront another equally compelling reality. This is the emergence of such fundamental changes in the pattern of economic activity in the industrialised world, as a result of technological innovation, that the traditional capitalist model will no longer be relevant to its needs.

Notes

1. In other words, involving a potential risk exposure several times that of the sums initially put up. Hence these investments are similar to the practice of 'trading on margin' (i.e. with borrowed money) which played such a ruinous part in the bubble that precipitated the Wall Street crash of 1929.

2. As revealed by the sensational collapse of the London-based Baring's merchant bank in 1995.

3. Commercial banks were still denied such latitude under the terms of a law (the Glass-Steagall Act) which was enacted in 1933 precisely to prevent the banking calamity stemming from the speculative excesses of the late 1920s from being repeated. However, political pressure from the banking industry to have this law repealed has been persistent since the early 1980s and may well succeed, particularly if the Republican Party gains control of both Congress and the White House.

4. The deal in this case did not initially stem from a takeover, but took the form of a 'leveraged buy-out' (LBO), where the management of the airline were pressurised by banks into borrowing $7 billion (double its market worth six months earlier – in a highly cyclical and competitive business) to buy back all the public equity and thus convert it into a private company (Anatole Kaletsky, 'The Lure of the Roller-coaster', *Financial Times*, 20 September 1989).

5. This is not to deny that the boards of many of the target companies were often all too deserving of criticism.

6. This figure exceeds the *annual* gross domestic product of all but three of the world's countries. While it certainly overstates the total volume of funds invested in the market (since a large proportion is turned over more than once in a day), it is still an indicator of the enormous growth in the volume of surplus capital available for investment around the world.

7. C. Doggart, *Tax Havens and Their Uses*, The Economist Intelligence Unit, London 1997.

8. See L. Thurow, *The Future of Capitalism*, Nicholas Brealey Publishers, London 1996.

7

Technological Nemesis

The preceding chapters have traced the origin and impact of some of the major influences tending to undermine the long-term sustainability of the capitalist system. All of these factors could be described as intrinsic to the system itself, in that their negative impact stems from its inherent tendency to generate an imbalance between the underlying demand for goods and services and the need for ever more outlets for profitable investment. Moreover, it has been suggested that in the absence of some spontaneous revival of the average rate of economic growth – to levels as least as high as those attained in the 1950s and 1960s – it will ultimately be impossible to avoid a global collapse in asset values, and hence of corporate enterprises, on an unprecedented scale.

The prevalence of these negative forces is of itself enough to cast doubt on the system's long-term acceptability to an industrialised world which has come to demand minimum levels of stability and security for the mass of the population. Yet these weaknesses are now being compounded by another profoundly destabilising influence. This is the accelerated technological change which is being experienced in the late twentieth century to a degree not seen since the advent of steam power ushered in the Industrial Revolution some two hundred years ago. This phenomenon is mainly associated with advances in electronics, commonly known as the information technology revolution.

It is already widely recognised that this development has been a major factor – combined with the intensifying competitive pressures experienced since the late 1960s – behind a sharp slowdown in the growth of demand for labour in the industrialised world in the closing decades of the twentieth century. As such it has been frequently referred to as a new industrial revolution, comparable in its disruptive impact on the labour force to the original industrial and agricultural revolutions of the late eighteenth and early nineteenth centuries. What is scarcely perceived at all – perhaps because it is without precedent – is that the new technology is having a comparable impact on demand for the other productive factor which has traditionally contested with labour for the spoils of capitalism, namely capital itself. This is happening, moreover, at a time when the global supply of both labour and capital is continuing to rise inexorably.

The startling implication of this twin trend is that, just as the final triumph of capitalism over feudalism in the nineteenth century was made inevitable by a technological revolution which greatly increased the demand for capital, so capitalism itself is now on the point of becoming outmoded because of a comparable technological upheaval which is weakening the demand for capital. One of the ironies of this development is that it has been driven to a great extent by state-financed research and development programmes (notably in the USA). Most of these were originally intended to further national defence interests,[1] although latterly such support has come to be viewed by governments as essential to the enhancement of national competitiveness in the global contest among Western industrialised nations for markets and jobs. This process, involving also the subsidisation of R&D programmes undertaken by private corporations in most sectors of the economy, has inevitably added to the competitive forces making for reduced costs, particularly of labour. At the same time it has spawned the development of new products serving as outlets for new investment, even though often these have simply served to displace existing ones fulfilling the same consumer demands.

To gain a fuller understanding of these epoch-making developments we must look more closely at the recent pattern of global utilisation of both these factors of production.

1. Labour Devalued

The problem of high and rising levels of unemployment has been a major preoccupation of governments in the industrialised world, particularly European ones, at least since the late 1970s. Prior to that point, for virtually the whole post-war period, it had been almost unanimously assumed that the problem of unemployment had been largely solved in the OECD countries, in that it appeared possible to sustain rates of economic growth, more or less indefinitely, at levels which permitted the absorption of the gently expanding adult population into the labour market. Consequently in that period the only issue for governments was to determine what should be considered the proper definition of full employment – typically deemed to correspond to an unemployment rate of 2–3 per cent of the workforce – so that policy could be directed at not exceeding this in order to avoid creating labour shortages and thus inflationary pressures.

During the decade of the 1970s itself, unemployment rates had begun to rise, approximately doubling in the OECD countries – from 3 to 6 per cent – in the course of the decade. However, the weight of official opinion, reflecting that of most economists, was that this could be regarded as a cyclical rather than a structural problem. In other words, it was the result of a temporary recession (albeit of rather longer duration than the occasional downturns experienced in the 1950s and 1960s) and could be reversed as economies resumed a more 'normal' growth path, something that it was assumed would be brought about through spontaneous recovery, assisted by the judicious application of the Keynesian tools of state intervention which were perceived to have been the essential buttress of post-war success.

It is a striking measure of the dogmatic attachment to this view, which still prevailed up to the early 1980s, that many academic and other economists insisted, almost as an article of faith, that there was no possibility that the introduction of new technology could lead to an aggregate rise in unemployment. This belief was based on the assumption, thought to be justified by post-war statistical data, that increases in aggregate labour productivity were always positively correlated with economic growth (in other words, aggregate productivity could rise only in periods of relatively fast growth).[2] This view in turn rested on the premiss that the investment needed to facilitate such productivity gains would only be undertaken by companies in periods of perceived market expansion. The possibility that they could see scope for profitable investment in cost-cutting under conditions of static demand simply did not occur to most economists. Very few even noticed that already in the 1960s, at least in Western Europe, the amount of extra employment generated by each percentage point of economic growth was steadily shrinking, as competitive pressures intensified the need to reduce labour costs.

.In retrospect the prevalence of such misperceptions in the 1970s appears to be just another instance of the fatal tendency of economists to adopt the facile assumption that any trend or correlation which is statistically identifiable over many years can be regarded as permanent – and hence the basis for an 'iron law'. More generally it reflected a failure to recognise the extent to which the prolonged period of rapid growth and 'full' employment of the post-war generation had, perhaps inevitably, reduced pressures to maximise efficiency. In particular, this meant that company managements could maintain satisfactory profit levels based on steady market growth and had relatively little incentive to try and extract maximum value from labour. Moreover, they generally perceived that it was not cost-effective to shed labour even during periods of market downturn because of the difficulty of finding more manpower when demand growth revived, as it invariably did quite quickly following the brief slowdowns of growth experienced in the 1950s and 1960s. By the same token full employment had put labour in an exceptionally strong bargaining position. Hence the balance of market forces was such that any stoppages resulting from disputes were likely to result in higher costs to employers through lost orders and markets than would result from conceding workers' demands.

In the course of the 1980s any notion that renewed high rates of unemployment were but a passing phase or that there could be no such thing as 'technological unemployment' was rapidly exposed as a delusion. This resulted mainly from an intensification of the competitive pressures already referred to, as average economic growth rates continued to decline. At the same time the scope for mitigating these pressures, and for re-investing profits which could not be absorbed by expanding capacity through takeovers and merger among competitors in the same industry, was limited – at least within national frontiers – by anti-monopoly legislation.[3]

Hence a conspicuous feature of industrialised economies from the early 1980s has been the tendency of established companies, in the service sector as well as manufacturing, to regard the application of cost-cutting new technology to their existing operations (without necessarily expanding capacity) as one of the most profitable ways to reinvest their accumulating profits. This has effectively turned on its head one of the most sacred assumptions of post-war political economy, namely that increased investment has a positive impact on employment (a still cherished shibboleth of the British Labour Party and trade unions). At the same time the resulting process of corporate 'downsizing' reinforced a gathering tendency on the part of governments quietly to abandon their commitment to full employment as an overriding goal of public policy.

The upshot of these tendencies has been a further increase in joblessness since the early 1980s, giving rise (particularly in Europe) to the phenomenon of 'jobless growth'. This has meant that, taking the 1974–94 period as a whole, there has been negligible growth in the numbers of employed people in the countries of the European Union at a time when the level of economic activity (GDP) has expanded significantly, albeit at a much slower rate than in the 1950s and 1960s.[4] Indeed in the most extreme case, that of Spain, employment actually fell by over 8 per cent over the period as a whole, at a time when the economy virtually doubled in size.

The practical inability of the economic system to deliver full employment was, not surprisingly, accompanied by increased questioning of the continued relevance or desirability of this objective. This was made all the more unavoidable by the very fuzziness of the concept, begging numerous questions about its definition in relation to full-time versus part-time employment, paid versus unpaid work, and the 'normal' length of time spent at work during a year – or during a lifetime. Yet while these ambiguities perhaps made it easier to brush aside the protests of those concerned at abandonment of the commitment to full employment, it did not make the spreading deprivation and alienation caused by increasingly endemic unemployment any more acceptable.

Perhaps the most egregious example of the rampant confusion and self-deception among mainstream economists on this subject is the continuing attempt of many to suggest that the answer to the problem of unemployment is to lower the price of labour until it reaches a 'market clearing' level.[5] The fact that such a prescription, based on the most simplistic application of supply/demand theory and ignoring the reality that the market-clearing price of labour may easily be below the minimum level of subsistence was largely discredited in the early nineteenth century (notably by Malthus), makes continuing advocacy of it at the end of the twentieth seem bizarre enough. Its survival at a time when businesses everywhere have, as noted above, explicitly adopted investment strategies based on 'downsizing' – or the elimination of labour through the application of advanced technology – can only be interpreted as another example of economists wilfully seeking refuge from reality in their textbooks.

Training: a non-solution

A more commonly peddled illusion concerning the problem of unemployment is that it is the consequence of the failure of the workforce to adapt to the changing demands of the competitive, global economy, in particular by acquiring skills in keeping with the new information technology. The obvious policy implication is that the resources devoted to training and retraining of the labour force need to be greatly increased. In Britain in particular this has been a continuing theme of political parties since the early 1980s as they have struggled to come up with a plausible answer to the intractable problem of unemployment.

Yet while it is true that there have been instances of specific labour shortages occurring during the period of sustained high unemployment since the early 1980s, a moment's analysis should make it obvious that such mismatches can only account for an insignificant proportion of total unemployment. This is indicated by the fact that in Britain (for example) the only relevant statistical indicator of labour shortages – that of the official count of unfilled vacancies – has shown a steep decline over the years relative to the number of registered unemployed and by 1996 was equal to only about 10 per cent of the numbers out of work, whereas in the era of full employment (e.g. the 1960s) the two indicators were roughly of the same magnitude. Moreover, given that governments have undertaken countless new training initiatives in the fifteen to twenty years since they first recognised unemployment as a structural rather than a cyclical problem, without any noticeable impact on the level of unemployment, the fact that they continue to give them such importance can only be taken as proof that they are completely bereft of ideas on how to solve the problem.

2. Capital: Devaluation Resisted

We have already noted the beginning of a decline in the growth rate of real demand for capital (i.e. fixed investment) in the industrialised world as early as the late 1960s – not only in absolute terms but relative to the growth of output. With the onset of chronic stagnation after 1973 this trend was accentuated, so that the recorded growth rate of fixed investment in the OECD countries actually fell below that of GDP over the subsequent period as a whole, whereas in the 1950s and 1960s it had (on average) comfortably exceeded it (see Figure 2). Inevitably this has contributed to a steadily rising capital surplus as the volume of funds available to invest has continued to grow, fuelled by an increase in both corporate profitability and the amount of savings channelled into securities markets.[6]

It is difficult to determine what proportion of this evident rise in the productivity of capital reflects a normal cost-cutting response to increasing competitive pressures in more stagnant markets or, on the other hand, a progressive switch to more productive technology – in other words, a long-term decline in what economists call the incremental capital–output ratio.[7] There are clear grounds, however, for believing that the latter has become a factor of growing importance. This is mainly because

- the advent of modern microelectronics (incorporating silicon and related technologies) has resulted in a significant reduction in the capital-intensity as well as the labour-intensity of many manufacturing processes, while greatly increasing their 'knowledge-intensity';
- an increasing proportion of final consumption is evidently for services such as tourism and entertainment, much of it comprising activities of relatively low capital-intensity and increasingly delivered by various forms of telecommunications (themselves based on relatively cheap microelectronic technology).

Paradoxically, another factor behind the slowdown in fixed investment may well be the artificial restraints to the introduction of new technology imposed by the increasingly oligopolistic structure of many global product markets. This traditional and well-documented tendency among big corporations[8] has naturally become more pronounced as stagnating markets and intensifying competition have led both to a greater concentration of ownership among giant transnational corporations and to stronger pressures to extract the maximum value from existing assets (notably in capital-intensive industries such as paper and petrochemicals). These pressures obviously conflict with the rapid introduction of new technology, which entails also the accelerated writing-off of existing plant and equipment, to the obvious detriment of corporate profits. In fact it is scarcely possible for companies to prevent technological change completely, however great their market power – if only because there is always the possibility of new sources of competition arising – so that companies must maintain a minimum degree of investment in research and development and hence are almost bound to utilise the results of this research to make improvements in their products. None the less the interest in controlling the speed at which new technology is introduced remains strong and is doubtless more effectively achieved as competition is reduced.

It is striking that little or no attention has been paid by economists to the tendency of demand for capital to fall – in contrast to their very conspicuous and long-standing concern at the decline in demand for labour.[9] Indeed, on the rare occasions when the question of the relative abundance of capital is discussed by economists it is common to find that there are at least as many arguing that there is a shortage of funds for investment as the opposite. Doubtless one explanation for this is that the symptoms of an excess supply of capital are less obvious to the general public than those of an oversupply of labour, which are manifest in rising unemployment and the social problems associated with it. Yet it is also true that the institutions of organised capital, with their powerful influence over the pattern of public debate on such issues – whether in academic circles or the media – have had a compelling interest in discouraging any attention being paid to the growing surplus of capital. Thus, for example, journalists often report a boom in the issue of new financial securities – such as the surge in international equity issues in 1996 – as reflecting a strong growth in demand for capital rather than the willingness of investor institutions to pay almost any price for new financial assets (including some of the most doubtful real worth) in their desperation to find outlets for their mountains of cash.[10]

Furthermore, it may be partly, or even mainly, out of awareness of the growing redundancy of capital that the chief protagonists of the financial sector have made such strenuous efforts to swell the ranks of those with a vested interest in sustaining its value. The least significant efforts to promote this cause have been those associated with the privatisation of state enterprises. It is true that in Britain, the first and most enthusiastic exponent of this policy, it was designed to encourage the maximum participation of individual small shareholders and proclaimed as a revolution of 'popular capitalism'. Subsequently, however, this was shown to be little more than an elaborate vote-buying scheme whereby members of the public were offered the chance to buy a modest number of shares in privatised utilities at a discount to their market value, permitting them to resell them immediately at a profit of a few hundred pounds.

Far more important is the world-wide effort to encourage the mass of the population to become investors in financial securities, either as individuals or through the medium of investing institutions such as the US mutual funds (known as unit trusts in Britain) or pension funds. Although in the United States this is a relatively long-established tradition, in the rest of the industrialised world it is quite a novelty. In Europe the change has occurred largely by promoting a gradual switch to providing pensions through funded schemes either managed by or on behalf of employing companies (known in Britain as occupational pension schemes) or else on an individual basis (personal pensions). Official propaganda has sought to justify this to the public on the grounds that

- the cost to taxpayers of state-funded schemes is no longer affordable, and
- the funded schemes can provide finance for productive investment and economic regeneration.

Of these two propositions the second is probably regarded as the least controversial, since it fits with a widely held perception that there is insufficient capital available for the amount of productive investment needed to generate a higher level of economic activity – and hence, it is assumed, a lower rate of unemployment. Yet, in the light of the evidence already cited that growth in the supply of investible funds has been outstripping the level of fixed investment by the corporate sector for many years (i.e. since well before the start of the information technology revolution), such an argument is clearly bogus.

In fact it is far more plausible to suppose that the impetus behind the switch towards funded pension schemes comes from politically powerful vested interests in the financial sector who are anxious to strengthen and perpetuate the importance and profitability of their own 'industry', thereby also increasing the size of the 'wall of money' which helps to prop up the market value of financial securities and other assets. This trend at the same time tends to expand the constituency of those disposed to support economic policies favourable to owners of such assets – including low interest rates, low taxes and, above all, official intervention in the markets to underwrite asset values (and the balance sheets of major financial institutions) whenever these are endangered by the prospect of a major sell-off. Naturally those who promote such increasing flows of funds into the financial markets do not care to dwell on the likelihood that the supply of them may be rapidly outstripping the demand, and that there is a consequent risk of serious losses to investors and the collapse of financial institutions.

A notable recent example of this danger is provided by the huge losses (amounting to some £8 billion) incurred by the Lloyd's insurance market in London in the late 1980s and early 1990s. These losses, which at one point appeared to threaten the very survival of Lloyd's at the centre of the international reinsurance market, were at first attributed to a combination of incompetent underwriting (not unmixed with fraud) and exceptionally heavy claims arising from an unusually large number of natural and unnatural disasters. Yet it has subsequently emerged that the main factor was in fact a doubling of market capacity between 1984 and 1988 as the number of wealthy individuals investing in the market soared on the back of the huge redistribution of income in their favour (in Britain and elsewhere) which accompanied the 1980s' boom. As in the case of banks confronted with a similar influx of capital which they are compelled to invest, the inevitable result was a drop in prudential standards and eventual disaster. Unlike the banks, however, members of Lloyd's were unable to look to the state as 'insurer of last resort' to bail them out, precisely because their traditionally huge profits have always been justified on the grounds that they accept unlimited liability for losses.

There is thus growing evidence of a long-term difficulty in finding outlets for the rapidly expanding volume of capital available for investment at rates of return which can be regarded as adequate based on realistic valuations of the potential income stream to be generated. Consequently any measures designed to encourage even more people to save for their retirement through the medium of financial securities will simply mean that the eventual market correction needed to bring asset prices into line with underlying worth will bring ruin to even more people – even if in the short run it might help sustain price levels by expanding the demand for securities (according to the 'wall of money' principle).

Just as the information technology revolution is leading to the emergence of knowledge-intensive production and thereby reducing the demand for investment capital relative to the level of output, it has also begun to undermine the traditional method of valuing companies, leading to much greater uncertainty and volatility surrounding the market price of company shares. This is resulting from a transformation in the nature of the asset base of capitalist enterprises, such that 'software' (including both technical know-how and managerial expertise) is becoming as important if not more important than 'hardware' in generating value for shareholders. Since this software is closely related to human capital – that is, the presence within the organisation of individuals with key capabilities – it cannot be classified as a fixed asset on which accountants can put a predictable long-term value, since the individuals concerned may leave the company at short notice or lose their capacity to keep ahead of rival technologists linked to competing firms.[11] Similar problems of valuation obviously apply to the growing number of companies in the entertainment business, such as football clubs, quoted on the stock exchange. For here again their short-term market worth depends heavily on the commitment and success of a few talented individuals, while a longer-term valuation can only be a matter of guesswork.

The most obvious way of trying to combat this uncertainty has become the use by a growing number of companies of very large financial rewards either to secure or to retain the services of key individuals. Although long familiar in the entertainment field, this practice was pioneered in the financial services industry in the 1980s. The packages offered typically comprise – in addition to a large basic salary – a substantial initial payment (or 'golden hello') on joining the company, further payments conditional on the executive concerned not leaving the company ('golden handcuffs'), including performance bonuses, share options in the company and generous pension arrangements. The level of remuneration involved, which in an increasing number of cases amounts to well over $1 million a year (not only in US but also in British and other European corporations) has aroused growing public criticism of what are widely perceived as symptoms of unacceptable corporate greed, particularly in the context of growing unemployment and economic insecurity among the mass of the population. Yet, given the ever greater difficulties of maintaining shareholder value in face of the remorseless demands of the capital markets and the lack of scope for investing accumulated corporate profits in fixed assets, it is entirely logical for companies to use some of their surplus reserves to sustain the increasingly vital resource of human capital and at the same time to stimulate it to push corporate shareholder value to the highest level possible.

Creative accounting

The difficulty of defining the book value of key executives and other 'intangible' assets (such as product brands or other forms of 'goodwill') points to another tempting way for companies to try and push up the market value of their shares. This is through the various techniques of 'creative accounting', which enable companies to show their financial performance in the most favourable light possible. The devices which can, quite legally, be deployed to do this in Britain – including off-balance sheet finance (permitting liabilities to be understated), capitalisation of current costs (so that they appear in the balance sheet as assets) and changes in depreciation policy so as to improve the profit and loss account – have been well documented.[12] At the same time there is evidence, necessarily anecdotal, that a growing number of companies (at least in Britain) are resorting to illegal falsification of accounts – in ways which auditors may not easily detect – to boost their reported profits.[13]

It is impossible to tell how far such methods have been a factor in the general tendency to market overvaluation of shares – although in mid-1997 it was authoritatively reported that a collective failure by US corporations to account for the recent huge allocation of stock options to senior executives and other employees may have resulted in an overstatement of their earnings by as much as 20 per cent, in the absence of which there would have been even less justification than there was for the rise in the stock-market index by 35 per cent over the preceding twelve months.[14] On a rational view of the long-term interests of the financial sector in not damaging confidence in the market's credibility, one might expect the regulatory authorities to make strenuous efforts to check any systematic attempts to distort reported accounts. On the other hand, given the impact of intangible factors in extending the scope for subjective valuation of companies, and above all the relentlessly growing pressures to push up shareholder value at any cost, there are stronger grounds than ever for treating company financial statements with suspicion.

In fact, however much care may be taken in such valuation, there is a growing risk of miscalculation as the proportion of intangible assets in balance sheets inevitably rises. In these circumstances a corresponding threat arises to the well-being of some companies which may be subject to speculative takeover by others without a soundly based understanding of their true market worth. Examples of this effect have been the acquisition of publishing houses in the USA and Britain by groups which have been prepared to pay inordinately high prices apparently based on lists of authors whose earning capacity has been seriously overestimated and, perhaps most egregiously, the $5 billion takeover of Columbia Studios (one of the major Hollywood film companies) by Sony Corporation of Japan in 1989 – a move which has not only left Columbia financially crippled but has helped to push up both the costs and market value of other Hollywood studios to the point where they are finding it ever harder to make an acceptable return on capital.

The potential significance of these developments for the future of capitalist enterprise would be hard to overstate. For whereas speculation has always been prone to predominate at a stage of the business cycle when investment in productive assets looks less attractive, it now appears that by the very nature of many income-generating businesses all investment decisions are becoming inherently more speculative. If this is indeed so, it can only mean that financial markets are destined to become more and more volatile, even in the unlikely event of a long-term resumption of rapid growth.

Revolutionary Implications

The conclusion that follows inescapably from these developments is that the incremental demand for both labour and investment capital in the modern world is in long-term decline, relative to the overall level of economic activity, and that this slackening of growth in demand for both will continue as their productivity continues to rise. Since the global supply of labour is destined to continue growing at least as fast as at present until well into the twenty-first century, there can be little doubt that the excess of supply over demand will increase – in both absolute and relative terms – especially if economic growth rates continue to decline in the world's major markets (or simply remain close to their historic average). In the case of capital, it is even more certain that supply will continue to outstrip demand unless and until one of two possible events occurs: either a sustained revival of global GDP growth to levels only previously seen in the 1950s and 1960s or a massive collapse in asset values (at least as severe as that of the early 1930s).

As will be shown in Chapter 12, it seems highly improbable that a revival of growth will occur at a fast enough rate – although by definition the possibility cannot be completely excluded. As for a financial market crash, this would certainly have the effect of choking off the supply of profits for reinvestment. Since, however, it would also kill the demand for investment, and would likewise result in a catastrophic contraction of personal incomes and of the economy as a whole, it could obviously not be regarded as a solution to the problem – except in the sense that a nuclear holocaust may be viewed as a solution to the problem of overpopulation. On the other hand the increased volatility in the valuation of companies because of the growing importance of software and other less durable assets in determining their market worth only increases the seeming inevitability of such an outcome.

For labour the long-term consequences of this process are already manifest, in that we have for several years been witnessing its progressive devaluation – except in the case of the few highly skilled individuals who create software or are otherwise seen as crucial to sustaining shareholder value in their companies. The result has been not only a widening gap between the highest and lowest paid workers but a general relative decline in levels of pay at the bottom end of the scale. This phenomenon is particularly marked in the United States, where average real wage levels in the mid-1990s are actually lower than in the late 1970s.

There is as yet no sign of capital being devalued in the same way, despite a demand–supply imbalance comparable to that of labour. On the contrary there is clear evidence that the cost of capital is still tending to rise everywhere. This is to be explained partly by the very fact that the bargaining power of labour has been weakened by rising unemployment and that consequently it has been possible to impose a reduction in its share of value added – by around 2 percentage points since the 1970s to 65.6 per cent in the OECD as a whole[15] – to the benefit of profits and hence to the rate of return on capital. At the same time the globalisation process, by enabling capital to seek out the highest returns available anywhere in the world, has clearly tended to raise its 'opportunity cost'.

Unquestionably, however, the decisive factor in preventing a devaluation of capital such as to reflect its growing superfluity has been the continuing deployment of the machinery of state and of taxpayers' money to manipulate capital markets and maintain asset values. The methods used, as already described, range from state orchestration of stock-market buying to sustain share prices (perhaps not confined to Japan), to tax incentives for investing in securities and thinly disguised subsidisation of bank profits (through discounted sales of public debt) so as to maintain market liquidity. Yet above all these in importance is the overarching commitment of the state, in its capacity as lender of last resort, to provide an effective guarantee against the insolvency of the financial markets as a whole.

It is perhaps not necessary to point out that the reason why state power and resources continue to be used to maintain an artificially high market valuation of capital – even in the face of a steadily worsening fiscal crisis – is the political dominance of the vested interest associated with capital, which has enabled it to mobilise both public resources and the mass media in support of its interests. In contrast organised labour, always much less powerful than organised capital, has been rendered weaker and more fragmented than at any time since the 1930s by recession and globalisation, and hence quite unable to prevent the further weakening of its position stemming from the technological revolution.

Thus it seems no exaggeration to suggest that the position of labour in the industrialised world is now fully analogous to the one in which it found itself in Britain during the Industrial Revolution two centuries ago. At that time it was new technology, applied both to agriculture and manufacturing, which devalued both traditional farm labour and that employed in cottage industries, neither of which could compete with steam power, undermining the livelihood of most of the then overwhelmingly rural population. Yet then at least the emerging industries offered the displaced workers alternative employment, albeit at the heavy social cost of transforming them into an urban industrial labour force. The new industries were, moreover, able to expand rapidly based on the development of new markets for the vastly cheaper products they were able to turn out. Today, however, there is no sign that the new industrial revolution based on information technology could unleash a comparable explosion of new demand. If this is so, any suggestion that employment in the traditional sense could remain the mechanism for income distribution on any kind of stable or equitable basis appears wholly unrealistic – at least under anything resembling a free-market regime.

It is more and more widely recognised that this conundrum demands an answer, since it is socially and politically untenable to allow the economic marginalisation of a growing proportion of the population of the industrialised countries – not to mention those in a far worse plight in the former Communist countries and the Third World. Yet most proposals for dealing with it are essentially adaptations of the present tax and benefit systems prevailing in OECD countries, involving an increase in taxation to be used for the subsidisation of wages.[16] As such they fail to do more than suppress some of the symptoms of unemployment (by cutting the official total of jobless), while inevitably keeping those thereby brought back into work on very low income levels. Worse still, such 'welfare-to-work' schemes (including the much-trumpeted one of the incoming British Labour government in 1997) may simply serve to depress the level of wages of low-paid workers while shifting the burden of unemployment around among different members of the more disadvantaged sectors of the work-force. To this extent the only true beneficiaries of such schemes may prove to be those companies and their shareholders whose profits are in the process subsidised by the taxpayer.

What remains far less clear is precisely how the impact of the new industrial revolution will unfold in relation to capital, whose primacy in the economic system was effectively established by the first industrial revolution. The essential reason for this was that the scale of fixed investment needed to facilitate the mechanised mode of production (as well as other key developments of the steam age, such as railways) was only possible through the concentration of large quantities of capital which had for the most part to be mobilised through capital markets mediating the funds of many different private investors. The requirement to offer investors a profit sufficient to offset the risk of losing their investment in the event of the recipient enterprise's failure has created both the resources (in the shape of retained profits) and the necessity for continuous expansion of investment and production, although this process has had an unavoidable tendency to be interrupted by the periodic failure of demand necessary to sustain adequate levels of profitability. Hence the classic cycle of boom and bust.

Now, however, the prospect looms that, even when the cycle is allowed to reassert itself through a long delayed shake-out of asset values in financial markets, there will never again be more than limited demand for capital for fixed investment. In such circumstances competitive financial markets will probably cease to have more than a marginal role in sustaining economic activity. To try and prevent this happening, however, the corporate sector can be expected, with the full support of OECD governments, to continue using all their ingenuity to find new ways of absorbing the unremitting flood of surplus capital. The main techniques being adopted, and their chances of continuing success, are considered in the next chapter.

Notes

1. Including the space programme, which arguably had as much to do with pure prestige in the Cold War rivalry with the Soviet Union as with actual defence requirements.
2. See UK Manpower Services Commission, *Review and Plan*, London 1978.
3. Although fear of a hostile takeover bid – whether from a foreign competitor or from a company or investor with no existing presence in the sector – also became a powerful spur to cutting labour costs so as to sustain a company's profitability, and hence its share price, at high levels.
4. Indeed if we exclude Germany – for which the statistics are distorted in an upward direction by the effects of the country's reunification in 1990 – there was no net increase in total employment in the countries of the European Union over the period (source: OECD).
5. See S. Brittan, *Capitalism with a Human Face*, Fontana, London 1996.
6. This can be viewed as a validation of the Marxian 'law' of the tendency of the rate of profit to fall (*Capital* Volume 3).
7. In other words the average value of output generated by each additional unit of fixed capital employed. This is not to be confused with the more easily measured aggregate capital–output ratio, which actually showed a tendency to rise in certain countries, including Britain, during the 1960s and 1970s, probably reflecting a declining level of capacity utilisation.
8. See J.K. Galbraith, *The New Industrial State*, Hamish Hamilton, London, 1967.
9. See C. Giorno, P. Richardson and W. Suyker, *Technical Progress, Factor Productivity and Macroeconomic Performance in the Medium Term*, OECD Economics Department Working Paper No. 157, Paris 1995. Typically, this article equates 'factor productivity' with labour productivity alone and hence avoids any consideration of the impact of changes in the productivity of capital.
10. Richard Lapper, 'Demands for Capital Grow', *Financial Times*, 27 September 1996.

11. C. Handy, *Beyond Certainty: The Changing Worlds of Organisations*, Hutchinson, London 1995.

12. T. Smith, *Accounting for Growth: Stripping the Camouflage from Company Accounts*, Century Business, London 1992.

13. See 'Well Cooked Books May Not Be so Rare', *Financial Times*, 4 February 1997.

14. Barry Riley, 'Vertigo as Wall Street Assesses its Options', *Financial Times*, 25 June 1997.

15. Source: OECD.

16. See Council of Churches for Britain and Ireland, *Unemployment and the Future of Work: An Enquiry for the Churches*, London 1997.

8

Coping with the Capital Glut

We have already noted, as a self-evident fact, that the availability of investible funds has risen almost continuously in real terms since World War II, and that from around the early 1970s the growth of fixed investment opportunities has slowed down. However, although the slowdown in fixed capital formation can be quantified with reasonable precision, the same is not true of the trend in availability of capital for investment. This is because of the lack of comprehensive and reliable statistics on the global assets of investing institutions or individuals. This is scarcely surprising in view of the natural inclination of investors to conceal the level of their holdings – an endeavour in which they are nowadays greatly assisted by the increase both in the number of offshore financial centres (by definition shrouded in secrecy) and the ease with which funds can be transferred to and from them. At the same time the enormous diversification in the number of available investment instruments makes indicators such as the volume of deposits held at financial institutions largely meaningless in this context.

Nevertheless, some indication of the huge scale of the increase in investible funds since 1990 may be gained from one of the few relatively comprehensive time series available from an authoritative source, the OECD.[1] This shows that the value of financial assets held by all investor institutions in member states (comprising mainly insurance companies, pension funds and investment companies) increased by no less than $9,800 billion (9.8 trillion) or 75 per cent between 1990 and 1995. The average annual increase of $1.96 trillion was equal to around 10 per cent of the aggregate national income (GDP) of the OECD countries during the period.

For the purposes of our analysis, however, it is less important to pin down precisely how much the volume of investible funds has grown than to know that it has clearly outstripped the growth in investment opportunities – and to consider what is implied by the continuation of such a trend. In this chapter we therefore examine the evidence in terms of the proliferating symptoms of an over-supply of capital and the efforts of the corporate sector (with the full support of governments) to take remedial action. In the light of the discussion in the last chapter it is clear that such action is needed, from the perspective of capitalists, to avert an effective devaluation of capital within the market economy. This task is, of course, a twofold one in that it requires

- the identification of profitable new outlets for investment to absorb the growing supply of capital, and
- the maintenance of an acceptable rate of return on the stock of capital already invested as well as on new investments.

It will be readily apparent that, as long as the growth in real demand for investment capital is tending to weaken while the rate of return sought by investors remains high, the fulfilment of these mutually interdependent objectives is bound to prove ultimately self-defeating. This is because the inevitable consequence of maintaining a high return on the capital stock as a whole is that yet more investible funds will be generated for which outlets must be found. Moreover, as already noted, in a globalised economy increasingly geared to anarchic speculation there is a natural tendency for investors to push their demands for return on capital higher still. Hence the effort now needed to sustain the market value of capital resembles the futile labour of Sisyphus (the character in Greek mythology con-demned for ever to push a boulder to the top of a hill only for it to roll back to the bottom again and again).

Expanding the Outlets for Investment

As we have already observed, the processes of global economic liberalisation and financial deregulation in the 1980s served to boost the scope for more or less speculative investment in a number of areas such as the foreign-exchange market. In fact there can be little doubt that the political impetus behind the whole process of liberalisation stemmed precisely from the pressing need to create new investment opportunities rather than from a sudden conversion to the virtues of free competition – a point underlined by the evident relaxation of anti-trust policy by the US Justice Department under the Reagan administration. Likewise one may even wonder whether the general rapid increase in the level of public deficits and indebtedness did not owe as much to a perception of the potential offered by the state as an investment outlet for private capital as it did from a serious conviction that cutting taxes would stimulate growth. As it turned out, in fact, the greatest scope of all for developing such new outlets for private investment has been provided by the state sector.

Public-sector debt

The biggest and seemingly most reliable public-sector outlet for private investment has become the public-sector debt market in the OECD countries themselves. As noted earlier, these countries collectively have not recorded a budget surplus since the early 1970s, with many individual countries (notably the United States, France, Italy and Canada) being in perpetual deficit for the past twenty years. The failure of virtually all governments not merely to reduce these deficits but to prevent them from getting bigger has resulted in an aggregate OECD government borrowing requirement averaging $650–700 billion a year in the 1990s, compared with an average of around $500 billion a year in the 1980s and a mere $100 billion annually in the early 1970s (in constant 1994 prices).[2]

A striking aspect of this phenomenon is that, for all the rhetorical denunciation of budgetary deficits (particularly in the US Congress), they do not appear to be considered as great a problem as when they first began to rise steeply in the mid-1970s. At that time there was considerable talk of the supposed danger of the public sector 'crowding out' the private sector from the capital markets, a suggestion which in the 1990s would be obviously absurd at a time when all parts of the global economy are awash with funds. On the contrary one might conclude that in the eyes of the financial sector the state has now assumed the role not only of lender but also of borrower of last resort. Whether or not this chronic situation is now in fact officially regarded as serious is far from clear, notwithstanding the ritual expressions of concern. What is clear is that the resulting debt service burden – having tripled as a share of national income (to 3 per cent) between 1975 and 1995 in the OECD area – cannot continue to be viewed with indifference if eventual monetary meltdown is to be averted.

Privatisation

The need to restrain the growth of public debt and the perceived constraints to dealing with the deficit by increasing taxes are forcing governments to look for new ways of raising revenue and of providing finance for necessary public services. It is a truism that the only available source of such funding is the private corporate sector. An obvious irony of this situation is that the lower taxes and proliferating subsidies applied to private corporations have themselves been a major factor aggravating this fiscal gap, which they are now being called on to fill from their otherwise superfluous profit flows. Despite this the current political consensus in the 1990s is that the private sector should be induced to fill this gap by way of profit-generating investment rather than through taxation.

The word 'privatisation' – which was not to be found in the Oxford English Dictionary before the mid-1980s – is popularly understood to signify the sale of state-owned assets to private investors or companies. In particular it is associated with the major public utilities, which in most countries the state has traditionally owned and operated, as well as other commercial activities in which it has a substantial stake. In analysing the evolution of latter-day capitalism, however, it is more useful to view it as a general tendency to introduce private capital into the financing and running of economic activities hitherto provided and financed predominantly, if not exclusively, by the state. This takes a number of different forms.

The sale of state assets   As we have observed in the case of Britain – where the Conservative administration pioneered the practice after its landslide election victory in 1983 – selling off state enterprises to private investors has generally been justified to public opinion primarily as a means of (a) relieving taxpayers of the burden of funding allegedly loss-making enterprises and (b) facilitating their modernisation and enhanced efficiency through the introduction of private capital. The fact that many of them were in reality quite profitable under state ownership – and in any case were perforce made profitable *before* they could be privatised – was a point easily glossed over in presenting the case to a public long attuned to the incessant media refrain of 'private enterprise good, public enterprise bad'.

Yet whatever the theoretical merits or demerits of privatising state enterprises as presented to the public, there is no doubt that its main purpose as perceived by more informed opinion was and remains that of helping to plug the hole in state finances which has been growing ever wider since the mid-1970s. As such the economic benefits have been viewed with considerable scepticism by much of the political establishment, in that, since these assets could only be sold once, the proceeds would do nothing to solve the problem of a long-term structural deficit. This point can be graphically illustrated by pointing to the fact that the total net proceeds of all the British state sell-offs in the 1984–96 period (after allowing for the cost of debt write-offs and other sweeteners) was no more than around £60 billion in 1996 prices – which compares with the national budget deficit of £50 million in one year alone (1993). On this view, therefore, such an exercise in 'selling off the family silver' (to which it was famously likened by the former Conservative prime minister Harold Macmillan) could only be regarded as a measure of desperation.

In contrast to the extensive airing given to these rather dubious grounds for privatisation of public assets, the one more or less solid justification for it (if only from the perspective of private capital) – that it provides a much needed outlet for otherwise redundant investible funds – is seldom, if ever, mentioned. Yet if proof were needed that such sell-offs are more to do with promoting the interests of investors (including their well-paid advisors and merchant banks in the City of London and elsewhere) than those of taxpayers, it is surely provided by the case of British Rail, one of the last major public corporations to go under the hammer in Britain (only completed in 1996). As in virtually all other countries, the railways in Britain had for the most part ceased to be profitable before World War II – largely due to the advent of motorised road transport. Certainly since they were taken into public ownership in 1947 they have been consistently loss-making – even if a few services within the network as a whole have recorded surpluses – and have only been kept going by virtue of state subsidies.

Not surprisingly, therefore, in view of private investors' need to make a market return on capital, railway privatisation was only made possible by a substantial increase in state subsidies – officially admitted to be more than double the cost under public ownership. Since there was thus a substantial extra cost to the taxpayer, and no clear prospect of any benefit to railway users,[3] it is impossible to reach any other conclusion than that this was seen solely as a benefit to investors (as well as the usual army of consultants and financial engineers advising on the sale) underwritten by the state. Such a display of official irresponsibility (not to say corruption) in face of a public-sector deficit and debt which had already reached unsustainable levels is a measure of how far governments are now prepared to subordinate all other considerations to that of sustaining the value of capital.

The scope for private investors to buy up state assets is by no means confined to the Western industrialised world. Indeed, as will be shown more fully in later chapters, the bankruptcy of the state is an even more immediate prospect in most developing (or Third World) countries and is a palpable reality in nearly all of the former Soviet bloc. In these circumstances it has been easy for Western business interests, abetted by the World Bank and International Monetary Fund (which are effectively controlled by OECD governments), to compel such countries to sell state enterprises to foreign investors in return for new loans. This process, it may be added, is hardly new, being strongly reminiscent of the machinations by which the British government gained control of the Suez Canal from the Khedive Ismail in 1875. However, despite being able thus to compel bankrupt Third World and ex-Communist governments to sell such assets to them at what may appear to be knock-down prices, Western financial institutions must confront the very real risks of investing in such politically and economically unstable countries. On the other hand the very fact that such investments are essentially speculative – with a high-risk/high-reward element – makes them attractive to an increasing proportion of investors, especially if they perceive that it will be possible to get some lender of last resort (in other words, OECD taxpayers) to assume the risks in any major crisis (as indeed occurred in the case of the Mexican financial crisis of 1994–95 – see Chapter 10).

Private finance of infrastructure   In addition to taking over existing state enterprises and assets, the private sector is also looking for opportunities to make profitable investments in the field of public infrastructure, encouraged by governments which have dwindling resources available to fulfil their traditional role in this area. As a result there is an increasing incidence of initiatives to introduce private capital into both the construction and the running of such facilities as roads, hospitals and prisons which have long been viewed in most countries as the province of the state. At the limit in Britain this has even involved the sale to private investors of government office buildings, which are then leased back to the state.

Yet since the profitability of such investments obviously depends on their generating a market rate of return, and since this can only be assured by the government effectively guaranteeing a minimum level of revenue to the private companies involved, there is an obvious potential conflict with the interests of the taxpayer and the need to redress the chronic fiscal imbalance. The inherent difficulty of resolving this conundrum lies behind the persistent problems encountered by British governments (Labour as well as Conservative) in developing their Private Finance Initiative (PFI) to fund the development of such infrastructure, which they have proclaimed as a cost-effective solution to the growing funding crisis facing many public services. According to the ideological consensus, of course, where the operation of such facilites is transferred to a private firm the savings resulting from introducing the supposed efficiency enhancements which only the private sector can achieve should pay for the extra margin needed to cover the higher return on capital demanded. Yet the reaction of the Treasury and other public agencies involved, such as Health Authorities, suggests they do not actually believe their own rhetoric in this regard, and are consequently unwilling to guarantee the kind of income stream – through 'shadow tolls' on roads or other rental and management charges – demanded by investors.

Their reservations in this regard seem likely to have been prompted by the experience of the Channel Tunnel, the first and (to date) the largest of all privately funded infrastructure projects. Although this project was assigned to the private sector entirely at the insistence of the Thatcher government, the latter was unable to avoid providing government guarantees for the loans required, so that (following substantial cost overruns during construction and the subsequent massive shortfall of revenues in relation to costs) British and French taxpayers now face huge potential liabilities as the Eurotunnel corporation totters towards seemingly inevitable bankruptcy. The consequent tensions surrounding further PFI initiatives show that, notwithstanding the continuing profligate waste of public money in support of investor interests manifest in the privatisation of state enterprises and in other ways, there is a creeping recognition of the limits to the taxpayer's ability to act as spender of last resort.[4]

The privatisation of government In addition to the introduction of private capital into the building and operation of infrastructure there have been moves, notably in the USA and Britain, to entrust the provision of public services to private firms. This has been particularly noticeable in the prison service and in the field of local government, where services such as catering, garbage collection and gardening, traditionally provided by municipal departments with their own permanent staff, have been put out to competitive tender among mainly private companies. Naturally this approach has been justified on the grounds that it provides better 'value for money' for local taxpayers than non-competitive provision by the authorities themselves. However, both theory and practice suggest it is hard to make any significant improvement in either the cost or the quality of such inherently labour-intensive services. Hence the need here also to generate a margin of profit over and above actual cost – which is absent in the case of public provision – has put pressure on private operators to cut either wages or the quality of service.

Perhaps more alarming than the transfer of responsibility for public-service provision to private companies is the increasingly blatant tendency for supposedly democratic institutions to sell out the public interest to private commercial interests – or indeed to pretend that there is no distinction between the two. The most conspicuous example of this in Britain since the early 1980s has been the practice of local authorities – precluded from raising local taxes by central government's imposition of 'rate-capping' – of giving planning approval for land development by private business interests in return for money needed to fund works or operations of the local authority for which the latter has insufficient resources; this despite the fact that such decisions are supposed to be taken purely on environmental or planning grounds. Moreover, this form of officially approved corruption has often proved to have other negative consequences, as in cases where local councils' raising of cash by authorising retail developments on green-field sites away from town centres has been found to conflict with the government's later adoption of a policy of discouraging such developments – which are dependent on increased use of private cars – in favour of ones accessible to public transport.

Other new investment pastures

Naturally, however, the public sector is not the only area where the swelling flood of excess capital has been searching for new outlets. Indeed it has clearly been the main purpose of deregulating financial markets all over the world both to permit the creation of new investment outlets and instruments and to facilitate their exploitation by investing institutions and non-financial companies alike.

Hidden value in the non-profit sector A natural target for the omnivorous investor community in areas not previously open to them, in both the United States and Britain, has been the extensive field of mutual or non-profit organisations. Many of these were originally set up in the nineteenth century with the principal objective of providing low-cost services to participating members, mainly in banking, insurance and retailing activities. Since their foundation many have accumulated sizable financial reserves, although because of legal and other restrictions these have traditionally been invested in rather low-yielding assets. Since the early 1980s, however, such restraints have been eased, providing both the opportunity and incentive to convert them into regular capitalist enterprises.

As a result, in the United States many Savings and Loan institutions were acquired by commercial enterprises seeking to exploit their newly unlocked potential for profitable investment – as well as the federal government guarantee of their deposits, which thus helped to bring about the scandalous wave of S&L bankruptcies at the beginning of the 1990s (see Chapter 6). Likewise, since the 1980s legislation has facilitated the progressive conversion of Britain's building societies – hitherto all mutual organisations owned by their depositors and dedicated to financing residential building and house purchases – into quoted companies which are essentially no different from commercial banks. As such it was akin to privatisation – except that the assets already belonged to private individuals.[5] Yet unlike the case of real privatisations no one has ever seriously argued that this transformation served any purpose except the rather dubious one of giving the societies access to the mainstream capital markets, and conversely.

Mergers and acquisitions It is a familiar and essential characteristic of the capitalist system that strong companies take over weak ones, or that ones which are individually vulnerable to competitors or declining markets try to offset this weakness by combining their forces. It is also well understood that, to the extent that such mergers have the effect of restricting competition, they may work against the interests of consumers, just as cartels or 'trusts', made up of companies which are nominally separate, have tended to do where not prevented by anti-monopoly regulations. Because of the latter restrictions successful companies have tended to grow either by expanding their operations overseas or by diversifying into new product areas, thus avoiding the possibility of contravening anti-monopoly rules, which would result from increasing their share of their core product markets at home. The growth of such transnational or conglomerate corporations has been a particular phenomenon of world capitalism since the 1960s, as companies have increasingly seen their home markets stagnate and thus offer dwindling scope for further expansion.

Since the early 1980s the number and value of such mergers and acquisitions has mushroomed throughout the industrialised world, greatly stimulated, particularly in the United States, by financial deregulation.[6] It has also been significantly facilitated by a more permissive approach to anti-monopoly (or, in American parlance, 'anti-trust') controls. This has resulted, most explicitly in the United States, in a greater readiness on the part of the authorities to allow evidence of potential increased efficiency resulting from a merger to be used as a justification for it, even where it would clearly have negative consequences for competition.[7] The evident presumption of the regulators is that the beneficiary companies can be relied on to pass on at least some of the efficiency gains to consumers. This change of approach has been justified by the growing exposure of many industries to competition from foreign firms within their domestic markets. A conspicuous example has been the civil aerospace industry, where the merger of Boeing and McDonnell Douglas announced in 1996 is set to reduce the number of suppliers of large jet airliners in the United States to one, with only one other serious competitor in the world (Airbus Industrie of Europe).

One of the recurring features of such mergers has been the high price often paid for the target company – frequently 40–50 per cent above the market price prior to the bid – in order to gain control.

Typically this has been justified on the basis of rather nebulous claims of 'synergy' with the acquiring company, hints about the magical management skills of the acquiring company (often skilfully 'hyped' by an expensive public-relations firm), and ill-defined assertions as to the potential break-up value of the target company (which it might have been supposed could have been realised without the need for a takeover at all). Indeed the results of such mergers tend to bear out the suspicion that – like the 'greenmail' operations of corporate raiders in the 1980s – many of them are purely speculative exercises which often reduce rather than enhance shareholder value and indeed leave the merged group weighed down with an excessive burden of debt.[8]

Various other forms of trading in corporate assets have been developed or expanded since the early 1980s – with little other purpose, it would appear, than to provide outlets for the burgeoning 'wall of money' generated both by surplus corporate profits and by pension and mutual funds. A notable example has been the trend towards de-merging or flotation by large corporations of subsidiaries which are no longer deemed to fit in with group strategy, often through the mechanism of a management 'buy-out' or 'buy-in'.[9] It is perhaps significant that the justification for mergers and de-mergers is often based on conflicting management theories as to the relative merits of large-scale conglomerate corporations operating in different sectors or, on the other hand, of smaller, more specialist (or 'focused') organisations. While to the layman these apparently contradictory ideas may seem to be no more than ephemeral fads generated by the swelling band of management consultants and 'gurus' (usually presented in obscurantist jargon), to the financial community they are evidently essential props to investment strategies they might otherwise be hard put to justify.

The quest for high risk

A feature of capital markets of the past twenty years has been the growth in investment vehicles and instruments catering specifically for those seeking high-risk assets and the high rewards that are supposed to go with them. The main reason for this phenomenon is that it has become progressively harder for fund managers to sustain the kind of returns demanded by their clients in an increasingly competitive marketplace simply by investing in conventional stocks, particularly when many of the latter seem increasingly to offer limited earnings potential, as consumer markets continue to stagnate while the perpetually rising tide of new money entering the market pushes valuations ever closer to the limit of credibility. At the same time the willingness of investing institutions to take bigger risks is reinforced by the pervasive influence of moral hazard: a combination of the huge bonuses offered to their successful dealers and the belief that the state as lender of last resort will pick up the pieces in the event of failure – provided at least the institutions concerned are big enough for their collapse to pose a threat to the stability of the system as a whole. For such compulsive gamblers a growing range of outlets have been developed to feed their appetites.

'Junk' bonds and derivatives   A popular outlet for those in search of high-return, fixed-interest investments in the 1980s was provided by 'junk bonds'. These were issued by companies with a low credit rating and subordinated to other forms of debt, so that in the event of the companies' insolvency their holders would stand a greater chance of loss, for which they were compensated with a relatively high interest rate. These instruments were particularly widely used to help finance the activities of US corporate raiders in the 1980s and, despite falling out of favour when the market collapsed in 1989, were much in demand again by the mid-1990s as the flow of funds coming into the financial markets once again built to a flood. Derivatives are a class of complex instruments ostensibly designed to allow 'hedging' by companies otherwise exposed to risk of loss from the fluctuating market prices of currencies, commodities or other crucial elements in their cost structure. As such they can be said to serve a perfectly legitimate function in a market economy. However, because they are designed to minimise the 'front-end' costs to those taking up such contracts and therefore effectively allow them to place a bet which could result in their winning or losing a sum many times greater than their initial outlay, by 1996 the bulk of the vast funds they have attracted have reportedly been from institutions looking on them as high-risk, high-yield investments.[10]

Venture capitalism   One outlet of growing importance for those in search of high-risk/high-reward opportunities has become what are known as venture capital funds. These operate in a similar way to mutual funds except that all the money subscribed is invested in companies which are unable to meet the criteria needed to obtain a listing on a stock exchange. These typically comprise new businesses, often specialising in the development of supposedly unique products based on newly patented technology, which also have difficulty in raising loan capital on account of the inherent uncertainties involved and their lack of any record of commercial success.

While theoretically it seems easy to justify the existence of such funds as fulfilling a need which the mainstream financial markets are unable to meet, it may seem surprising that such facilities only started to appear in the United States in the 1960s and were virtually unknown anywhere else until the 1980s. Moreover, their exponential growth since then – with the volume of funds invested in them globally rising 75 per cent to $90 billion between 1987 and 1993 – has occurred despite the fact that the returns on them have been no higher than those obtainable on regular equity markets, although in theory it should have been higher to justify the undoubted extra risk.[11] All this suggests strongly that the phenomenon has been created by the growth in supply of investible funds rather than the demand for them.

'Emerging' markets   Until the 1980s the developing countries of Asia, Africa and Latin America (otherwise known as the Third World) were regarded as off limits to all but the most dedicated investors – or at least to those other than the few with sufficient local knowledge and influence needed to shorten the odds in their favour. This view was based on a well-founded perception that such countries suffered from a number of more or less common drawbacks – including small markets, unstable governments, weak currencies and at best unpredictable policies with regard to the freedom to transfer funds abroad. Moreover, since the few Third World stock markets were nearly all very small and lacking in liquidity (not to mention in transparency or proper regulation), virtually the only realistic way of investing in these countries was through direct investment, involving the costly, time-consuming and risky business of starting a new operation from scratch.

Yet this perception has ostensibly been transformed since the 1980s, as investment institutions have begun to trumpet the potential profits to be made in many Third World countries, which they refer to as emerging markets. They have justified this to investors by reference to the alleged dynamism of certain Third World economies (particularly ones in East Asia), which are claimed to have immense growth potential in the supposed new global economy where they are projected to take an ever growing share of world markets from the decreasingly competitive economies of the OECD countries. The result has been a spectacular rise in foreign- investment flows into such Third World markets since the mid-1980s. Thus it is estimated that by 1994 annual capital flows of private capital (including port-folio as well as direct investment) from developed to developing countries had risen at least fivefold in real terms since the mid-1980s to around $175 billion.

What is most remarkable about this trend is that it has taken place at a time when the growth in Third World economies taken as a whole has actually been declining both in absolute terms and relative to that of the increasingly stagnant industrialised world (see Chapter 10). Moreover, even the relatively small number of countries – such as China and the East Asian 'tigers' – which have shown exceptional dynamism have done little to justify any great increase in investor confidence, other than liberalise capital movements to and from abroad and increase fiscal incentives and subsidies to foreign investment. Such problems as the limited liquidity and lack of transparency in financial markets and the unpredictable legal environment are not obviously less significant than previously, while the inherent fragility of many Third World economies makes the investment climate vulnerable to wild swings in government policy and market prospects. It is true that the privatisation of state enter-prises, often quite profitable quasi-monopolies, has provided some lucrative investment opportunities for foreign capital. Yet the very fact that the sale of these assets has occurred – usually under the duress of intensifying fiscal weakness and of demands made by the IMF or the World Bank in return for desperately needed loans – is surely a sign of general economic weakness rather than the rosy picture that so many investment institutions typically paint.

Indeed, despite some quite elaborate attempts to rationalise this new-found investor enthusiasm for the Third World, many fund managers make little attempt to conceal the fact that the flows of funds they have directed to these markets have been largely specu-lative – that is, based on a hope of high rewards to compensate for a high degree of uncertainty and risk. The crudity of this approach was put with devastating bluntness by a Wall Street fund manager caught up in the Mexican financial débâcle of 1994–95, who confessed, 'We went into Latin America not knowing anything about the place. Now we are leaving without knowing anything about it.'[12] Despite this well-publicised fiasco, which led some investors to start referring to Third World countries as 'submerging' markets, the inflow of funds has since resumed.

Maintaining the Return on Investment

It is a measure of the success of owners of capital in sustaining its value, in spite of the evident decline in the real economic demand for it, that over nearly twenty years since 1979 the total return (earnings plus capital appreciation) on all forms of investment (equities and fixed-interest securities) has not only comfortably exceeded inflation but has been greater than in any period of comparable length since the Industrial Revolution. Most strikingly, this means it has even surpassed (on an annual average basis) the results achieved during the post-war boom period of the 1950s and 1960s – notwithstanding the deteriorating performance of the underlying economy since then. It is perhaps not surprising, therefore, to find also that an increasing proportion of the total return on investments since the start of the 1980s has resulted from capital gains (an appreciation in the market value of the securities concerned) rather than earnings (dividend or interest plus reinvested profits), with the former accounting for as much as 75 per cent of total returns in the USA and Britain – compared with well under 50 per cent (on average) in the 1900–1979 period as a whole.[13] This clearly suggests that the rise in value has been driven more by an increasing flow of funds into the market and speculation that prices will continue to be pushed upwards – assuming the maintenance (or restoration) of benign economic conditions – than by the actual income stream produced by the securities.

In fact, it is clear that this sustained rise has been made possible primarily by a combination of devices designed (a) to extract more 'shareholder value' from the underlying assets represented by the securities, and (b) to create artificial market conditions tending to keep the traded price of securities above the level that might be justified by objective valuation of the underlying assets. These two broad approaches are of course complementary, since ultimately a rising market valuation of shares must be sustained by increased profits, or at least the appearance of such an increase. In the latter connection an important aid to the whole process is undoubtedly the application of the techniques of creative, or even false, accounting – made easier by the increasing scope for subjective asset valuation – referred to in the last chapter.

Enhancing the return on fixed investment It is, of course, an elementary objective of companies to raise the return on capital employed by improving efficiency and thereby lowering operating costs per unit of output. Increasing pressures on management to 'make the assets sweat' in this way have undoubtedly been a major factor contributing to the sustained rise in the value of equities. The success of corporations globally in this respect is indicated by the rise in rates of return on capital in the business sector since the late 1980s, so that in the OECD as a whole they averaged 15.5 per cent a year between 1990 and 1996, compared with 13.8 per cent in the decade of the 1980s[14] – even though output growth was much lower in the later period.

Increasing capital's share of value added A phenomenon closely linked to the rising productivity of capital is that of rising labour productivity. Whereas during the period of high economic growth and 'full' employment up to the early 1970s this process was often reflected in aggregate real wage rises as fast as or even faster than the growth of profits, the subsequent steep rise in unemployment has clearly undermined the bargaining power of labour (a process aided in Britain by anti-union legislation). The effect has been to enable capital to increase its share of corporate value added at the expense of labour, as witness the 16 per cent real decline in hourly wage rates in the USA between 1973 and 1993. Over the OECD as a whole this is reflected in a gradual recovery since the early 1980s in the share of profits (as measured by gross operating income) in corporate value added, mirroring the increased rate of return on capital.[13]

Another way of effecting a rise in capital's share of total value added (equal to gross domestic product) has been through a reduction in the share of the tax burden borne by companies. In fact, although corporate profits taxes in the OECD countries have risen as a proportion of GDP over the thirty years since 1965 (from 2.3 to 2.9 per cent), they have done so less than other direct taxes and their share of total taxation has fallen over the same period (from 8.9 to 7.5 per cent) – at a time, moreover, when the share of company profits in

GDP has risen quite markedly.[16] The tendency to cut corporate tax rates has been given great impetus by the 'globalisation' of markets, which has compelled governments to hold down corporate taxation in order to try to attract or retain investment and jobs. Likewise state fiscal resources have been deployed to support profits through various forms of subsidy, whether directly (e.g. through investment grants and incentives) or indirectly, as in the case of the de facto wage subsidies provided through the social-security system. Remarkably, in the European Union this has resulted in enterprises receiving more in state aid than they have paid in direct taxes.[17]

We may note in passing that, in pursuing a strategy aimed at pushing up both the rate of profit and the aggregate share of profits in overall value added, the corporate sector and the governments which are so beholden to it have tended to exacerbate the structural economic weaknesses which are themselves such major contributors to the intensifying pressures on corporations – a normal consequence of the business cycle under *laissez-faire* capitalism to which Keynes had drawn attention. For the effect of thus boosting the return on capital and raising its share of value added at the expense of both labour and the state has inevitably been further to depress demand for new fixed capital investment, as well as the growth of employment and consumer demand, and thereby also to increase the demands made on the state for welfare spending.

The mechanisms just described have clearly been important in raising or sustaining the market value of existing corporate investments. However, as suggested by the growing contribution of capital appreciation to the total returns on investment, manipulation of supply and demand in the securities market has probably become at least as significant.

The crudest approach to using state resources in support of the market value of assets is that of officially inspired buying of securities in the market. This technique is known to have been used from time to time by the Japanese government, through the agency of major banks, to prop up values on the Tokyo Stock Exchange. However, it is not an expedient likely to find much favour with most governments or financial markets – unless, at least, it could be applied covertly – since it would obviously tend to foster a perception that the market was rigged and that prices of securities were essentially artificial. Indeed this feeling may well help to explain the dismal performance of the Tokyo stock market in the 1990s, as

Japanese investors have persistently held aloof from buying back into the market despite its having halved in value since the peak of 1989. In Europe and North America governments have adopted less direct methods of encouraging investors to buy. Most of these take the form of stimulating an increasing flow of funds – the familiar 'wall of money' – into the markets, thus increasing the demand for securities and bidding up their prices.

Funded pensions   The growing importance of invested funds as a means of providing pensions for the retired has already been mentioned. Although these developed quite rapidly in the United States from around the end of World War II (encouraged by generous government tax incentives), this approach to providing retirement pensions has been a relatively recent innovation in much of Europe, where traditionally these have been financed by the state out of the compulsory contributions of those still working and from employers, supplemented by additional injections of public money where necessary (the 'pay-as-you-go' system).[18] As noted earlier, the progressive switch to funded schemes – based on tax-free investment in securities and other assets – has been justified partly on the grounds that state schemes are increasingly unaffordable, as governments are more and more subject to fiscal constraints. Yet whatever the original rationale, its impact in sustaining the market values of securities and other assets would be hard to overstate, since the system has created an institutionalised flow of new money into the markets – amounting to hundreds of billions of dollars a year – which all has to be invested in one kind of asset or another.

In the 1990s increasing doubts have begun to surface as to whether this will prove a viable method of delivering adequate pensions in the longer run. This is partly the inevitable consequence of schemes maturing, as a growing proportion of scheme members have entered retirement on full benefit (as compared with the early years after the creation of most schemes in the 1960s and 1970s) so that schemes' outgoings started to approach or exceed their receipts. At the same time, and partly as a result of the swelling flow of pension and other institutional funds into the market, soaring financial asset prices are making it harder to assure sustainable returns on new investment. As a result there has been an increasing shift on the part of private companies, particularly in the United States, away from providing 'defined benefit' schemes – under which pensions are based on a guaranteed proportion of the pensioner's final salary, with the companies themselves being required to make good any shortfall in the fund – towards 'defined contribution' schemes, which offer scheme members no guaranteed level of benefit on retirement and thus leave them fully exposed to the risk of any deficiency in the value of the fund. It remains to be seen whether in the long run employees will accept the added insecurity entailed in shouldering the market risk themselves, or indeed whether the whole concept of funded pensions will survive a substantial downturn in the financial markets.

Undeterred by such concerns, the US Advisory Council on Social Security went so far in 1996 as to recommend that social-security contributions should be invested in equity markets. Its proponents naturally presented this as a way of ensuring that state pension and social-security commitments could be met without raising taxes, just as they had done when the federal government switched from pay-as-you-go to funding for its own employees' pensions in 1986. Similar proposals for state pensions were advanced by the British Conservative government just before it was swept from power in 1997. Yet, coming at a time when stock-market indices had soared to levels which were by then widely regarded as unsustainable, these initiatives could also be construed as a desperate device to boost investor confidence that a new tidal wave of funds might soon arrive to sustain market values or push them even higher. Certainly it could scarcely be regarded as a means of securing long-term stability of pension values in the face of such obvious fragility in the financial markets – except with the support of a government guarantee of minimum pension levels in the event of the scheme's insolvency. Yet the potential cost of such a guarantee to the taxpayer could be even greater than that of the Savings and Loan débâcle of the early 1990s, as indicated by the persistent losses incurred by the US government's Pension Benefit Guaranty Corporation in bailing out private-sector pension plans even during the years of booming financial markets.[19]

Other incentives to equity investment A variety of other mechanisms for encouraging the flow of investible funds into financial securities, particularly equities, have been promoted by governments in recent years, all based (like pension funds) on the offer of tax breaks to investors or savers. They include personal saving schemes for retirement in the USA, the Business Expansion Scheme and Personal Equity Plans in Britain, schemes to promote stock-market investment by insurance companies in France, and tax breaks for Germans investing in privatisation issues. The obvious effect of such incentives is to offer prospective beneficiaries a substantial discount on the market price of shares – now in most cases in the UK amounting to 40 per cent (the marginal income-tax rate applicable to most of those who can afford to buy shares out of their current savings).

Buy-backs of shares   As equity prices have risen ever higher on world stock markets in the 1980s and 1990s, notwithstanding chronic economic stagnation in the industrialised world, they have continually pushed the market valuation of companies closer to the limits of plausibility in relation to underlying earnings potential or asset value. This phenomenon has faced company managers and boards of directors with the constant challenge of raising profitability still further in order to try to justify the rating imposed on their shares by the market. Yet as the unpromising economic climate continues to restrict the rate of return that can be looked for from new investment, while the high costs of taking over other companies likewise test the resourcefulness of managers and accountants in squeezing the necessary extra value from group assets, other ways of boosting shareholder value have had to be found.

According to the theory of capitalism, in a situation where the directors of a company feel unable to invest shareholders' funds at a satisfactory rate of profit they should hand the surplus back to shareholders in the form of dividends, thus enabling the funds to be recycled through the market into more profitable outlets. In reality such a response does not necessarily permit the maximisation of shareholder value, not least because dividends are often subject to relatively high rates of tax, so that such a strategy will seldom endear management to the financial markets. A popular way round this problem in recent years has become the buying back by companies of their own shares. Although largely outlawed until the early 1980s – precisely because of the scope it can give company managers for manipulating the value of their own shares – it has been greatly facilitated by regulatory changes since then, particularly in Britain and the United States.[20]

Its attraction is that it is not only a more tax-efficient way of distributing profits to shareholders than paying dividends – and thus constitutes yet another de facto subsidy to profits – but obviously tends to boost the level of earnings per share (as profits are spread across a reduced number of shares outstanding) and hence the all-important market rating – even though there may have been no improvement in the profitability of the underlying assets of the company. Indeed, since no one could suppose sophisticated investors to be capable of believing that any additional shareholder value had thereby been created, it may be assumed that many company managements consciously use buy-backs (or rumours of them) as a stimulus to speculative bidding up of their share price to a higher level than is justified by the fundamentals. It should be noted, moreover, that the ability of companies to buy back their shares played an important part in facilitating the speculative boom in corporate takeovers – and associated 'greenmail' – in the 1980s.

The ultimate expression of official concern to promote the artificial inflation of the market value of securities may well prove to be the abolition – or at least the sharp curtailment – of capital gains taxes. These were introduced in most OECD countries from the 1950s onwards so as to counter the distortion and unfairness resulting from the ability of companies and investors to avoid tax on investment income by not distributing profits in the form of (taxable) dividends but retaining it within the company and thereby allowing investors to be rewarded with (non-taxable) capital gains. From the time of their introduction there has been a general consensus that taxing such gains was desirable on grounds of both fiscal equity and economic efficiency. Yet since the late 1980s there has been an increasingly vociferous lobby in the US Congress – which has found echos in Britain – in favour of cutting or even abolishing them.

What makes this demand so remarkable is that it comes at a time when the fiscal crisis of the Western world is intensifying, although the inevitable effect of such a measure would be to diminish state revenues significantly – especially since, taken in conjunction with the ability to distribute profits by buying back shares largely free of tax, it would mean an end to the payment of taxable dividends. That it can now be seriously proposed must thus be seen as reflecting a heedless desperation among capitalists to sacrifice everything to propping up market asset values.

All the devices just described are ways of artificially boosting the rates of return on investments in response to unrelenting pressures to push them ever higher. Theoretically, of course, this problem might be resolved if these forces were somehow to abate, so that the market rate of return could fall to a more readily attainable level. However, history suggests unambiguously that the only way this can happen under a competitive market system is by means of a destructive 'crash' rather than an orderly retreat to lower returns. Moreover, now that investment in equities and other financial assets has come to play such a central role in determining the level of pensions, a major decline in the returns to such investment would in any event have dramatic social and political implications.

Hence a sober assessment of these various stratagems must surely conclude that, for all the undoubted ingenuity of the financial manipulators, it can only be a matter of time before the forces of economic gravity reassert themselves and the reality of systemic financial failure must be faced.

Notes

1. *OECD Institutional Investors – Statistical Yearbook 1997* (first year of publication).

2. Figures derived from OECD data.

3. In fact official surveys have shown that the quality of service has got worse since privatisation despite the higher subsidy.

4. This point has even been recognised by the right-wing *Economist* (28 January 1995) notwithstanding its generally unqualified enthusiasm for privatisation.

5. Indeed the conversion of the mutual Trustee Savings Bank into a quoted joint-stock company in 1987 was promoted by the government – which had statutory responsibility for the bank but did not own it – in the same way as the privatisation of the public utilities.

6. Reaching a peak of $349 million in 1988 (source: Securities Data).

7. J.F. Rill and A.P. Victor, *Here's to a More Significant Role for Efficiencies in US Merger Analysis,* Report to the Business and Industry Advisory Committee of the OECD, 1996.

8. *Financial Times* Survey of International Corporate Finance, 22 May 1996.

9. This involves existing senior managers of the subsidiary concerned (or, in the case of a buy-in, highly reputable outsiders brought in to run the company) being lent money to buy a large proportion of the equity of the new company, while other investors take up the rest, with a view to eventual flotation.

10. Bank for International Settlements, *International Banking and Financial Market Developments*, February 1997. By the end of 1995 the total amounts at risk in the derivatives market totalled over $50 trillion (around double the GDP of the whole world).

11. OECD, *Financial Market Trends*, February 1996.

12. Quoted in the *Financial Times*, 27 January 1995.

13. Source: *Global Financial Data*. The conclusions are based mainly on US and British market statistics, but are broadly reflected in the trends in other financial markets for which historic data do not go back as far (with the exception of the very special case of Japan).

14. Source: *OECD World Economic Outlook*, June 1997. The 1990–96 average rate of return was even higher than that recorded over the decade of the 1970s, despite the fact that GDP growth in the 1970s was on average nearly double that recorded in 1990–96.

15. Source: ibid.

16. It is true that social-security contributions, of which employers (i.e. companies) continued to account for nearly two-thirds, has been the fastest growing component of tax revenue, rising to over 25 per cent of the total by 1994. Yet since this amount has been charged against corporate profits before calculating their share of GDP it merely serves to emphasise how dramatic the increase in the latter has been.

17. D. Puga, 'Recipe for Reform: Regional Policy for an Enlarging European Union', *Centre Piece* (magazine of the Centre for Economic Performance, London School of Economics), Autumn 1997. The data relate to 1988–90.

18. The US had no social-security system at all until 1936, and there has always been a certain political bias against pensions or other benefits funded directly by the state – as distinct from state subsidies to private funding.

19. It has only recorded a surplus in one year since its creation in 1974.

20. Through the Companies Act of 1981 in Britain and regulations issued by the Securities Exchange Commission in the United States in 1979 and 1983. The practice still remains largely illegal in continental Europe.

9

Wider Symptoms of Disintegration: I – The Wreckage of Soviet Communism

The growing weakness of the industrialised market economies as they struggle to reconcile their contradictory internal pressures is compounded by economic disasters in the rest of the world to which they are increasingly incapable of responding. The result of this impotence is growing instability, which serves to increase the degree of uncertainty and risk in the global investment climate. In particular, the sudden collapse of the Soviet empire in the 1980s has confronted the Western world with a challenge it has thus far proved singularly unable to meet.

From the end of World War II to the mid-1980s it was a more or less unchanging assumption of Western governments that the Soviet Union (together with its satellite and client states, mainly in Eastern Europe) represented the major threat to the security of the capitalist world. This belief was based both on the perception that the USSR was a totalitarian communist state dedicated to promoting the overthrow of capitalism and on recognition of its capacity, as a nuclear power and possessor of sophisticated technology, to obliterate the West physically. As noted by numerous commentators, this assumption not only guided the strongly interventionist foreign policy pursued by its rival superpower, the United States, supported with varying degrees of enthusiasm by its allies among the other Western industrialised countries; it also provided the justification for a huge and highly lucrative armaments programme in the USA and for other state-backed initiatives deemed to be of 'strategic' importance (such as the space programme and research and development in a number of sectors).

While the notion of the Red menace seemed all too plausible in the 1950s and 1960s – as the Soviet Union demonstrated a continued ability both to rival Western technology (notably in space travel) and to foster anti-US forces in countries such as Vietnam – by the early 1970s signs of economic weakness were already apparent. This was particularly true of East European satellites such as Poland and Hungary, where political dissatisfaction with low living standards, as well as with continued Soviet domination, was strong. This was reflected in an increased eagerness to borrow money from the West and to acquire Western technology – a desire which was matched by the enthusiasm of Western companies and governments (led by Chancellor Brandt's administration in West Germany) to meet it. Doubtless the latter was also in part a symptom of incipient concern in the OECD countries to find new markets to compensate for the saturation of those in the West, which was further exacerbated by the recession of the mid-1970s. As a result substantial loans were made by Western banks to Eastern Bloc countries during the 1970s, mainly for the supply of equipment and technology – as they were, for similar reasons, to many Third World countries. Just as in the latter case, however, both lenders and borrowers – in their eagerness respectively to sell and to acquire the goods concerned – failed to consider carefully enough just how or whether the loans could be repaid.

The rising debt-service obligations resulting from these loans – and the consequent need from the late 1970s to impose greater domestic austerity in order to meet them – was unquestionably a factor behind the renewed political discontent in the region, culminating in the overthrow of the Gierek government in Poland and the ensuing upheavals in 1980–81. A more important reason for this turmoil, however, was the growing economic crisis in the Soviet Union itself, resulting in its diminishing ability to meet its commitments to the satellite states, particularly in terms of cheap energy supplies. These problems were exacerbated by the disastrous war in Afghanistan, beginning in 1978, and the subsequent re-intensification of the nuclear missile race with the USA following the election of President Reagan in 1980. In fact the imminent bankruptcy of the Soviet Union was probably discernible by the authorities well before the death of President Brezhnev in 1982, although only after the accession to power of Mikhail Gorbachev in 1985 was it officially acknowledged to be a reality.

Different factors have been cited to explain this economic

breakdown. Supporters of US policy, particularly under the Reagan administration, claim that by stepping up the arms race in the early 1980s the USA finally stretched the resources of the 'evil empire' to breaking point and thereby achieved victory for the West in the Cold War – although the same commentators tend to deny that this effort could have had any negative effects on the US economy. In reality the latter was hardly unscathed by the conflict, which had required successive US administrations to devote huge fiscal resources to defence-related spending (including the space programme). Once the post-war boom receded, the cost of this became increasingly hard to bear in the face of demands for more spending on social and other more politically appealing programmes. Thus by the 1980s the effort was contributing substantially to the growing fiscal and debt burdens of the USA and its allies – even as it yet remained a crucial prop to the profitability and growth of a large part of the corporate sector. In a sense, therefore, the outcome of the contest between the two superpowers may be likened to one between a pair of traditional prizefighters, where victory goes to the last one to collapse from exhaustion.

Yet although the defence burden did become more and more intolerable in the dying days of the Soviet era, the country's inability to sustain it can only be explained in terms of more fundamental flaws in the organisation of the economy. These would almost certainly have caused it to collapse in any event – even though this would probably have been delayed if the Afghan war and the intensification of the arms race had not occurred.

Although the precise nature and extent of the weaknesses in Soviet economic management were for long concealed from Western observers by the veil of secrecy cast over the whole system before 1985, it is now clear that its central deficiencies were:

- reliance on planning based on administratively determined priorities and quantitative targets without any reference to market demand signals;
- lack of meaningful systems for measuring or controlling costs – particularly at enterprise level – and a consequent inability to relate prices to true costs of production and distribution; and
- closed, dictatorial structures of management and administration, resulting in pervasive corruption, systematic suppression of criticism, and distortion of the facts about economic performance.

The development of such a dysfunctional system, and its survival for so many decades, can only be understood in the context of a society based on the principle of rigid adherence to a monolithic ideology. Indeed the power of this indoctrination has been such that even by the mid-1990s, after ten years of *glasnost* (openness), many highly educated officials in the former Soviet Union find it very difficult (as the author has observed at first hand) to accept that the system's inherent inefficiencies were bound to lead to economic ruin and that it must in consequence be abandoned.

Objectively, however, there can be no disputing the reality of this ruin and of the social breakdown and disorder that have accompanied it. All over the ex-Soviet empire this is manifest in such phenomena as

- crumbling public infrastructure and services;
- enterprises (agricultural and industrial) whose capital stock has not been renewed for decades and is run down to the point where it can now barely function at all;
- enterprises without money to pay more than a fraction of their current costs, including staff salaries, so that they only survive at all thanks to fraud and misappropriation of resources; and
- increasingly corrupt public officials, prevalence of organised crime and a general breakdown in law and order.

Although the failings and potentially disastrous consequences of the Soviet economic system had been consistently pointed out by Western propaganda, it seems clear that its quite sudden collapse after 1985 took the governments of the 'free world' largely by surprise. This was evident from the disconcerted reaction of the Reagan administration to President Gorbachev's radical proposals for disarmament at the Reykjavik summit in 1985, and even in the generally confused response of the Western allies to the dismantling of the Berlin Wall in 1989 and the subsequent rapid moves towards German reunification. More importantly, there seems to have been little awareness at the time of the collapse of just how extensive was the economic decay which had precipitated it – and correspondingly little idea as to what the West could or should do about it.

It is scarcely surprising, particularly in view of the strongly right-wing political tide still running in the capitalist world at that time, that there was an outpouring of triumphalist rhetoric from US and European leaders celebrating the evident demonstration of the superiority of the capitalist system. Indeed, given the mounting problems facing the Western market economies (described in earlier chapters), the fall of Communism was an especially welcome opportunity to engage in ideological point-scoring. Yet given the reality of the West's own chronic economic weakness – particularly in terms of slowing growth rates, high unemployment and soaring public indebtedness – its ability to capitalise on the situation by offering large-scale aid in support of a revival and transformation of the ex-Communist economies was severely constrained.

Indeed the leadership of the Western world has been hard put to frame an appropriate response to the unexpectedly sudden demise of Soviet power ever since the dissolution of the USSR in 1991 – despite an ostensibly strong political will to help the process of reform and promote the enhancement of living standards in the former Soviet bloc. The self-interest of the European Union in particular in pursuing this goal has been obvious from the outset. For the potential danger to the security of Western Europe from a large, impoverished and unstable group of countries on its eastern flank is all too readily apparent – and indeed has been chillingly demonstrated on a relatively small scale by the conflict in the former Yugoslavia.

Despite these manifest dangers the Western effort to help redress the plight of the 'economies in transition' has been pitifully small. In the immediate aftermath of the collapse there was considerable idealistic talk of a 'Marshall Plan' for the countries of the East along the lines of the brilliantly successful programme of US aid to Europe in the 1940s and 1950s. In fact, it has been suggested, perhaps with some justification, that in the absence of a genuine ideological orientation to the market economy and a legal and cultural climate favouring private business there is little prospect of anything resembling the Marshall Plan achieving more than limited success in the ex-Soviet empire. Arguably, therefore, it was appropriate to insist, as the Western donor community has done, on the need to begin by devoting significant resources, in the form of technical assistance, to effecting a radical change in the bureaucratic Leninist culture still prevailing.

Yet precisely because of these ideological and institutional limitations, as well as the state of total financial and infrastructural collapse of all the countries of the former Soviet Union, it seems bizarre that the donors should have at the same time required them rapidly to implement economic policies based on a combination of extreme liberalisation and rigid monetary orthodoxy – as a precondition of receiving any Western aid at all. The essential features of this approach have been rapid moves to

- decontrol prices or else – where markets are effectively (and unavoidably) dominated by state monopolies, as with energy and other public utilities – increase prices to reflect costs of production and distribution;
- remove all barriers to imports other than relatively low tariffs;
- remove all restrictions on capital movements to and from other countries;
- fully liberalise the financial sector, entailing the right of all private sector companies to establish banks;
- privatise state-owned enterprises;
- balance the state budget; and
- impose high real interest rates and restrict credit creation in order to contain inflation. In line with the precepts of the International Monetary Fund this is often done in conjunction with manipulation of the exchange rate so as to try and maintain it at a fixed level and thereby enable it to constitute a 'nominal anchor' against inflation.

To the extent that countries have actually attempted, under duress, to implement the full range of these drastic policy shifts, their combined impact has been quite devastating, especially on the distorted and weakened economies of the former Soviet Union itself. Rapid adjustment of prices to reflect real costs, while obviously desirable as a long-term goal, has meant an inevitable sharp cut in real personal incomes, while the simultaneous imposition of a severe credit squeeze has further stifled domestic purchasing power. Combined with full exposure to foreign competition – made more burdensome in most cases by an increasingly overvalued national currency, as the 'nominal anchor' exchange-rate policy fails to prevent continuing inflation (albeit at a lower rate) – and the loss of traditional export markets in the rest of the former Soviet Union, these developments have rendered productive activity largely unviable. The result is that a large proportion of agricultural and industrial enterprises have effectively ceased production, while most of those that have not are technically bankrupt and only continue to trade by systematically withholding payment from their creditors (including their own employees) – in a way which would be treated as illegal in normal market economies. Coming on top of this, privatisation seems at best an irrelevance, at worst a stimulus to stripping the few remaining assets of the companies concerned. A graphic, but not untypical, example of the combined effects of these policies is the fact that in 1995 the single biggest export from Georgia – just one of the fifteen independent republics created by the dissolution of the USSR in 1991 – was reportedly scrap metal looted from collapsed industrial enterprises (many of them 'privatised').[1] Statistically these tendencies are reflected in a decline in gross domestic product of at least 35 per cent in all former Soviet republics since 1990, with the majority witnessing a fall closer to 50 per cent.

Inevitably the creation of such poor prospects in the productive sectors of the economy means that the only viable forms of activity are trade and speculation, notably in foreign currency. At the same time the effective absence of any exchange controls serves to facilitate capital flight, although in any event the high profitability of cross-border trade and the consequent strong incentive to corruption of customs officers means that in any case it is quite easy to move foreign exchange abroad. In these circumstances hyperinflation and the total collapse of the national currency are only avoided by raising real interest rates even higher and deploying official foreign-exchange reserves to achieve an artificially stable exchange rate.

The general climate of lawlessness has been exacerbated by the failure to establish a framework of legislation – governing such basic matters as property rights, corporate accountability and bankruptcy – as well as the means to enforce them, such as are generally recognised in the West as essential to the minimally adequate functioning of a market economy. The result has been the wide-scale incidence of banking fraud, often at the expense of small savers, for which there is no legal redress and which governments often seem content to ignore. One of the most notorious examples of this was the 'MMM' scandal in Russia in 1994, when what turned out to be a straightforward 'pyramid' scheme[2] was allowed to continue advertising for new investors on state television even after it had declared its inability to repay existing depositors and where the founder and chief executive of the company was able to secure immunity from prosecution by having himself (fraudulently) elected to parliament. More recently (in 1997) the eruption of a similar scandal in Albania brought this poorest of European countries to the brink of civil war.

In such an economic and ethical environment it is small wonder that a large proportion of the population feels constrained to resort to crime and illicit trade as the only means of survival. This trend is all the more inevitable in that illegal parallel markets were already well developed in the declining years of the Soviet Union, often involving senior state and party officials in de facto organised racketeering. In giving a further stimulus to this tendency, the 'reform' process insisted on by the West has not only created a climate of economic and social insecurity but, by driving an ever greater proportion of activity underground, has removed it from the purview of the tax authorities and rendered the state even more bankrupt than at the point of the Soviet Union's collapse.

The adoption of such an approach – referred to by its advocates as 'shock therapy' – is all the more astonishing in that there is no historical precedent anywhere in the world for it succeeding, in terms of transforming poor countries into prosperous ones by exposing them to unrestricted competition with much stronger economies. Indeed it has been a central presumption of policy towards the 'developing' world ever since World War II (enshrined in the General Agreement on Tariffs and Trade) that economically backward countries must be granted offsetting support and privileges vis-à-vis the industrialised market economies if they are eventually to become internationally competitive and thereby raise their living standards. Moreover, as noted in earlier chapters, from the earliest phase of their industrialisation none of the industrial market economies of the West has ever allowed itself to be wholly exposed to unbridled market forces.

The ostensible broad justification for imposing a more swift and radical change in the Eastern bloc countries has been based on the view that their economic state was so distorted at the time of Communism's collapse that they were not susceptible to gradual reform and must therefore be exposed to sudden and total recasting. Yet the essentially metaphysical basis of this assertion is attested by the inability of its proponents to find either a theoretical or empirical justification for it. Rather they are reduced, as in a recent World Bank apologia for shock therapy, to citing the aphorism of a distinguished non-economist, the playwright president of the Czech Republic, Vaclav Havel, that 'it is impossible to cross a chasm in two leaps' as a serious argument in its favour.[3]

A still more baffling question for any objective observer must be why the capitalist West should have persisted with the attempt to impose such extreme *laissez-faire* policies even after the predictable result – the making of a bad economic situation worse and creation of dangerous social tensions – has become manifest. For although the avowed aim of US and European policy is to convince the people of the former Communist states of the benefits of the market economy, it is hard to believe they are unaware that shock therapy has, on the contrary, created widespread and profound disillusionment with the market system – such that there is even growing support for a reversion to the Soviet model of economic management despite its disastrous record.

The Relative Success of Eastern Europe

Defenders of the shock-therapy approach often attempt to suggest that certain ex-Communist countries have actually succeeded in stabilising their economies, and even achieving a measure of growth, by pursuing such radically orthodox policies. Perhaps the most commonly cited examples are Poland and the Czech Republic, where economic growth has turned clearly positive since around 1993.[4] However, to the extent that this success is real and durable – which is in any case open to doubt – it can scarcely be attributed to adoption of anything resembling the standard shock-therapy prescription, from which both countries have deviated in some important respects.

In particular, both countries have retained a large measure of state ownership and control of the banking system. This in turn has enhanced the ability of the authorities to maintain stability within the financial sector as a whole, intervening far more decisively than their counterparts in Russia and other countries of the former Soviet Union to ensure the closure or takeover of the numerous small private banks which were opened in the early phase of the reform process but (in the majority of cases) failed as a result of mismanagement or fraud. Moreover, the state's continued dominant role in the banking sector has undoubtedly played an important part in enabling both governments to ensure that the privatisation of non-financial state enterprises has not been allowed to have such a disruptive impact on output and employment as has occurred elsewhere in the 'transition' economies.

In the case of Poland this has evidently been an important factor behind the very slow pace of privatisation of the larger industrial enterprises, making it possible to channel funds to businesses which might in many cases have been forced into liquidation if made wholly dependent on private-sector sources of finance. In the Czech Republic it has meant that, despite what was once acclaimed as a very successful mass privatisation of most of the economy, the state has retained a large measure of de facto control of the corporate sector, both through equity stakes held directly by the big four banks in many privatised enterprises and through the investment funds which they set up to act as channels for the millions of individual share owners created by mass privatisation (the equivalent of mutual funds or investment trusts in the West). Consequently the pattern of ownership and control in the Czech economy resembles the corporatist structure traditional in Germany and other West European countries (not to mention Japan) far more closely than the extreme *laissez-faire* model which is preached by the zealots of shock therapy and is being imposed with such disastrous effect on most countries of the former Soviet Union.

At the same time both Poland and the Czech Republic have largely eschewed the standard shock-therapy prescription for monetary and exchange-rate management, having either abandoned, or never applied, the policy of fixing the exchange rate as a 'nominal anchor' against inflation.[5] Instead they have been able for the most part to keep the their currencies somewhat undervalued against major Western currencies despite having rates of inflation that are relatively high by OECD standards. Their ability thus to maintain a reasonable degree of currency and price stability has also been enhanced by their continuing use of exchange controls to curb destabilising outflows of money – again in defiance of the shock-therapy model. Hence, in contrast to virtually all countries in the former Soviet Union, they have for the most part ensured their currencies remain relatively undervalued and thereby given themselves a more competitive cost structure appealing to foreign investors.[6]

It is also striking that, despite their rejection of certain key elements of the standard 'reform' prescription laid down by the International Monetary Fund for former centrally planned economies, both Poland and the Czech Republic have continued to enjoy relatively generous support from the foreign donor community. In this they differ sharply from most countries in the ex-Soviet bloc, including Russia itself, which have been compelled by international donors to swallow the full dose of austerity and liberalisation despite starting from a much more unfavourable position than those states bordering on Western Europe. Yet, because the effect of this has been a continued fall in output and the transfer of more activity to the parallel economy, they have been quite unable to reduce their budget deficits in line with the demands of the IMF and in consequence have failed to meet the conditions laid down for receiving significant quantities of aid.

China: The Great Exception

A still more remarkable anomaly, however, is presented by China, a country which, despite being still avowedly Communist and making no pretence whatever of practising democracy, is yet treated by the West as being in transition to a market economy. This is because of the 'open door' policy it has pursued since the late 1970s, involving the provision of generous incentives to foreign companies to invest in joint ventures in China, at the same time typically transferring technology and know-how to the Chinese partner. Such deals have been very attractive to many foreign companies because of both the low cost base in China (especially of labour) and the potentially huge and undeveloped Chinese market, contrasting strongly with the largely saturated ones in the OECD countries. The country has also benefited from the existence of the large and wealthy Chinese diaspora in other East Asian countries with a strong predisposition (cultural as well as financial) to invest heavily in the mother country. The result has been very rapid growth, averaging some 8–9 per cent a year in the fifteen years up to the mid-1990s.

In the present context the most striking feature of China's recent economic development is the fact that it has received vast financial support from Western donors[7] and commercial banks despite following policies largely at variance with the principles of shock therapy, as imposed on nearly all former Soviet bloc countries. Thus although it has largely abandoned centralised planning, there has been virtually no privatisation of state enterprises and the economy remains dominated by the public sector.[8] Indeed, aside from micro-enterprises, virtually the only businesses under effective private control are foreign joint ventures (although the local partner in such cases is often state controlled). Equally, foreign trade remains largely under government control and subject to administered prices, while even internal trade remains subject to official intervention. Likewise, although there has been some liberalisation of domestic prices (especially in the agricultural sector), this is bound to be of limited significance in an economy still dominated by the public sector, where enterprise managers inevitably remain exposed to government pressure to limit price increases (despite official protestations to the contrary). At the same time, moreover, the financial sector remains almost totally state dominated, which also helps facilitate the government's continuing tight control of capital flows out of the country.

The truth is that China's phenomenal growth since the late 1970s has been largely the result of the authorities' willingness not only to permit but to encourage the growth of what amounts to a parallel free-enterprise sector (but within the formal economy) without substantially reforming, let alone phasing out, the existing state-owned sector. Their determination to do this is most vividly symbolised by the fact that the tax regime applying to foreign joint-venture companies is actually more favourable than that governing purely national enterprises (even more so in the Special Economic Zones set up in various coastal cities specifically to attract joint ventures).

It must be said that there are many grounds, at the time of writing, for doubting whether the relative economic success of Poland, the Czech Republic or China can be sustained, particularly in the face of an increasingly stagnant and more competitive global economy. Equally there is no denying that other former Eastern bloc countries which have substantially departed from the shock-therapy prescription, such as Romania, have been far less successful in bringing about economic stabilisation or growth. Nevertheless it ought scarcely to be a matter of dispute that the economic performance of those economies in transition which have largely avoided imposing the radical measures of liberalisation and strict financial orthodoxy demanded by Western aid donors has been distinctly less disastrous than that of virtually all those ex-Communist countries which have struggled vainly to adhere to the impossibly rigid model precribed by Western donors.

Despite this seemingly obvious inference, there remains a solid weight of rhetorical support for shock therapy among the most prominent Western economists, as well as from the major donor institutions themselves. This typically takes the form of claims that

- Those countries which have achieved some degree of growth and stabilisation have done so by dint of following the shock-therapy prescription. A common tendency is to exaggerate the extent and success of privatisation – even though very often the process amounts to no more than a nominal transfer of ownership in enterprises without significant assets, or else the virtual gift of businesses or assets to senior officials and their families.

- In so far as it is conceded that China's relative success has been accomplished with the retention of a state-dominated economic model, this has been justified by its exceptionally large rural labour surplus being available for redeployment into new market-oriented enterprises without causing an imbalance in the existing productive sector. Since other economies in transition lack this advantage, the argument runs, shock therapy is needed to stimulate a shake-out of resources in inefficient state-owned industries as a prerequisite to economic regeneration (this despite the fact that after several years of shock therapy and falling output there is now substantial de facto unemployment and surplus labour in the former Soviet Union).

- In those countries, including Russia and nearly all other states of the former Soviet Union, where the imposition of shock therapy since 1991 has been accompanied by a continuing fall in output, devastated living standards and the virtual collapse of law and order, the decline will soon be reversed as stabilisation is achieved and the conditions for profitable investment are created. Many advocates of this view have annually proclaimed since the early 1990s that Russia's GDP growth would turn positive 'next year' and continue to do so despite the failure of their earlier predictions – perhaps in the belief that it is bound to happen sooner or later, if only because there must be a limit to how far it can fall.

The obstinate adherence of the Western establishment to a view so evidently at odds with objective reality calls for some explanation, especially as its insistence on doing so now poses a clear and growing threat to civil peace in a part of the world where nuclear weapons remain a potential danger. Their position seems all the more perverse in that the experience of Germany and Japan after World War II, when both countries achieved miraculous economic revivals with the help of massive injections of US aid – or, in the case of Japan, acceptance of its right to export freely to the West while heavily protecting its own domestic market – has long been thought to demonstrate the benefits of providing economic support to a defeated enemy – in contrast to the ruinously vindictive reparations imposed on Germany after the First World War. Thus the economic terms of surrender being imposed on Russia and its former allies are more akin to those of the Versailles Treaty than the Marshall Plan.

One possible inference is that the former Soviet empire is being more harshly treated because the leadership of the West secretly fears a resurgence of the Russian military 'threat'. Yet such a hypothesis is hard to square with the much more indulgent treatment accorded to China, even though the latter could be considered just as plausible a military menace and retains strong ideological and political differences with the West, not least because of its rejection of democracy and its appalling human-rights record.

In the final analysis it is hard to reach any other conclusion than that the West's insistence on clinging to the shock-therapy dogma is dictated largely by its own looming fiscal bankrutpcy and the related need to divert an ever growing proportion of state resources to propping up the market value of capital in the wider global economy. For governments which feel consequently compelled to cut spending on vital public services and infrastructure at home are bound to find it difficult, in political as well as practical terms, to devote much of their taxpayers' money to rebuilding the run-down infrastructure of the former Soviet bloc, particularly since the cost would run to hundreds of billions of dollars. Yet it is clearly awkward to have to make such a reason public, as it would entail proclaiming the West's own economic weakness to the world. At the same time it might well be seen as politically embarrassing to support strategies based on extensive state intervention abroad while proclaiming the virtues of *laissez faire* at home. For these reasons it is considered more expedient

- to impose on the ex-Communist countries such severe conditions for receiving aid that they will inevitably be unable to meet them and hence not qualify for significant donor support; but at the same time,
- to invent specious reasons for allowing exceptions to the shock-therapy rules in cases where this seems politically or commercially desirable.

Whatever the true rationale for the pursuit of the shock-therapy strategy, by 1997 the practical contradictions of trying to sustain it had become grotesquely obvious, even though this fact was scarcely acknowleged by the mainstream media in the West. Thus the Russian government – under the Western-approved reformist duo of Anatoly Chubais and Boris Nemtsov – had so far lost control of the state finances that it was forced to declare its budget invalid and go back to parliament with new proposals to fill the gap, while at the same time the World Bank – in an unprecedented move – felt obliged to provide a $10 billion loan to help the government meet the huge arrears in state wages and pensions.

As we shall see in the next chapter, a similar refusal to face economic reality – accompanied by a comparable systematic perversion of the truth – is being applied to justify the industrialised world's failure to address the even greater catastrophe of the Third World – and for similar reasons.

Notes

1. *Georgian Economic Trends*, published by European Union (TACIS) September 1996.

2. A fraudulent practice whereby the funds from new depositors, lured by promises of high returns, are used to pay out to existing ones instead of being invested in income-yielding assets. Although illegal in Western market economies, these have been allowed to operate in a number of former Soviet bloc countries besides Russia – often, it appears, to the personal benefit of senior government officials – but seemingly without eliciting any demands from Western donors for their suppression.

3. *From Plan to Market. World Development Report 1996*, World Bank, Washington DC.

4. Hungary, although in a similar economic condition, cannot be considered a comparable case since its 'reform' process began much earlier (in the 1970s) and has been much more gradual, thus avoiding any need for shock therapy.

5. See *Economic Transformation in Central Europe: A Progress Report*, Centre for Economic Policy Research, London 1993. The damaging consequences of maintaining an uncompetitive exchange rate have also been recognised in Lithuania, which in 1997 announced its intention to abandon this policy in favour of one of progressive devaluation.

6. In fact, the Czech government's shift to a strong exchange-rate policy in pursuit of lower inflation from 1996 has only served to underline the dangers of such an approach, since it has resulted in a widening trade deficit, declining output and increasing disenchantment among foreign investors.

7. It has consistently received twice as much as Russia in loans from the World Bank throughout the 1990s.

8. An announcement in 1997 of the government's intention to move towards privatising state enterprises – which if genuine will inevitably take years to implement – is evidently a response to the increasingly intolerable financial burden incurred by the state in funding their losses rather than to pressure from foreign donors.

10

Wider Symptoms of Disintegration: II – Third World Catastrophe

As the West seeks to grapple with the problems of the collapsed Soviet empire, it is also finding it increasingly hard either to ignore or to cope with the equally intractable ones of the rest of the world outside the industrialised OECD countries. The nations concerned, accounting for over half the world's population (three-quarters if China is included), comprise mainly former colonies of OECD countries in Asia, Africa and Latin America. They have commonly been referred to collectively as either the Third World or developing or less developed countries (LDCs), and this convention is followed here, even though it is certainly arguable that they are not a sufficiently homogeneous group to be covered by any meaningful definition of such terms. On the other hand the fact that a limited number of 'developing' countries may have attained, or be close to attaining, the living standards of industrialised (OECD) countries scarcely constitutes a reason for claiming, as some have done, either that the term 'Third World' never amounted to a meaningful classification or that it is rapidly ceasing to do so.

At all events what is indisputably true is that the vast majority of the countries commonly identified as belonging to the Third World have only emerged from direct colonial dependence on one or other of the industrialised countries (the First World) since World War II – although in the case of Latin America this happened over a hundred years earlier. Scarcely less disputable, but officially denied, is the fact that they have remained largely dependent economically (if not politically) on the corporations and states of the rich industrialised world – notwithstanding their nominal status as sovereign independent countries.

In fact it is evident that, for all the rhetoric about 'self-determination' and international brotherhood which accompanied the decolonisation of the Third World, independence has not yet led to any fundamental change in the relationship of the 'liberated' countries with the industrialised world – even though most of the posts in government and business once held by Europeans are now filled by local people, and the developed world's influence over them is exercised less formally than in the colonial era, often by private commercial interests rather than through government channels. Arguably indeed, as suggested earlier, the decolonisation process resulted as much from the imperial powers' desire to shed the costly and politically embarrassing burden of administering these territories as from the demand of their inhabitants to be rid of their demeaning status as subject peoples.

It is by no means clear that it was ever the serious intention of the departing colonial powers to create nation-states which stood a reasonable chance of attaining economic independence to match their nominal political sovereignty. Had it been so they might have made more of an effort than they did to create entities having the size and resources capable of supporting the minimum necessary infrastructure for a modern state – entailing more gradual progress to decolonisation – instead of creating a large number of small and impoverished states (particularly in Africa, the Caribbean and the South Pacific) which could never hope to generate the necessary revenue themselves. That they preferred the latter course is probably attributable to a combination of a wish to perpetuate dependency through fragmentation (particularly in the case of France's disengagement from its African possessions) and alarm at the potential cost of continuing to support territories without significant fiscal resources of their own (perhaps more applicable to the British attitude).[1] In either sense the decolonisation process could be likened, in the jargon of present-day corporate management, to the demerging of unprofitable subsidiaries or outsourcing of operations which it is no longer cost-effective to retain in-house. Following the same analogy, there was never any likelihood that the parent company's dominance of the market could be challenged as long as it retained effective control of the technology, sources of capital and distribution channels.

For as long as the Cold War lasted the need to retain such effective dominance was seen to be as much political as economic. US foreign policy, with varying degrees of support from its allies, was dedicated to the 'containment' of the supposed threat of Soviet influence expanding across the globe – even though this was often illusory, since the Soviet Union never had the resources to compete with the West as a source of economic largesse, and as time went by was progressively less able to impose itself even on neighbouring countries such as Afghanistan. Hence the objectives of the industrialised world in the post-colonial era were not essentially different from those followed by the individual imperial powers, and by Britain in particular, before the granting of formal independence – namely, to retain effective economic and political control at minimum cost.

The perception that such was the reality behind the liberal rhetoric gave rise to the denunciation of 'neo-colonialism' by post-independence Third World leaders such as Kwame Nkrumah of Ghana – though their hostility did not prevent most of them from succumbing to the blandishments of international corporations where these were accompanied by large personal pay-offs and other favours. In any event such complaints were largely lost, in the immediate post-colonial era, amid a more general consensus that independence would bring a boost to economic development in Africa and Asia. Even Latin America, which remained obstinately backward a century or more after its liberation from colonial rule, was proclaimed to be on the brink of a breakthrough to a higher level of development, as notably under the US-inspired Alliance for Progress initiated in the early 1960s.

This generally positive climate of belief in the need for, and possibility of, rapid economic development in the Third World led to the emergence of a whole new branch of economic study – 'development economics' – dedicated to identifying the most effective strategies for enabling the LDCs to catch up with the advanced nations of the 'North'. At the same time it spawned a steadily expanding number of development aid institutions and programmes with the ostensible purpose of channelling finance and technical assistance to LDCs in support of the development process. These included a variety of agencies under the aegis of the United Nations (UN Development Programme, Food and Agriculture Organisation etc.), the World Bank and a number of regional development banks, together with national aid agencies of the individual donor countries. Together these bodies, along with the numerous academic institutions and consultancy organisations which advise and support them, constitute what is often referred to as the aid 'industry'. Since the 1960s it has been instrumental in disbursing over 0.3 per cent of the OECD's aggregate gross national product a year (equal to over $50 billion in 1993) in development aid of one form or another.[2]

Yet for all the extensive resources of money, time and talent expended in pursuit of the ostensible goal of raising the living standards of the Third World closer to those of the industrialised countries, there has been little indication of a sustained movement in this direction for the vast majority of the developing nations. On the contrary, all the evidence points to the conclusion that the relative economic condition of the Third World as a whole has experienced a net deterioration since the early 1960s, compared with that of the OECD countries. Thus the most authoritative statistical indicators show that average income (gross national product per head) in the Industrial Market Economies (roughly equivalent to the OECD) grew at a broadly similar average rate to that of the Lower and Middle Income Economies (the rest of the world apart from the Soviet bloc) from 1960 to the mid-1980s – so that the ratio of the former to the latter remained in the range 16–18:1 throughout the period. However, by 1994 this ratio had jumped to around 24:1, reflecting the fact that growth in income per head in the Third World has declined even faster than in the industrialised countries between the two periods – from over 3 per cent a year to under 1 per cent.[3] This has occurred despite the fact that some countries – notably China and a number of other, smaller nations in East Asia – have achieved quite spectacular growth in national income per head (6–8 per cent or more a year) since the early 1980s, in contrast to the more general Third World trend (the growth of income per head in Africa, the Middle East and Latin America combined was close to zero over the ten years to 1994).

Such measures of comparative human welfare – based on methods of computing national accounts which cannot adequately take cognisance of informal, non-monetary economic activity nor, in a world of perennially distorted exchange rates, properly reflect relative purchasing power – may justly be queried. However, even if this means that the official data cited above significantly overstate the gap between 'First World' and Third World living standards, it does not invalidate the evidence that there has been no closing of this gap over the last thirty years or more. Moreover, other indicators of the economic performance and prospects of the LDCs, taken together, show beyond dispute that the plight of much of the three-quarters of the human race who inhabit them has got worse over the last twenty years and is now, near the end of the twentieth century, as fearful as at any time since its beginning.

Unserviceable debt

The most telling indicator of the failure of development strategies in the vast majority of LDCs has been the intractable burden of external debt they have incurred since the mid-1970s. From under 20 per cent of aggregate gross national product in 1974, this had risen to 40 per cent of GNP by 1994. The factors leading to the build-up of this debt have to some extent mirrored those behind the growth in the public-sector debt burden in the OECD countries, in that they are born of governments' desire to plug a hole in their budgets combined with a desperate need on the part of financial institutions as well as governments themselves to believe that the debt will ultimately be repayable out of extra output generated either by the loan itself or by a subsequent rise in the general level of economic activity. Yet from the outset LDCs have been even more prone to the unsustainable accumulation of debt because of their lack (in most cases) of anything resembling genuinely responsible governments and the susceptibility of their rulers to the influence of profit-seeking foreign bankers and business interests, while the representatives of the 'aid industry' also had a strong institutional bias in favour of increased lending. The latter was indeed accentuated in the case of the largest of all the development finance institutions, the World Bank, by the avowed policy of its longest-serving president, Robert McNamara (1968–78), of maximising loan disbursement.

The resulting tendency to engage in inappropriate borrowing from abroad – often based on considerations of personal or institutional gain rather than ones of real economic benefit to the recipient country – did not have conspicuously adverse consequences up to the mid-1970s, largely because the prolonged global post-war boom was still continuing and enabling most Third World countries to service their debts, which in any case were still generally quite modest. Yet the final end of this boom with the 1974–75 recession proved to be even more of a watershed for Third World development than it did for the economies of the industrialised world.

Remarkably, however, the first reaction to this downturn in the OECD countries was that it heralded an era of growing economic prosperity among LDCs, or at least those on which the developed world was believed to be dependent as major suppliers of key commodities. This perception was based largely on the success of the Organisation of Petroleum Exporting Countries (OPEC) – whose members were all recognisably from the Third World – in using their power as an effective cartel to push up the price of oil sharply and thereby effect a massive transfer of income to themselves from the rest of the world. The view that other commodity producers could emulate OPEC and engineer a sustained real increase in the price of metals – or even soft commodities such as coffee – gained wide currency, as speculation drove up commodity prices to dizzy heights in the mid-1970s. Within a few years the naïveté of this notion had been fully demonstrated, as the stimulus of market forces induced both savings in usage of many commodities (including petroleum) and the opening of new sources of supply. Worse still, the long-term shift in the economic climate of the OECD countries from high growth to relative stagnation became an additional negative factor depressing demand for commodities and other exports from LDCs, so that those not in possession of significant oil wealth soon found themselves markedly worse off than before the mid-1970s' commodity boom.

In truth, the extent to which most bankers ever sincerely believed in the potential wealth of commodity-producing LDCs may reasonably be doubted. For the most important consideration in their eyes in the mid-1970s was to find any justification, however flimsy, for lending money to willing borrowers in a climate where it was still thought permissible to assume that, in the words of one of the leading US bankers of the day, 'countries cannot go bankrupt'.[4]

Already by the end of the 1970s such lending to so many irresponsible governments had in fact brought several LDCs to the brink of insolvency. The reality of the 'debt crisis', however, was largely ignored until the threatened default by Mexico on its $70 billion debt in 1982. Because of the potential threat to the global financial system of allowing a major default to occur, there has never been any question, then or since, of declaring any country bankrupt – although many of them should properly be defined as technically insolvent on even the most generous accounting criteria. Not surprisingly, given this combination of complacency and impotence on the part of the donors, successive new loans and 'reschedulings' have failed to give most LDCs the capacity to reduce their existing debt burden. Indeed they have not even been able to prevent the remorseless growth of arrears, year after year, to be added to the total and a consequent threefold rise in their accumulated external indebtedness between 1980 and 1994 to almost $2 trillion – equal to more than 160 per cent of their export earnings (nearly double the ratio recorded in 1980). Moreover, even though the softening of terms on much of this debt has restricted the rise in the average ratio of debt-service to export earnings over the period (from 13.2 to 16.6 per cent), it still means that their debt-service liabilities by 1994 were equal to around four times their annual receipts of new development aid.

Monetary collapse and capital flight

As many LDCs have become progressively less able to meet their external financial commitments since the mid-1970s, their currencies have inevitably become chronically weak and have depreciated rapidly against the US dollar and other hard currencies. The resulting high rates of inflation have tended to induce a vicious circle of hyper-inflation and depreciation. While moderate inflation has proved to be consistent with quite rapid growth and rising real incomes, above a certain level it is liable to induce a serious loss of confidence on the part of businesses of all kinds.[5] This not only discourages productive activity and stimulates more lucrative but economically damaging speculation instead; it also promotes the flight of capital out of the country into more stable currency areas, where owners can be more confident it will retain its value. The end result of such a process of monetary decline is to render the country concerned totally dependent on continual financial flows from abroad and thus subject to the dictates of foreign institutions and powers in all matters of economic management.

The rise of parallel markets

In a climate of such monetary instability there is a natural tendency for a growing proportion of commercial transactions to be conducted in foreign currency or in kind (barter), particularly if the authorities try and impose a significantly overvalued exchange rate in defiance of the dictates of the market. The result is that more and more business occurs outside the formal economy in parallel or 'black' markets. A major adverse consequence of thus driving so much economic activity underground is a corresponding reduction in the tax base, while at the same time it discourages those firms remaining in the formal economy, which may find it hard to compete with parallel market operators unless they themselves resort to similar illicit practices.

Degradation of the public sector

The dwindling tax base resulting from both the rise of parallel markets and general economic stagnation has inevitably precipitated a decline in state revenue. This has in turn reduced governments' capacity to maintain the basic functions of the state still further, leading to:

- failure to keep public officials' pay at adequate levels – so that even senior civil servants' salaries are typically equivalent to no more than $50 a month, with the result that either they neglect their official duties in order to earn a living from parallel employment or business activities, or else they are readily susceptible to corruption;
- deterioration of physical infrastructure, such as roads, power supply and telecommunications, adding greatly to the cost and inconvenience of productive and commercial activities as well as diminishing the general quality of life; and
- decline in the availability and quality of basic public services, such as health and education, with inevitably negative consequences for the social and economic fabric.

The population explosion

Excessive population growth is the most tangible symptom of Third World countries' economic predicament, and a serious handicap in their efforts to escape from it. This is not because the LDCs' current population levels are necessarily unsustainable, but because they have failed to generate the economic resources needed to cope with the expansion that has occurred. Unlike the developed North, where rapid population growth in the nineteenth century was a symptom of rising prosperity, the Third World's population explosion has largely preceded industrialisation. Hence in sharp contrast to England at the time of the Agricultural and Industrial Revolutions, where the traumas of economic change (horrendous as they were) could be partly relieved by the absorption of surplus rural population in rapidly expanding manufacturing industry, growing rural population density in the Third World has become a serious impediment to agricultural modernisation due to excessive fragmentation of land holdings and the consequent difficulty of raising rural productivity and living standards through the introduction of modern farming techniques.

Environmental decay

Increasing rural overpopulation and the poverty that goes with it are a major source of environmental degradation in Third World countries. Overgrazing of pasture (notably in sub-Saharan Africa), the destruction of forests by more and more land-hungry peasants practising slash-and-burn farming (a common phenomenon in Latin America) – as well as because of the growing demand for wood fuel in the absence of other sources of energy – and the cultivation of unterraced slopes are major contributing causes of the ever-increasing problem of soil erosion.[6] This not only creates a vicious circle of declining land productivity and further rural impoverishment but leads to wider environmental damage through increased flooding and even (as is now widely believed) climatic change. At the same time the influx of surplus population into urban areas tends to create huge agglomerations of 10 million people or more (such as Mexico City, Calcutta, Jakarta and Lagos) where the lack of means to provide adequate infrastructure leads to indiscriminate and increasingly intolerable pollution of air, water and land.

Rising lawlessness, revolution and secession

Few could be surprised that the spreading economic, social and environmental decay has produced a progressive breakdown in law and order in many Third World countries, just as it has in the former Soviet Union. The precise causes of this in each particular case may vary, although it can hardly be without significance that in many LDCs there has never been much respect for the law on the part of governments themselves, with open abuses by rich and powerful individuals frequently going unpunished and a blatant lack of impartiality on the part of the judicial system. Combined with rising social deprivation, this has often been a recipe for the growth of quasi-revolutionary movements with the avowed aim of protecting the most vulnerable communities from officially sanctioned oppression, even though very often the resistance movements themselves then resort to the same brutal methods as those employed by government forces. This has been a particular feature of Latin American countries (notably Colombia, Peru and Mexico) in the 1980s and 1990s, where the death squads and drug-trafficking syndicates linked to the ruling establishment are frequently mirrored by rebel organisations.

Elsewhere conditions have degenerated to the point where civil war has effectively broken out, as in at least six countries in Africa, including three – Somalia, Sierra Leone and Liberia – where the state has more or less ceased to exist.[7] At the same time an increasing number of countries have been afflicted by regional secessionist movements, often expressing discontent with the performance of central government and its undue subservience to particular sectional or ethnic groups – a phenomenon almost as widespread in Asia (e.g. Turkey, the Philippines, Sri Lanka) as in Africa. Attempts by the international community to resolve these conflicts, usually through the agency of United Nations peace-keeping forces, are often confounded by the difficulty of disarming guerrilla soldiers who understandably perceive the possession of a Kalashnikov rifle to be their only potential source of livelihood. The problem is frequently compounded, moreover, by the role of arms traffickers (mainly representing manufacturers from developed countries) in plying all sides with weapons.

It goes without saying that the twin phenomena of civil chaos and economic decay tend, if unchecked, to interact in a downward spiral of insecurity and hopelessness. Moreover, their effects all too easily spill over into neighbouring countries, which are often too weak to counter the threat. A good example of this is the development of huge uncontrolled contraband activities in Afghanistan – as a result of years of civil war – which has attained such a scale that it has had the effect of driving many productive enterprises in neighbouring Pakistan out of business, further exacerbating that country's already fragile economic position.[8]

The refugee explosion

Another vivid demonstration of the social and economic breakdown afflicting so much of the Third World is the rapid surge since the early 1980s in the numbers of those seeking to leave their homes in poor countries in search of a better life in richer ones, including some of the better favoured Third World states. Measuring the scale of the problem is difficult, not least because of the illegal character of most of the migration involved. Yet the millions of Latin Americans who attempt, in mosts cases unsuccessfully, to enter the United States each year across the Mexican border, the hundreds of thousands of 'boat people' annually attempting to enter the European Union from North Africa and points south, and the tenfold rise in the number of people seeking asylum in Britain between the beginning and the end of the 1980s all testify to the exponential rise in the number of those feeling they have little to lose by risking all in abandoning their own countries for a new life somewhere else.

A slightly different phenomenon – the refugees displaced by famine, war and the threat of genocide – has also been increasing sharply since the early 1980s, particularly in Africa. According to official statistics the total number affected – including the large numbers in Europe displaced by the civil upheavals in the former Communist states – rose from around 10 million in 1985 to 26 million in 1995.[9] Arguably such enforced mass migrations are an even more direct reflection of social and economic breakdown, even though some (such as in the cases of Angola, Afghanistan and Cambodia) may be viewed more as hangovers from earlier Cold War conflicts.

The Failure of 'Reform'

Faced with such overwhelming evidence of this burgeoning catastrophe in the Third World, the response of the OECD countries has been a mixture of deception and inactivity. The end of the Cold War, combined with the pressures of their own fiscal crisis, have prompted a tendency to hold down resources devoted to aid for the Third World, partly so as to permit the diversion of resources to meet the new demands from the ex-Soviet bloc.[10] At the same time, as in its approach to the latter, the international donor community – led by the World Bank and the International Monetary Fund – has insisted on subjecting debtor countries to rigorous programmes of economic austerity, combined with extensive deregulation of the economy, comparable to the 'shock therapy' model inflicted on the former Soviet bloc, as the price of rescheduling their debts.

The imposition of such 'structural adjustment' on countries whose economic problems stem largely from the misrule of the corrupt and unaccountable oligarchies which had been responsible for running up the debts in the 1970s, usually with the backing of donor country interests, has been widely seen even in the industrialised world as being both illogical and unjust – even though many opponents of the policy seem unable to propose a better alternative than to write off most existing debt and grant further loans to the same rulers or their equally profligate successors. Many of these critics have also pointed out that most of the evidence from the more successful developing countries – such as South Korea, Taiwan and Singapore (the so-called Asian Tigers) – is that selective state intervention, subsidy and protection have been a much more effective recipe for development than the *laissez-faire* approach being demanded of the debtor LDCs under the standard structural adjustment formula.[11] The views of such critics had been largely vindicated by the mid-1990s, when it had become obvious – even to the high priests of neo-classical orthodoxy in the World Bank and the IMF – that the donors' prescription was not working. Thus in Ghana, one of the first countries in Africa to embrace the World Bank/IMF course of treatment in the 1980s, people were still dying in riots of protest at new austerity measures in 1995, twelve years after its 'recovery programme' was launched.

Official recognition of the failure of structural adjustment is evident from the effective abandonment by the World Bank of the fiction that most if not all heavily indebted LDCs can be expected ultimately to repay their debts while following the dictates of structural adjustment. On the contrary, the Bank finally in 1996 started to plead with the bilateral donor governments (represented by the Paris 'Club') to forgive at least 80 per cent of the official debts owed to them by the very poorest countries – a move which may also have been prompted by the Bank's desire to keep intact another polite fiction: that its own loans are always repaid on time.

Such belated realism is also reflected in a growing acceptance by the Bank that without donor funding of their current budgets the administrations of many of the smaller and poorer LDCs, particularly in Africa, will effectively cease to function. Hence by 1996 it was discreetly orchestrating the financing by donors – including charitable non-governmental organisations (NGOs) – of programmes such as the state health care system in Sierra Leone (and comparable basic services in other African countries) which the government was no longer able to finance. By the mid-1990s this lead was being followed by other donors, with Britain (for example) agreeing to provide direct budgetary support to Zambia, mainly for the payment of salaries to officials of the Ministries of Health and Education. In fact a similar policy had been followed by France in relation to its former African colonies more or less since their 'independence', although it has become progressively harder for it to find the resources to meet their needs.

Another weakness of the post-independence development model implicitly recognised by such donor moves to get more closely involved in the day-to-day running of Third World administrations is that the attempt to force traditionally unaccountable regimes to act responsibly by attaching conditionality to aid packages – such as demands for spending cuts, or even improvements in the respect for human rights – is simply not workable. For it presumes that dictators, such as the notorious ex-President Mobutu of Zaïre, who have no domestic political compulsion or any other reason to promote the enhancement of their people's economic well-being, can be induced none the less to do so by the offer of aid – or the threat to withhold it. Yet repeated experience has shown that such patron–client relationships between aid donors and Third World autocrats tend to be both corrupting and ineffective. For when such dictators incur the withdrawal of donor support by their failure to respect the conditions of aid extended to them, they themselves suffer few consequences of such sanctions – in contrast to the mass of their impoverished fellow citizens. For the latter are often adversely affected by resulting decline in the quality of public services such as education and health care, whereas the leaders themselves are able to send their children to private schools in Britain or pay for medical treatment in Swiss clinics.

The significance of such developments is not merely that they reveal official acceptance that the basic assumptions underpinning the original structural adjustment approach are essentially bogus. They also imply a recognition that the theoretical premiss of the post-imperial order – that most ex-colonies could be enabled to fend for themselves as economically independent states – is ultimately untenable. Such a conclusion, although unpalatable to many both inside and outside the Third World, is actually in line with proposals made in the early 1980s by the respected Brandt Commission on

International Development for establishing, in effect, a permanent flow of aid transfers from the developed to the developing world.[12]

Despite such growing doubts, the established vision of 'development' is far from being abandoned. On the contrary, the leaders of the industrialised world are still anxious to hold out the prospect of attaining developed-country status as something to which LDCs can aspire if they follow the right policies. Yet their efforts to promote this vision smack increasingly of desperation.

Thus much hyperbole has been expended in promoting the example of the supposedly dynamic East Asian 'Tiger' economies and China, even though, as noted above, their sustained rapid growth since the late 1970s has owed much to interventionist economic policies which are a negation of those advocated by the international donor agencies. Moreover, to the extent that they have successfully taken advantage of the trend to globalisation, they have done so mainly by relying on the exploitation of cheap labour – as well as on imported capital and technology, much of which is provided by Japanese and Western companies fleeing higher costs at home. For these reasons the durability of their success remains in doubt, as demonstrated by the setbacks suffered by the economies of Korea and Thailand in face of the downturn in OECD markets for their exports since 1995.

A more telling manifestation of the industrialised world's approach to the Third World since the 1980s has been the US-inspired attempt in the 1990s to convince the world that Mexico can be classed as a fully developed country. This has taken the form of the admission of Mexico to the OECD (the industrialised countries' club) and to the newly established North American Free Trade Area (NAFTA) as a theoretically equal partner of the United States and Canada. The justification for this was the country's supposedly miraculous transformation since 1988 – under the leadership of President Carlos Salinas (a US-trained economist) from an unstable, debt-ridden, state-dominated economy into a deregulated, market-oriented one with a more or less hard currency. Yet the reality behind this myth was soon to be brutally exposed. At the end of 1994, the very year in which Mexico had been admitted to the OECD, the Mexican peso suddenly halved in value on currency markets as investors lost confidence in the government's will or ability to sustain it in the face of a ballooning balance-of-payments deficit. Total monetary collapse was only averted by a combination of a vicious credit squeeze –

which precipitated such a severe banking crisis that the government was obliged to resume control of most of the domestic banks it had but recently privatised – and an international rescue operation led by the US Treasury and the IMF to arrange stand-by loan facilities for Mexico of $50 billion (equal to a normal year's aid transfers by the OECD to the entire Third World).

Subsequently it was found that there had been widespread bank fraud and official irregularities accompanying the whole process of privatisation and liberalisation, as well as racketeering and violent crime involving those at the highest level – revelations which resulted in the outgoing President Salinas apparently becoming a fugitive from justice outside the country. At the same time civil strife has increased in those parts of the country suffering increased deprivation, first as a result of the liberalisation process and then from the consequences of the extreme austerity imposed following the subsequent financial collapse. In short, once the mask had slipped there was little to suggest that Mexico – a de facto one-party state for nearly seventy years, with little more than a veneer of representative institutions – had advanced much beyond the stage of economic and social instability and irresponsible government traditionally associated with Third World countries.

The failure of this experiment was a blow not merely to those promoting a vision of Third World development through rapid growth based on a *laissez-faire*, neo-classical model. It also caused serious embarrassment to those financial institutions assiduously fostering the belief that 'emerging' markets offered a promising investment opportunity – in their increasingly desperate quest for credible outlets for their growing mountains of excess capital. By the same token it probably dashed the dawning hopes of the OECD governments which make up the donor community that they could induce the global private investor institutions and the TNCs to fill the gap which their own fiscal weakness had left them increasingly unable to fill.

Yet such is the dire need felt by the leaders of international big business and their political counterparts to maintain public faith in these perceptions that there is no sign of their drawing the obvious lesson from the Mexican débâcle – any more than from the equally spectacular failure of shock therapy in Russia. Indeed even more improbable fantasies continue to be peddled as to the potential of other developing countries, such as that China is set to become the world's largest economy within twenty years – even though it presently has less than one-tenth of the gross national product of the United States.

A Common Thread

Our study of the unfolding economic catastrophe in both the ex-Communist countries and the Third World, and of the industrialised world's response to it, serves to underline the central weakness in the global economic structure which is preventing any effective moves to avert disaster: the remorseless demand to sacrifice all other objectives to that of meeting the ever more voracious demand for profit from the continuously swelling and increasingly redundant mass of capital. As has been suggested, however, the need to re-dress the proliferating human disasters arising from the attempt to sustain this unsustainable burden is now becoming even more com-pelling. The question that must therefore be answered is whether there is a conceivable way out of this impasse which will allow these conflicting demands to be reconciled.

Notes

1. Such is one possible interpretation of the report of the British Royal Commission on East Africa (1955), as implied in Basil Davidson, *The Story of Africa*, Mitchell Beazley, London 1984.

2. Although since 1990, responding to the pressure of their own mount-ing fiscal deficits, the share of the OECD countries' GDP devoted to development aid has fallen below 0.3 per cent.

3. Data derived from World Bank, *World Development Report 1984, 1995, 1996*, Washington DC.

4. Walter Wriston, President of Citicorp. That a senior financier could get away with such an utterance in the light of numerous earlier debt defaults in Latin America and elsewhere – going back to the nineteenth century – is a measure of how far prudential standards had by then degenerated in the face of moral hazard (see Chapter 5).

5. Although there have been some temporary exceptions to this general rule, such as Brazil in the 1960s and 1970s and Turkey in the 1990s.

6. It should be added that the uncontrolled application of modern, ex-tensive farming techniques also frequently results in environmental damage.

7. Although the recent holding of elections in Liberia (1997) may portend a return to some form of civil order.

8. *Financial Times*, 5 August 1997.

9. Source: United Nations High Commission for Refugees.

10. While the share of GNP devoted by OECD countries to aid has remained more or less constant, an increasing proportion of it is effectively devoted to refinancing existing official debt and therefore cannot be considered additional aid.

11. See Stephen C. Smith, *Industrial Policy in Developing Countries: Reconsidering the Real Sources of Export-Led Growth.* Economic Policy Institute, Washington DC 1990.

12. *North–South: A Programme for Survival,* Pan Books, London 1980.

11

A Crisis of Legitimacy

Throughout the preceding analysis of the evolution of latter-day capitalism we have had cause to refer to the widespread incidence of fraud, corruption, organised crime and abuse of power (both at corporate and government level) as highly significant influences on the changing pattern of the world economy since the 1970s. While it is undoubtedly true that such phenomena have always been present in capitalist economies (as well as non-capitalist ones), there are grounds for believing that their incidence has grown in recent years to a point where they constitute a threat to the survival of the system itself and to the continuation of political support for it. One of the most conspicuous causes of this alarming trend is the growth in the unaccountable power of large private corporations – in inverse proportion to the decline in the power of supposedly democratic governments. While for ideologues of the New Right this may be a matter for celebration, there are signs that it is beginning to sap the belief of the political and business establishment itself in the legitimacy of the system. Moreover this sense of unease is inevitably being reinforced by the failure of the attempted *laissez-faire* revival to resolve the deep-seated economic crisis.

A more detailed analysis of what lies behind these tendencies and an assessment of the emerging reaction to them is thus crucial to our understanding of the longer-term prospects for the global capitalist system.

The Spread of Lawlessness

Since statistical data on the incidence of economic crime are, as might be expected, either inconclusive or completely lacking, the evidence for its growth is largely impressionistic. It consists mainly of an apparent increase in the level of press and media reporting of such abuses.[1] Yet while this may not be conclusive, the perception that such a deterioration has occurred appears all the more plausible because of the progressive removal of restraints to such criminal activity and indeed increasing incentives to engage in it.

Fraud

At one level the apparent growth in the incidence of fraud since the early 1980s is attributable to much the same cause as are other crimes against property such as burglary and armed robbery: namely, the increased difficulty in making an honest living brought about by chronic economic stagnation, reduced employment opportunities and, in many occupations (particularly in the United States), declining real levels of income. Yet over and above these broader influences growth in commercial fraud, including tax evasion, has been driven by specific pressures deriving from the particular tensions of the financial asset markets and the measures of deregulation introduced to try and relieve them.

In earlier chapters it has been shown how progressively intensifying pressures to push up recorded profits have led to growing recourse to methods of creative accounting and financial manipulation, which are used (often quite legally) to give a misleadingly favourable picture of companies' financial position. To a large extent this may be seen as an expression of normal market pressures to raise the rate of return on shareholders' funds – albeit in a climate where, inevitably, it has become progressively harder to do so. Yet it is also surely a product of the unprecedented set of circumstances which have created a vast surplus of capital for which most of the potential investment outlets are purely speculative. As is now widely recognised, this environment is one in which financial institutions are under strong pressure to offer fabulous incentives to those who can make huge short-term profits by gambling with other people's money, such that the temptation to manipulate markets – or simply to cook the books – is all too irresistible.[2] What few of these critics have felt able to confront is the disturbing reality that this tendency is only accentuated by a climate of competitive deregulation in which different financial centres are effectively encouraged by their national authorities to compete for business by not asking too many questions.

Corruption

As noted in Chapters 9 and 10, corruption has become a central mechanism in the functioning of the political and economic systems of the former Soviet Union and the Third World. Until recently this phenomenon was largely disregarded in Western official circles, where it was typically viewed as an inevitable symptom of transition from backward, pre-industrial societies to modern developed economies – or, in the case of the ex-Communist states, from bureaucratic dictatorship to market-oriented democracy. It has even been quite common to hear it suggested that the taking of bribes by government officials in these countries can be viewed with equanimity to the extent that it at least indicates an understanding of how market forces operate in a liberal economic environment.[3]

In the 1990s, however, such complacency has given way to increasing alarm on the part of significant sections of the international establishment. This stems partly from a belated recognition that the economic costs and distortions arising from corrupt practices are imposing an unsustainable burden on much of the developing world – and are leading to a political backlash even in those countries (mainly in East Asia) which have (at least up to 1997) managed to sustain rapid economic growth, notwithstanding a high incidence of corruption. This is an issue of particular concern to development agencies such as the World Bank as they seek to check the rise in the number of their non-performing loans, many of which have clearly been the result of corrupt deals, usually involving equipment suppliers or consultants from developed countries as well as officials of the recipient government (if not staff of the lending agencies themselves).

At the same time a number of private-sector bodies have begun to find less tolerable the need to pay ever larger bribes in order to win, or even get shortlisted for, contracts in Third World countries – a requirement which not only adds to their costs but makes it highly unpredictable whether they can get any business at all in certain countries. One result has been the creation (in 1993) of a world-wide pressure group – Transparency International – aimed at combating corruption, and a recommendation by the OECD to its member governments (in 1994) on steps they should take to 'counter illicit payments in international business transactions'. One remarkable revelation to emerge from these initiatives has been the fact that in many countries (particularly in continental Europe) bribes paid by national companies to foreign governments in pursuit of contracts are treated as tax deductible by the domestic authorities – even though such actions would be criminal offences if they related to officials of their own government.[4] While for obvious reasons there are no statistical measures of the incidence of corruption, these unprecedented developments may be taken as an unambiguous indication that it has been growing significantly in recent years.

A similar inference seems justified from the movement to penalise corrupt businessmen and politicians for actions largely within their own countries. The most spectacular example has been Italy, where the *mani pulite* (clean hands) campaign spearheaded by magistrates with overwhelming public support in the early 1990s led to the conviction of many senior politicians and businessmen and effectively destroyed the two political parties (the Christian Democrats and Socialists) which had enjoyed a virtual monopoly of power at national level since World War II. Similar but less far-reaching purges have been seen in Japan, France and Belgium since the early 1990s. Even in Britain, where there has long been a fairly general, if naive, assumption that politicians and other public servants are largely above such venality (at least at national, as opposed to local, level), a plethora of abuses have lately been brought to light, notably the 'consultancy' services provided by members of parliament to corporate and other interest groups.

It was suggested above that the growing reaction against such corrupt acts probably reflects a marked rise in their incidence and a belief that it is now out of control. On the other hand the growing intolerance of such practices, at least in some countries, may also be ascribable to a more acute awareness that in times of increasing fiscal stringency the waste and loss to the public purse resulting from them can no longer be tolerated as they were in the past, implying that such laxity might have remained acceptable but for the onset of recession and the looming threat of fiscal bankruptcy.

Such an interpretation in turn prompts one to question whether these developments may not be the start of a process of exposure and collective rejection of the 'corporatist' ethic which constitutes the basis of latter-day capitalism. The essence of this philosophy, manifested first and foremost in Keynesian principles of economic management, was that state power and public money may legitimately be used to subsidise and foster private enterprise, selectively or not, where this is seen to be in the interests of sustaining 'general equilibrium'. The term 'moral hazard' is generally used by economists, as in the present work, to refer to the dangers this approach poses for the management of banks underwritten by the state acting as lender of last resort (see Chapter 5). Yet it could properly be applied to the consequences of the whole panoply of supports offered by governments to private businesses in order to induce them to undertake specific investments, create jobs or do whatever else may be defined as required by the public interest.

To the extent that adherents of the neo-liberal right are concerned by the recent upsurge in corruption, their favoured explanation for it is that it is mainly a symptom of excessive concentration of power and taxpayers' money in the hands of a bureaucratic state. Such a view seems somewhat surprising in so far as the power of governments is also alleged by the same school of opinion to have been greatly curtailed since the beginning of the 1980s. It is also hard to sustain in view of increasingly frequent reports of corruption within a purely private-sector context, with well-documented instances of executives of major corporations (notably giant car manufacturers) paying and receiving bribes for the exchange of company secrets or in return for the placing of orders.

In contrast, left-leaning opinion claims that the 'new corruption' is more the product of the growing influence over the processes of government among unaccountable private-sector entities, whose wealth has not only greatly increased relative to that of debt-ridden governments but whose power to suborn the latter has been greatly enhanced by the very processes of 'liberalisation' advocated by the right. To the extent that this phenomenon has indeed coincided with widespread deregulation of the economy and the encouragement of much greater involvement of the private sector in the activities of the state, it is unquestionably a more plausible explanation.

Yet arguably this is a false dichotomy, since whether corrupt acts are initiated by public officials or private businessmen, they are really both sides of the same coin. This is the all too normal propensity to regard the state and its resources as belonging to no one – and therefore essentially fair game – rather than as belonging to everyone and thus the responsibility of each individual. Such an attitude, which is understandable in countries with little or no tradition of responsible government or public service, is likely to have been strengthened in countries which have such a tradition by the prevailing ideology of individualism and corresponding denigration of the state. At the same time the growing tendency to view it as a convenient milch-cow to be used for advancing particular sectional or corporate interests is clearly becoming more pronounced as economic austerity and insecurity make it harder to advance these interests while playing by the rules.

Organised crime

The fact that the term 'organised crime' has become increasingly hard to define in the late twentieth century is itself a measure of how pervasive and significant it has become. For most people it has conjured up a sterotype of Sicilian mafiosi or New York or Chicago mobsters (as traditionally portrayed by Hollywood), whose defining characteristic is the use of violence and fear to try to impose their will and maintain control of criminal empires based on the profits of gambling, prostitution, drugs and other vice-related activities. Yet while such an image is evidently still valid for a large part of organised criminal activity – especially with regard to drugs – it is seriously oversimplified. For the evolution of the global economy, and of financial markets in particular, has made it easy for the proceeds of organised crime – which are estimated to have reached no less than \$1,000 billion globally in 1996[5] – to be converted into investment capital and assets which appear to the casual observer, and often even to the expert scrutiny of market regulators, to be as respectable as that of the most venerable banking institutions of Wall Street or the City of London.

This 'legitimisation' of a significant part of the activities of organised crime has naturally been accompanied by a certain sanitisation of the criminals themselves. That is to say that the transformation of the vast profits from their traditional activities into ostensibly conventional investment businesses has enabled their leaders to abandon the machine gun in favour of the chequebook and to use lawyers, accountants and other pin-striped professionals instead of thugs to attain their ends.[6] Their ability to do this, while maintaining almost total anonymity, has been greatly facilitated by the extensive deregulation of international financial markets. At the same time their capacity to deploy their vast accumulated wealth to subvert and control legally constituted corporations, not to mention regulatory and other government agencies, has inevitably become a distorting influence in the markets, although the extent of this is naturally difficult to document. Indeed there was a strong suspicion, as noted earlier, of the involvement of organised crime in the fraudulent bankruptcy of Savings and Loan institutions in the scandal which cost US taxpayers over $100 billion at the end of the 1980s – as well as some of the 'greenmail' activities (in some cases amounting to legalised loansharking) which led to damaging distortions in the balance sheets of companies being made takeover targets.

In a climate of progressively greater liberalisation – combined with weak official commitment to observance or enforcement of the law and continuing (if not increasing) legitimisation of the use of public funds to support private commercial interests – it was only to be expected that such 'white-collar' organised crime would expand and flourish. The question obviously arises, however, of how far its influence can be tolerated before it threatens to damage genuine entrepreneurship on a large scale. The existence of a criminal 'under-world' has, of course, been characteristic of virtually every human society throughout history and may well have to be regarded as a phenomenon that can never be wholly eliminated. As such, provided its influence is confined to a very limited sphere of economic activity, its existence may yet prove compatible with a reasonably stable society. However, where it attains enough power to subvert legitimate enterprise and legally constituted authority at the highest level it then clearly becomes a threat to social, economic and ultimately political stability, discouraging most would-be law-abiding state functionaries, business people, community leaders and others from performing effectively – or often even from remaining part of the particular community if they have an opportunity to move to somewhere more stable.

Such is undoubtedly now the condition of virtually every country of the former Soviet Union and probably of the majority of those in the Third World as well. In the latter countries, however, the vested interest of legitimate business has probably never been strong enough to offset the power of organised crime or of those more traditional elites which have always been in a position to override the law. This reflects the fact that many of them still retain a somewhat feudal structure of society in which personal ties based on tradition tend to count for more than either legal contracts or the criminal code. In the light of this observation it is startling to consider the implications of organised crime making major inroads into the economic fabric of industrialised countries such as Britain and the United States, whose great success over the last three centuries has been largely built on a rejection of feudal values in favour of the rule of law administered by a more or less impartial judicial system. Hence any erosion of this tradition in the 'bourgeois' nations of the industrialised world would amount to an enormous step backward in the perspective of their history.

Protecting the criminals

As noted more than once in earlier chapters, a dominant theme of the official response to chronic economic stagnation since the mid-1970s has been that of deregulation. Even though it has been inescapably clear since the late 1980s (if not before) that this would not produce the stimulus to economic recovery its advocates had predicted, the official consensus in favour of maximum relaxation of restraints on freedom of enterprise has remained intact. Indeed it has become an axiom for most concerned commentators, politicians and business leaders that it is an irreversible process which an individual state can only challenge on certain pain of seeing production and investment drain away from it along with the value of its currency.

Yet there can be little dispute that such widespread relaxation of restraints has had the effect of making it easier for companies and individuals either to act in ways that are against the public interest (even if not actually illegal) or else to evade detection or conviction in cases where they have broken the law. Without doubt the most positive stimulus to wrongdoing provided by the authorities of different countries has been their encouragement of the proliferation of offshore financial centres (OFCs), where total secrecy and anonymity of bank-account holders is generally guaranteed. The major factors behind this trend have already been described (see Chapter 6). How far those OECD governments which have connived at it (even though they could collectively have prevented it) did so with the conscious purpose of weakening the regulatory control over their own corporations and citizens – rather than in response to ad hoc pressures to assist development in territories that otherwise lacked a significant economic base – is far from clear. What is certain is that they have greatly enhanced the ability of perpetrators of fraud, corruption, tax evasion and other criminal activities to cover their tracks.

The most obvious symptom of this growing anarchy is the by now familiar activity of money laundering, whereby the cash proceeds of crime (including, naturally, the vast but unquanitifiable gains from fraud, corruption and tax evasion) are converted – through the mediation of banks – into financial assets which can then be more readily used for 'normal' investment purposes. There is no doubt that banks are in a position greatly to restrict such laundering and also to bring criminals to justice by reporting dubious transactions to the authorities, as they are constantly urged to do by governments and law-enforcement agencies. Yet once again the promotion of international competitive deregulation by the self-same governments makes a mockery of their exhortations, since bankers are only too aware that if they get a reputation for thus aiding the authorities in pursuit of criminals all they will achieve is to deny themselves a share of trillions of dollars worth of business. This perception is clearly all the greater in a climate where, as in Russia, criminal organisations are themselves effectively allowed to set up banks.

In fact the ambivalence of the authorities towards these developments is striking – and nowhere more so than in the United States. On the one hand the US government is constantly admonishing other governments, particularly those harbouring offshore financial centres, to take stern measures to prevent money laundering by criminal organisations (especially suspected drug traffickers) and 'international terrorists'. Yet at the same time the use that has been made by the CIA of such offshore centres to facilitate its own clandestine subversive activities in Central America and elsewhere is well documented.[7] Indeed such is the continuing paralysis of leading OECD governments in face of the clear threat posed to their authority – not to mention the solvency of the state itself – by the existence of these centres that there is by now bound to be a suspicion that governments of OECD countries are themselves significantly infiltrated by the criminal interests who are the main beneficiaries of the OFCs' creation.

The uncertain commitment of the US authorities to deterring illegal or anti-social actions by private business is also manifest in some of the changes to company legislation enacted by a number of states since the 1970s. Many of these have had the effect of extending limited liability so as to render company directors largely immune from civil actions for damages – with the result that in some states the cost of any negligent act by management, including any consequential litigation, now falls exclusively on shareholders' funds. This permissive attitude stems from a combination of the lowering of regulatory standards by states as they compete for company registrations – leading to Delaware, one of the smallest of the fifty states, being host to a far larger number of company head offices than any other state – and the huge influence of corporate donations on the political process (see below).[8]

Loss of Accountability

Just as it has become easier for companies and individuals to pervert the course of the economy by criminal behaviour, it has become harder for the would-be law-abiding to establish responsibility for malfeasance by either private or public bodies – or to obtain redress for wrongs they may have suffered or to hold governments to account for abuses perpetrated in the public's name.

Corporate governance

The conspicuous increase since the early 1980s in the number of well-publicised cases of major financial wrongdoing in OECD countries, many involving well-known corporations or businessmen, is an important factor behind incipient public concern at the way large private companies are managed and at the extent to which they are or should be accountable to the wider community. Other reasons for such concern are perceptions of the growing power of corporations to damage the public interest through either an over-zealous pursuit of short-term profit, the personal greed of directors, or sheer incompetence. This is typically manifested in such events as large-scale 'downsizing' of workforces, environmental disasters (such as explosions at chemical plants or marine oil spillages from tankers) and, especially in the United States, the granting of what appear to be exorbitant remuneration packages to senior executives (particularly where most of their lower paid employees have been forced to accept a pay freeze, if not an actual cut).

More generally there is an emerging recognition, even among

prominent members of the establishment, that large corporations wield enormous power in modern Western societies, both through the inordinate influence they can exercise over government policy – often by nakedly subverting the democratic process – and through the enormous impact their actions can have on the economic fortunes of particular local communities, or even of entire countries. In the words of one of the leading US advocates of improved corporate governance, 'the US corporation is overweeningly powerful and accountable to no one.'[9] Yet most of the debate surrounding this issue within the business and political establishment is concerned with how to make companies more accountable to their shareholders, the owners of the business, whose opinions are routinely disregarded or manipulated by the effectively all-powerful chief executives, with or without the connivance of the other directors. The fact that the consequence of increased shareholder power might be an intensification of the pursuit of short-term profit, and hence even more anti-social management of companies from the standpoint of the public at large, is seldom emphasised.

What no mainstream commentator or political party has yet begun to contemplate is the possibility of any change in the regulatory framework which might actually put real pressure on corporations to take account of the public interest. There is one simple and rather obvious reason for their failure to do so. This is the impossibility of devising mechanisms for subordinating privately owned corporations to the public interest without undermining the central principle of property rights. In their effort to avoid addressing this issue, however, numerous establishment figures have been given to pontificating on the theme of 'corporate responsibility' and even the importance to national economic well-being of re-establishing 'trust'. The most widely canvassed variant of such ideas is that of an approach based on balancing the interests of 'stakeholders' (including employees and consumers) in determining key decisions on the running of companies.[10]

Yet none of these formulations offers a plausible basis for effecting any change in the structure of corporate control which would not leave ultimate authority with shareholders or boards of directors acting as their representatives (in line with standard company law). Indeed it is ironic that the application of the stakeholder principle in the United States – where it has been enshrined in 'stakeholder laws' (requiring boards of corporations to take account of non-shareholder interests in shaping their decisions) in thirty-eight states – has had the effect of giving company boards and chief executives greater protection from their shareholders (e.g. in fending off an unwelcome takeover bid on the grounds that it would not be in the interests of employees or customers) without making them any more genuinely answerable to such other interest groups or the public at large.[11]

Hence we are left in precisely the same dilemma as that confronted by earlier epochs in dealing with this issue. For, as noted by the eminent historian R.H. Tawney in considering the debate over property rights in the England of four centuries ago, 'If property be an unconditional right, emphasis on its obligations is little more than the graceful parade of a flattering, but innocuous, metaphor. For, whether the obligations are fulfilled or neglected, the right continues unchallenged and indefeasible.'[12]

It is precisely the need to challenge the notion of an unconditional right of property and to insist on the public accountability of its owners – taking account of the immense power of corporations to influence the welfare of society – which now demands to be grasped. The justification for doing so is surely all the more compelling in view of the huge privileges and protection now provided to the private corporate sector by the state. These supports – beginning with the right to limited liability conceded in the mid-nineteenth century and culminating in the state's assumption of the role of lender of last resort in the Keynesian era – have become indispensable to the present-day corporate sector. Yet the implied contract linked to these favours clearly must be that the corporate sector will in turn provide the economic well-being which the community requires.[13] Hence it seems inconceivable that in a modern economy the presumption that private companies (whether truly answerable to their shareholders or not) can be the ultimate arbiters of our common economic destiny will be found tolerable indefinitely. Indeed future generations may well marvel that they were allowed so much latitude for so long.

Accountability of the state

Whereas in law private companies are not even theoretically accountable to the general public for their actions (provided those actions are themselves lawful), the state under modern democracy is clearly understood to be not only the guardian of the public's interest but answerable to it through its elected representatives. It is true that even in some of the most economically advanced countries of the Western world there is still a widespread popular tendency to view the state as inherently hostile rather than as an expression of the views and interests of the mass of citizens. Such perceptions are partly, no doubt, attributable to the fact that universal suffrage is still quite a recent phenomenon in nearly all these countries, dating in most cases from no earlier than the end of World War I (with women's suffrage being instituted still later than this in many of them), and that the folk memory of the state as an oppressor representing only the rich and powerful is still strong.

Nevertheless the notion that governments are trustees for the public interest and are therefore accountable to the electorate is by now implicit in the constitutions of all OECD countries. It follows that the public should in principle be kept informed of what they do in its name and that they should be expected to lose office if they are seen to abuse this trusteeship or otherwise transgress their mandate. It has, moreover, been the peculiar conceit of the Western industrialised countries that their brand of liberal democracy – underpinned by rights of free speech, free association and the rule of law – is the model of government the rest of the world should aspire to.

Measured against such a presumed standard of responsible government, the record of many OECD governments has demonstrated increasing irresponsibility in recent years. As already mentioned, this has been in part the result of the all-pervading culture of deregulation since the early 1980s and the associated rise in the scope for and incidence of financial wrongdoing. Yet it is also clearly a function of the much greater financial resources which have been brought to bear on winning political support for private corporate interests. This is most obviously true of the United States, where the legal restraints on the scale of funds that can be utilised by political parties in the electoral process are minimal and where the sums provided by corporations to congressional candidates alone grew from around $40 million in 1978 to $150 million in 1988 and appear to have risen to at least four times the 1988 level by 1996. Yet in Europe also – where there are much tighter legal limits placed on the level of political funding – the growing number of scandals in recent years involving illegal, covert donations to political parties is evidence of a similar trend. At the same time the meteoric rise of the political public-relations and 'lobbying' industry is another indicator of the growing value attached by private business to winning political influence.

Since it is noticeable that corporate political donations are often distributed among different, notionally opposing, parties it is clear that their purpose is usually related at least as much to gaining favourable consideration for government contracts – or for a particular sectional interest such as the brewing or motor industries – as to lending support for a broader political cause. This in turn points to the continued, and indeed growing, importance to business of decisions regarding government expenditure and taxation, notwithstanding the supposed efforts to 'roll back the frontiers of the state'.

The huge growth in corporate spending designed to influence the policies and decisions of governments can also probably be ascribed in part to the mounting surplus of capital being generated by the profits system. As noted in earlier chapters, this massive flow of funds – which is not being allowed, as would be dictated by traditional capitalist rationale, to self-destruct through the natural operation of the business cycle – has to find an outlet in more or less speculative forms of investment. Against this background it would be entirely logical for companies to view contributions to political parties and other expenditure designed to buy influence as simply another form of investment. Indeed in a climate where investment is becoming necessarily more speculative, the rate of return on such political outlays may well be considered as predictable as most other prospects.

A much more explicit element in companies' profit projections is the amount of state funding they receive in support of specific investments, even though understandably they do not care to emphasise this in public. These receipts are the obverse of corporate payments to political parties, although if a company is large and powerful enough it can probably extort government subsidies to its investments irrespective of whether it has contributed to party funds. Perhaps the most conspicuous example of this in Britain has been the Ford Motor Co., which was widely reported to have demanded and received a grant of many millions of pounds under the threat of moving the main operations of Jaguar Cars (a formerly British-owned company it had acquired in 1989) to the United States. Again in 1998 it managed to extract some £50 million more in government grants as the price of producing a new model at its assembly plant on Merseyside rather than in Germany or the USA.

The most singular aspect of such subsidies to the profits of giant corporations – which are commonplace in all countries as each fights to attract and retain employment-generating investment within its own borders – is that frequently the government refuses to disclose to taxpayers how much of their money it has spent on them, ostensibly on grounds of 'commercial confidentiality'. Nothing could better illustrate the extent to which the principle of democratic account-ability has been undermined by the creation of a pattern of economic 'globalisation' which is designed to subordinate all other interests to those of the private corporate sector. Ironically, those who seek to defend this dispensation usually do so on the grounds of the stimu-lating benefits of freer international competition that it confers on rich and poor countries alike – notwithstanding the distorting effects of such subsidies on competitiveness. Other attempts at rationalising it have been based on the notion that corporations are themselves component parts of democracy and that it is quite legitimate for them to subvert the constitutional channels of democratic accountability.[14]

The evidence of this chapter points to a common factor in this rising tide of malfeasance and misappropriation of public resources. This is the desperate struggle to find ways of supporting the value of capital in defiance of the ineluctable forces tending to devalue it. However, it is scarcely possible any longer to ignore the damage this has inflicted on the fabric of the state and the basic social order which underpins it. If this tendency is not to end in catastrophe it must be recognised that organised capital has become – together with, but to an even greater extent than, organised crime – a para-site so voracious that it is killing the body it feeds off.

Notes

1. Unrelated surveys carried out by journals such as *Business Week* and the *New York Times* point to a signifcant rise in the proportion of major US corporations convicted of illegality between the early 1980s and early 1990s. See R. Monks and N. Minow, *Corporate Governance*, Blackwell, Oxford 1996, p. 30.

2. See Bank of England, *Currency Stability Review* No. 2, February 1997.

3. As noted in *Transparency International Newsletter*, September 1996.

4. Astonishingly, this practice seems unlikely to be wholly outlawed by the OECD convention on combating international corruption that appeared close to finalisation at the end of 1997.

5. *Financial Times*, 14 February 1997.

6. The application of the more traditional approach is quite common in the Far East, however, where the Japanese *sakaiya* still commonly manage to extort protection money from large companies – by, for example, threatening to disrupt their annual general meetings.

7. Mark P. Hampton, 'Where Currents Meet: The Offshore Interface Between Corruption, Offshore Finance Centres and Economic Development', *IDS Bulletin*, April 1996, Institute of Development Studies, University of Sussex.

8. R. Monks and N. Minow, *Power and Accountability*, HarperCollins, New York 1991.

9. Robert Monks, paraphrased in Martin Dickson, 'Sharpening up the Cutting Edge', *Financial Times*, 15 July 1996.

10. See G. Kelly, D. Kelly and A. Gamble, eds, *Stakeholder Capitalism*, Macmillan, London 1997.

11. Monks and Minow, *Corporate Governance*.

12. R.H. Tawney, *Religion and the Rise of Capitalism*, Penguin Books, Harmondsworth 1961.

13. In the view of the eminent Justice Louis D. Brandeis of the US Supreme Court, expressed in 1932, the granting of the privilege of limited liability by any state of the union could only be justified on the presumption that it would confer some benefit on the public.

14. See Adrian Lithgow, 'Lobbyists Have a Role to Play in Democracy', *Sunday Business*, 18 August 1996.

12

Can the Profits System be Saved?

The evidence presented thus far provides obvious grounds for doubting the durability of the existing world economic order on the eve of the twenty-first century. This is suggested not only by the symptoms of growing instability and widening social deprivation but also by the general weakening of the authority of the state, rising levels of criminality, more pervasive official corruption and, in a growing number of countries in virtually every continent, the effective collapse of civil order. The central conclusion to emerge from our examination of these phenomena is that the fundamental cause of this intensifying global malaise has been the impossibility of sustaining high enough economic growth to support the value of capital assets at the levels demanded by a competitive market, while at the same time meeting the income and welfare requirements of the mass of the population (including those of the state acting as collective provider of basic services).

Such an insight is hardly new, since it was the inescapable lesson of earlier capitalist crises that 'market imperfections' are bound to result in periodic excess of supply over effective demand such as to precipitate sharp contractions in profits, output and incomes. What is seemingly without precedent, however, is the enduring tendency since World War II to believe, or at least to pretend, either that this cycle has been effectively eliminated or that it is just about to be. Such hubris was originally induced by the ascendancy of Keynesian economic strategies for a generation after 1945, when the prolonged boom led to a general presumption that the elixir of eternal economic youth had at last been discovered. We now know that, while Keynesian interventionism may have played an important role in sustaining the boom for so long, it could not prevent it coming to an end and is certainly not a sufficient explanation of why it happened at all. Yet despite this discovery the view has persisted among mainstream economists, including the neo-classical opponents of Keynes who have dominated official thinking since the late 1970s, that more or less perpetual rapid growth is attainable if only the right policies are pursued.

We have already observed the compelling reason for government and business leaders to maintain this stance in defiance of objective analysis, namely that the consequences of accepting the inevitability of the boom and bust cycle under capitalism are by now untenable, both financially and politically, for those who seek to sustain the profits system. Hence, despite the deepening stagnation of the world economy since the mid-1970s, official opinion has clung to the hope that growth will revive and thereby permit the liquidation of debt – both public and private – which has been allowed to accumulate in order to try to stave off still deeper crisis. Indeed it ought scarcely to be a matter of dispute that unless there is a sustained revival of growth rates to levels consistent with both a reversal of the upward spiral of debt and the satisfaction of the financial market's voracious demand for higher profits, then a cataclysmic collapse of the market values of financial assets and securities will be unavoidable.

Since, therefore, a sustained resumption of growth in the Western industrialised countries must be regarded as indispensable to the survival of the profits system, it is entirely understandable that the protagonists of the system refuse to entertain the possibility of its failing to occur. But, while deploring such mindless determinism, we must avoid committing the comparable error of assuming, based on the trends of the period since the post-war boom collapsed in the mid-1970s, that such a revival could not occur. Such caution is all the more appropriate in that the question of the origins of growth remains the central unresolved conundrum of market economics. Hence it is in principle no more plausible to maintain that a revival of growth will not happen just because there is no obvious reason for expecting one than that there will be such a revival because the health of the economic system demands one. It thus behoves us to consider the evidence carefully before attempting a balanced judgement.

Patterns of Demand

Serious analysis of long-term growth prospects in a market economy must start from consideration of the outlook for final demand. We may therefore dismiss from the outset any suggestion that, in line with Say's Law,[1] supply may be expected to 'create its own demand' – even though there are still a surprisingly large number of analysts (including both *laissez-faire* supply-siders[2] and faithful adherents of Marx's labour theory of value) who are still attracted by such deterministic fantasies.

Trends in private consumption since the 1970s

It was suggested in Chapter 3 that the crucial factor behind the slowdown in world growth since the early 1970s has been the relative stagnation of effective consumer demand for goods and services. It was also noted that this was mainly a consequence of the progressive saturation of developed-country markets for durable goods in particular – following a period of spectacular growth from around 1950, when they had for the first time become affordable by the mass of the population. Since then, despite occasional limited boosts to aggregate demand arising from the introduction of new products, such as colour television sets in the 1970s and video recorders in the 1980s, private consumption has generally continued to stagnate.

Yet the persistence of this stagnation has not been for want of efforts to stimulate the appetites of consumers. Expenditure on advertising in most OECD countries rose by well over 5 per cent a year in real terms in the 1980s – at least double the average rate of economic growth. At the same time there have been yet greater extensions of the boundaries of taste and decency in the effort to attract more custom. If the so-called permissiveness of the 1960s was as much the result of commercial pressures as of more libertarian social attitudes, then this is surely even more true of the subsequent decades. For the latter period has witnessed a proliferation of ever more explicit displays of sex and violence in the mass media – facilitated in the USA by the abolition of restrictions on pornography in 1973 – as well as other forms of crude sensationalism based on openly mendacious journalism. At the same time, legalised gambling has been greatly boosted by the expansion of casinos – notably in the USA, where their establishment in states which had previously banned them has been openly justified as a means of generating revenue and employment to replace that lost from declining industries – and in Britain such innovations as the national lottery (promoted by the authorities and openly advertised, even though this remains prohibited for other forms of gambling). Likewise legal restraints on Sunday trading have been significantly eroded in Britain and are coming under pressure in other countries as well. All this has been allowed to occur in disregard of the demonstrably damaging social effects arising from many aspects of this cultural degradation.[3]

Disconcertingly, such tendencies have received the blessing of both governments and media moguls, on both sides of the Atlantic, who loudly profess support for 'born again' Christianity and a return to Victorian or 'family' values. This willingness to sacrifice cultural and social values to material considerations – as well as that of 'politically correct' critics to defend it – might even perhaps be compared to the cultural decline of the Roman Empire, where ever more barbaric forms of public entertainment were used by the authorities to distract and debauch the increasingly demoralised and discontented populace.[4]

A more traditional method of trying to boost effective demand for certain products is 'planned obsolescence'. This long-recognised phenomenon of the consumer society is based on the principle of trying to ensure that products incorporating a given level of technology – whether consumer goods or capital equipment – are rapidly superseded by new models incorporating more advanced technology and with an apparently superior capability. To be successful it obviously requires both that improved technology can be constantly introduced into the products concerned at relatively low cost to the producers and that competition among them – or among distributors – is restrained as far as possible. One area in particular where today such conditions favour this kind of market manipulation is that of personal computer hardware and software. The result has been that consumers often find that they must replace products every few years simply because they are no longer compatible with other systems to which they must be connected, or because replacement components are no longer available, even though otherwise they could remain serviceable for many years.

At the same time, consumers have been encouraged, or even quite aggressively pressurised, into borrowing more money to facilitate increased spending. In the United States the propensity to borrow has been further stimulated by allowing interest payments on a wide range of personal loans to be treated as tax deductible. In Britain in the 1980s finance companies were tacitly permitted to encourage borrowers to circumvent its more restrictive tax concessions – allowing tax deduction only for interest on house mortgage loans. This they could do by taking out second mortgages which, although ostensibly for extension or improvement to their homes, were in reality often destined mainly for the acquisition of consumer goods. Likewise in Japan a very high level of personal borrowing was induced by an enormous surge in real-estate values in the 1980s, only to be followed – as in the USA, Britain, Scandinavia and elsewhere – by a massive pile-up of bad debts once the credit boom turned to bust and property values accordingly collapsed. The consequence in almost all the countries concerned has been to lift the total volume of household debt to unprecedentedly high levels, as a proportion of national income, with particularly large increases in the ratio occurring in Japan (from 23 per cent in 1980 to 60 per cent in 1990) and Britain (from 38 per cent in 1980 to 80 per cent in 1990).

This process, which was greatly assisted by the widespread financial deregulation of the 1980s, has naturally had longer-term negative consequences not only for the solvency of a large number of borrowers but for the future growth of consumer demand. For by inducing consumers thus to mortgage their future purchasing power, the deregulated financial institutions have effectively appropriated a greater share of household expenditure in the shape of debt-service payments – at the expense of those sectors of the economy supplying goods and non-financial services.[5] Moreover, an increasing proportion of this growing personal-sector debt in the 1980s was for purchases of real estate, often at highly inflated prices – as most people came to believe, not least because of the associated tax breaks, that this was an investment which was bound to appreciate or at least maintain its value in real terms – rather than of consumer goods and services.

The great increase in personal debt and debt-service obligations would seem largely to explain the steady decline in household savings ratios recorded in the seven major industrial economies (the Group of Seven)[6] since 1975. This has taken place notwithstanding the continued rise in average real disposable (that is, net of tax) incomes over the period, which would normally be expected to result in a rising proportion of incomes being channeled into savings. On the other hand, thanks to a high proportion of residual savings being invested in financial assets that have been rapidly appreciating in value (particularly in the USA), this decline in the savings ratio has not been reflected in any squeeze in consumer purchasing power. Yet while the true significance of this 'wealth effect' on consumption is hard to determine,[7] there is an obvious danger that any major fall in securities markets will have a disproportionate negative effect on consumer demand.

Reduced provision by the state or social services generally (including health and education) is undoubtedly another important negative influence on the growth of consumer spending. Indeed the increasing need for individuals to spend some of their own money on services such as health care and education, as state funding has been reduced, may be seen as a disguised form of taxation. It is of course true that such individual spending on these services is recorded as consumption for national accounting purposes. However, since the outlays involved are effectively a diversion from one channel to another of consumption which was already being paid for – albeit on a collective basis – they clearly do not contribute to a net increase in aggregate demand or output.

The net effect of these conflicting influences on consumer demand has been that the growth of private consumption expenditure in the OECD countries has slumped to progressively lower average levels since the 1970s. Hence in the first half of the 1990s it was rising at just over half the rate recorded in the 1970s (1.8 per cent a year compared with 3.5 per cent).[8]

Portents for the Future

There is thus every reason to suppose that the still continuing global macroeconomic trends of the two decades since the mid-1970s constitute a self-reinforcing downward spiral which can only result in still further decline in the growth rate of aggregate output and income. The question therefore to be posed is: what can conceivably occur, either spontaneously or as a result of official policy, to free the world economy from the deadly combination of saturated consumer markets, dwindling demand for both labour and capital in the wake of the information technology revolution, and the inescapable need for capital to keep pushing up the share of profit in national income?

As far as existing government policies are concerned, the signs are certainly not promising. Indeed the narrow concentration of debate among policy-makers on the issue of how to curtail swelling welfare spending commitments (the biggest and most intractable component of the fiscal burden) suggests that the most likely changes in policy will only serve to make things worse. Thus the switch from state to private individual pension provision can only mean the diversion of a higher proportion of personal incomes into savings – particularly if, as has been seriously suggested, such private provision is made compulsory (which would be an even more thinly disguised form of tax increase) – and thus weaken consumer demand growth still further.

In truth, however, as long as governments remain committed to giving primacy to the profit-maximising objectives of the private corporate sector, there is almost certainly nothing they can do which will not result in a further deterioration. In these circumstances salvation can only lie in a more or less unplanned revival of rapid demand growth based on influences which it is impossible to foresee. Such a phenomenon would need to be capable of bringing back into use much of the vast reserves of presently unutilised capacity (of capital and labour) over a period of many years. Only by virtue of such a spontaneous turnaround would it be remotely possible at once to reduce the massive burden of debt – public and private – and to continue satisfying the insatiable demand of capital for increased shareholder value.

A Rebirth of Consumption?

In considering the possibility that the pattern of stagnant effective demand will change dramatically, many have speculated as to the possible sources of such a renaissance. Since we have recognised that it is inherently very difficult to identify the underlying factors that may cause growth to accelerate, or to foresee when such surges will occur, we should hesitate to dismiss such hypotheses too readily. On the other hand there is no doubt that a lot of such thinking is based on simple-minded economic determinism akin to a belief in Adam Smith's Invisible Hand, or else amounts to an ideologically motivated clutching at straws.

Thus when the implications of the information technology revolution in terms of the destruction of manufacturing and service employment first began to dawn on the world around the late 1970s, optimists could quite plausibly point to the potential for generating new products (including consumer goods) – and hence new jobs – which might flow from this phenomenon and thereby offset the losses of existing employment as well as stimulate a revival of growth generally.[9] The fact that as yet, some twenty years later, this potential shows no sign of being realised – or not on the scale needed to reverse the downward growth trend – may not mean that it will never do so. Indeed it remains true that the most likely catalyst for any strong revival of consumer demand is some form of technological breakthrough facilitating the supply of products or services for which there is substantial latent demand at prices which bring them within range of the mass of consumers – as was the case with motor cars (as well as other consumer durables) and air travel in the 1950s and 1960s.

Yet the impact to date of the information technology revolution on consumers' behaviour points to some strong grounds for scepticism. For despite continuous improvements in product performance and steep real price reductions of personal computers since they first became widely available in the early 1980s, they are far from being regarded as essential items for the majority of households, popular as they are with a growing number of enthusiasts. This may well be because for most consumers they do not fulfil an obvious need which is not already being met by other means. As a result, for all the enthusiasm for technology stocks and elsewhere in the investor community, many computer and software manufacturers have collapsed in the face of slow market growth and intensifying competition.

Likewise in a related consumer field, satellite and cable television, it is far from clear that there is sufficient potential demand to meet the vast increase in capacity made possible by the new technology. Indeed it seems *a priori* questionable whether in Britain (for example) people who already watch an average of three to four hours of television a day mainly on four terrestrial channels will have enough extra waking hours to do justice to the further five hundred satellite channels to be made available as a result of the introduction of digital technology, not to mention the proliferation of cable channels created on the basis of fibre-optic technology.[10] Indeed the anticipation of this problem has led to a probably inflated bidding up of the television rights of major sporting events, in a fiercely competitive battle to gain monopoly control of one of the few types of programming for which there is clearly strong demand – often with a seriously distorting impact on the economics of football and other major spectator sports. Meanwhile the mounting financial problems of many cable operators in the mid-1990s, particularly in Britain, indicates that the willingness of the public to subscribe even the quite modest amounts demanded to watch these new services is indeed limited.

This is not to deny the significance of technological innovation in electronics and telecommunications in stimulating an increase in consumption of certain products and services. In particular, it is clear that the development of digital technology has, by reducing the cost of telecommunications, led to a substantial rise in the real value of effective demand for these services, while a further boost has arisen from the introduction of new services such as the Internet. However, as already noted, based on the evidence to date there is no sign that the combined effect of these developments on aggregate consumption is going to be sufficient to achieve the necessary boost to overall growth.

Environmentalism: Less Opportunity than Threat

Another instance of the tendency of investors and big corporations involved in emergent industries to indulge in escapist fantasy is provided by the case of the environmentalist 'industry'. Since the 1970s the progressive increase in public concern at the threat to the environment posed by such phenomena as indiscriminate world-wide industrialisation and unchecked population growth has been widely seen as a potential constraint to economic expansion at least as great as that resulting from inadequate demand growth. This concern stems both from the loss of amenity caused by what is seen by many as 'overdevelopment' (typically identified as excessive building in rural areas and the pervasiveness of motor-vehicle traffic) and from damage to the 'biosphere', which is thought to be posing a more or less immediate threat to human health and, in the longer term, a danger to the survival of entire communities.

The ultimate significance of this issue in putting a physical restraint on economic growth is hard to determine, especially since one cannot discount the possibility that, with the aid of modern technology, environment-friendly ways of increasing output may eventually be devised. For the immediate future, however, it is clear that its impact is more likely to be negative, should governments feel compelled – if only by the force of public opinion – to restrict the growth of polluting forms of consumption, such as the use of motor vehicles or air travel, or to limit the scope for adding value to products (by means such as packaging) so as to curb pollution.

Yet, as with the information-technology revolution, there has been a determined effort to present this development as an opportunity at least as much as a threat. For, it is argued, the demand for environment-friendly products as well as goods and services needed to clean up the mess can reasonably be expected to offset the higher marginal cost of production in respect of existing business and the consequent negative effect on sales and profits. Yet brief reflection might suggest that this is likely to prove wishful thinking. For even if the effect of environmental pressures is to promote a switch to cleaner forms of consumption (such as electric-powered cars) there seems little reason to suppose that this would take place at such a speed as to boost effective demand much above the levels which might have been expected from normal replacement of the existing products – at least without the benefit of large state subsidies to accelerate the process. In the longer run one would expect, other things being equal, a return to relatively static levels of demand of the improved products – or even a reduction in cases where cleaner products could not be devised – rather than that consumers would buy the same quantity of polluting goods and services, and then pay for the additional cost of counteracting the pollution.

Illusory Potential of the Third World and the Former Communist Bloc

An inherently more likely source of future market growth than any new product or service yet devised to stimulate consumers in the industrialised world is provided by the countries of the Third World and the former Communist bloc. For clearly the one thing at least which these countries, comprising over 80 per cent of the world's population, do not suffer from is consumer market saturation. Unfortunately, as demonstrated by the experience of the decades since most of them gained independence after World War II, there are a number of reasons why it is likely to be very hard to exploit the theoretical potential of these 'emerging' markets as a catalyst for the revival of world growth, namely

- Average consumer purchasing power (per head) in most of the Third World, and indeed of the ex-Soviet bloc, is extremely low (no more than around 10 per cent of that of the industrialised world),[11] so that the huge latent demand cannot readily be translated into effective demand. Moreover, as already noted, since the early 1980s income per head in most of these countries has actually been growing more slowly than in the industrialised countries. Hence to the extent that excess capital from the OECD countries may be invested in these regions, it may well continue to be, as now, mainly in order to take advantage of low labour costs in an effort to gain a competitive advantage back in developed-country markets. The only consequence of such an approach would be (a) to reinforce the pressures to keep average Third World incomes and purchasing power low, and (b) further to depress OECD markets as more jobs are moved to poorer countries (or else real wages are held down to prevent this) in the intensifying global competitive struggle.

- Because of chronic economic and political uncertainty in many developing countries, along with an unpredictable legal and regulatory environment and problems arising from inadequate infrastructure, OECD investors will tend to demand an extra risk premium from any project they are being invited to invest in. Added to the high rate of return on capital already being demanded to sustain the market value of companies, this means that the potential return on projects in the Third World and the ex-Soviet bloc will often appear inadequate to attract foreign investors – unless there is some implicit guarantee from OECD governments or donors against serious loss. Yet as indicated by the Mexican débâcle of 1994–95 (and then the East Asian 'meltdown' of 1997–98), the huge cost to developed countries' taxpayers of potential bail-outs will prove unaffordable if these are required by many countries.

Sadly, it may well prove that the most lucrative field of demand for OECD companies in the non-OECD countries remains that of armaments. Indeed there are signs that, with reduced military spending by the industrialised countries after the ending of the Cold War, Western arms suppliers are looking eagerly for opportunites in new areas of conflict in disturbed regions of the Third World and ex-Communist states (such as Bosnia). Yet these new outlets can scarcely compensate for more than a tiny fraction of the business lost through the ending of the major missile and aircraft programmes once justified by the Cold War.

It is true that, as made clear earlier, the long-term pressures tending to devalue capital have begun to increase the willingness of investors and bankers to seek greater risk in the speculative hope of high rewards. It has also been noted that this motivation continues to drive their enthusiasm for venture capital funds – notwithstanding their rather uninspiring performance to date – and for funds investing in the supposedly emerging markets of the Third World. From this standpoint the fact that investment funds are increasingly managed by highly paid individuals driven largely by considerations of short-term speculative gain is undoubtedly positive for the chances of getting funding for whatever may prove to be the consumer success stories of the future. For this means, as noted in the last chapter, that fund managers have a powerful incentive for taking risks in the knowledge that as long as the value of their funds keeps rising they will be fabulously rewarded, whereas a collapse will normally lead to nothing worse than the loss of their jobs. Clearly, on the other hand, this ethos of 'heads I win, tails I don't lose' can only prevail as long as there is sufficient confidence either that the financial system as a whole can remain solvent (and investor losses thus be kept within bounds) or that governments will be both willing and able to bail it out.

Moreover, in the feverish investment climate characteristic of the 1980s and 1990s it is even possible that the existence of this huge excess supply of capital will actually damage, or indeed already has damaged, the chances of many promising new product markets achieving the sustained growth that is needed to restore a stable and soundly based recovery of the economy as a whole. This is because the overenthusiasm of investors – born of sheer desperation to find profitable outlets for their surplus funds – may induce either excessive expansion of capacity in relation to demand growth potential or else overvaluation of the companies involved. In either case the effect may be to destabilise the latter financially – through undue pressure to maximise short-term profits and associated speculative takeover interest – with the end result that the businesses concerned may be distorted and the successful development of promising new product markets thereby prevented or delayed.

But if, notwithstanding such negative factors, a case can be made for expecting more significant new market opportunities to emerge, it must be recalled that this needs to happen on a more or less unprecedented scale if more than a fraction of the trillions of dollars of investible funds looking for a secure home is to be absorbed by fixed investment. Thus it will not be enough to bring out a few new consumer products or services each year, with the prospect that the market for them will reach saturation a few years later. Rather there is a need for a high level of new fixed investment to be sustained over several years.

Retreating to Determinism

Confronted with the obstinate refusal of growth to revive, a significant number of economists and others have been inclined to flirt with quasi-metaphysical theories which supposedly give grounds for expecting a spontaneous recovery in the global economy irrespective of the revealed current tendency of market forces. According to such theories economic growth is governed by very long cycles (of fifty years or more), which their advocates claim can explain the ups and downs of the world economy at least since the Industrial Revolution, and that these unfold more or less independently of any 'man-made' events or influences such as world wars, political changes or innovations in technology.[12] To anyone who recognises economics to be a social science – and hence inherently subject to the unpredictable actions and reactions of ever-changing human society – such attempts to subject it to a series of rigid laws of motion can scarcely seem worthy of a moment's consideration. That some respectable academics have allowed themselves to take such theories seriously is thus only of interest as an indicator of how far some will go to avoid addressing the harsh realities of systemic failure.

An even more desperate response of some economists, manifested in 1997[13] to the failure of the longed-for growth revival to materialise, has been to claim that it is actually happening but that somehow the statistics have failed to record it – or are inherently incapable of doing so. The main basis for these rather nebulous assertions appears to be that the large productivity gains resulting from the information technology revolution must be resulting in higher levels of output – or that, at the very least, the benefits to consumers resulting from the increased efficiency and convenience of the goods and services affected (such as that provided by cash-dispensing machines) ought to be reflected in a higher rate of economic growth than that actually recorded – rather than in an increased capacity surplus.[14] These claims have been advanced mainly by Wall Street economists – with the blessing of none other than Chairman Alan Greenspan of the Federal Reserve Board (the US central bank) – in an effort to convince the investor community that the huge surge in stock prices (which had doubled in just over two years since 1995) did not overstate the true value of the underlying assets. The most bizarre aspect of these arguments is that they amount to a repudiation of one of the most elementary tenets of market economics, namely that the only activities that count for the purposes of measuring total output or income are those that are actually paid for and can thus be valued in terms of a common monetary unit of account.[15] As such they seem unlikely to convince serious investors that there is any hidden real value in corporate equities. Rather their significance lies mainly in demonstrating the extent to which highly qualified economists are now prepared to sacrifice their intellectual self-respect in order to serve the interests of a beleaguered financial establishment.

Conclusion: No Way Out

If we concede that it is difficult, if not impossible, to give definitive explanations for why particular past surges in economic growth happened when they did, we must also concede that the possibility of another one occurring 'spontaneously' in the near future cannot be excluded. Yet the analysis presented in this chapter unquestionably indicates stronger grounds for expecting it not to occur. Moreover, this conclusion is reinforced by consideration of the huge scale of the growth needed to reverse the slide to disaster.

To put this in perspective, it should be noted that, even though the growth rates recorded by OECD countries since the mid-1970s – averaging some 2.5 per cent a year – have been low by the standards of the 1950s and 1960s, they appear to be very much in line with the norm for industrialised countries over the hundred years prior to World War II. Despite this, as we have seen, they have been insufficient to prevent either a growing underutilisation of both capital and labour or, largely because of this capacity surplus, a rapid rise in both public and private indebtedness. It follows that a revival of growth will have to be sustained at a rate high enough to permit the elimination of both the capacity surplus and the existing debt, while at the same time being consistent with continued high returns on capital, if a disastrous fall in financial asset values is to be avoided. It is difficult to estimate exactly what the minimum average growth rate needed to meet all these requirements would be. Yet there can be no question but that it would have to be at least as high as the 5 per cent average real rate recorded in the 1960s – and perhaps even higher, assuming a continuing rise in the productivity of capital and labour. Furthermore, it would probably need to be sustained at that average level for at least ten to fifteen years before something like balance was restored.

Many have until recently argued that the supposedly dynamic economies of East Asia – which have consistently recorded such high growth rates since the early 1980s – could provide both the example and the 'locomotive' power to restore sustained dynamism to the world economy. However, the record of Japan – whose model of development they are seeking to emulate – gives little ground for optimism, since it has gone from being the the fastest growing industrialised economy in the 1970s and 1980s to one of the slowest growing in the 1990s, as it stagnates under a mountain of bad debt. In fact, as noted in Chapter 10, there have been increasing signs since 1995 that South Korea, Thailand and other Asian 'tigers' are likewise set to move to a lower growth path because of problems not dissimilar to those affecting Japan.

Thus an assessment based on historical evidence and analysis of the more recent conjuncture of economic forces leads us to the conclusion that only a veritable miracle could avert an eventual (and perhaps quite early) world-wide financial and economic collapse such that the organs of state (whether national or international) will be too impoverished to prevent. For in order to continue paying for the consequences of the surplus of capital – by bailing out insolvent institutions (and countries) and otherwise subsidising profits – as well as that of labour (through higher welfare bills), governments would be forced to raise taxes substantially. Yet this could now only be done at the cost of either sharply reducing corporate profits, thereby undermining asset values anyway, and/or further squeezing personal incomes, thus engendering still weaker consumption growth and greater social deprivation. Faced with such an insoluble dilemma, political attention must soon begin to focus on alternatives to the profits system.

Notes

1. Named after its original propounder, Jean-Baptiste Say, the early-nineteenth-century French economist and follower of Adam Smith.

2. See G. Gilder, *Wealth and Poverty*, Basic Books, New York 1981.

3. Notably with respect to the impact of television violence on the incidence of violent crime. See R.H. Frank and P.J. Cook, *The Winner-Take-All Society*, The Free Press, New York 1995.

4. J.L. Hammond and Barbara Hammond, *The Bleak Age*, Pelican Books, West Drayton 1947.

5. In line with the rising personal debt burden, household debt-service (interest) payments rose steeply in most OECD countries during the 1980s, so that in several of them by 1990 this item of expenditure accounted for over 10 per cent of GDP – double the ratio recorded in the late 1970s in many cases (source: OECD).

6. Accounting for some 70 per cent of the world's GDP.

7. Bank for International Settlements, Annual Report 1997

8. This rate of decline has been only slightly slower than that of national income (GDP) as a whole. Indeed, since private consumption constitutes the main component of GDP (accounting for some 60 per cent of total expenditure in the OECD countries), its decline must be considered the principal factor contributing to the slide in overall economic growth.

9. See Central Policy Review Staff, *Social and Employment Implications of Microelectronics*, London 1978.

10. In fact, consumer surveys carried out in 1997 indicate that the amount of time spent watching television by the average Briton (still the highest of any European country) has actually declined since the late 1980s – at the very time the number of available channels has begun to increase rapidly.

11. Based on World Bank estimates of real 'purchasing power parity' in 1994, which are an attempt to adjust for the fact that comparative figures of GDP per head – showing average Third World incomes at barely 5 per cent of OECD levels – are distorted by exchange rates.

12. The best-known of these theories is the 'Kondratieff' long-wave cycle (so-called after the Russian economist who first developed the concept), which achieved a considerable vogue even among academic economists after large-scale unemployment had reappeared as a lasting phenomenon in the OECD countries in the 1970s – although the theory actually dates from the 1920s.

13. Just as the present work was being finalised.

14. See 'The Productivity Boom is Still a Mystery', *Business Week*, 25 August 1997; 'No End of a Boom', BBC Radio 4, 8 August 1997.

15. A very strong case can in fact be made for developing a calculus of economic welfare going beyond this traditional system of national accounts, thereby seeking to reflect more accurately the true extent of benefits and costs arising from the changing scale and pattern of economic activity – as has been urged particularly by environmental economists. See P. Ekins, *Wealth Beyond Measure*, Gaia Publications, London 1994. Since, however, such measures would incorporate non-monetary benefits and costs, they could hardly have any relevance to the growth of shareholder value.

13

Political Paralysis

Amid so many signs that the existing world economic and political order is becoming unsustainable, it is remarkable that there is so little overt questioning of its ideological basis. This anomaly clearly calls for some explanation if we are to make a realistic conjecture as to the likely political reaction to the multiplying disasters that now seem inevitable. In seeking one, it is appropriate to examine the impact of the upheavals of the post-1973 period on the main political interest groups and schools of thought in the Western industrialised world, particularly in the light of the post-war legacy described in Chapter 2.

The Trauma of the Left

The evaporation of the post-war certainties which until the early 1970s had seemed so durable was a phenomenon that the forces of the political left in the industrialised world have found particularly hard to come to terms with. This was undoubtedly because the leaders of left-wing political parties and their counterparts and natural allies in the realm of organised labour perceived themselves, with good reason, to have gained immensely from the institution of the mixed economy model in the post-war era. For it had not only led to enormous improvements in the living standards of their working-class constituency in terms of higher real earnings, job security and social welfare; it also gave the socialist party and trade-union leaders themselves a greatly enhanced and more influential position within the political establishment, as the representatives of the working masses whose interests were now for the first time generally accepted as of prime political importance.

As long as these conditions lasted it is small wonder that few on the left felt inclined to rock the boat. Thus although a minority of radical ideologues continued to point to enduring inequalities as well as inherent instability in the capitalist system, the vast majority of the left's supporters were not inclined to challenge an economic order which was permitting such palpable improvements to their lives. For their part, most leaders of the left felt even less incentive to seek radical change of a system which appeared able to deliver such a satisfactory outcome. Indeed, as it began to seem that the post-war boom could be extended indefinitely thanks to Keynesian economic policies, many started to cherish the belief that 'mixed-economy capitalism' was as far down the road to socialism as it was necessary to go, and that the only issue to be debated in future would be that of the distribution of the fruits of the supposedly everlasting boom.[1] Such was the basis of a broad political consensus of left and right which marked the 1950s and 1960s.

Hence the leadership of the left was psychologically ill-prepared for the collapse of this boom in the mid-1970s. Their general reaction was to assume that the recession was simply a temporary aberration which would quickly give way to a return of growth, thus obviating the need for them to re-examine their long-held belief in the capacity of the mixed economy to deliver sufficient growth and employment opportunities to keep most of their followers happy. Many were persuaded that the unprecedented combination of high inflation and low growth, or stagflation, in the 1970s demonstrated that this inflation was actually the cause of recession and, even more irrationally, that labour's demands for higher wages were the principal cause of inflation. Consequently the labour movement, particularly in some European countries, was induced to support policies of wage restraint, partly on the assumption that this was a way of averting mass unemployment, which was again starting to pose a real threat. By the end of the 1970s, however, a renewed plunge into recession and a consequent surge in unemployment – notwithstanding some success in cutting inflation – shattered these illusions, and with them what was left of the post-war Keynesian consensus.

Such a moment of crisis naturally appeared to many on the more extreme, Marxist left as the opportunity they had been waiting for, vindicating their prophesies of inevitable capitalist collapse. Yet they too were soon to discover they had been left behind by history. This was because of two profound shifts in the political landscape which had been going on for some time but in 1980 were still not widely recognised.

The first of these was the decline, in numerical terms, of the traditional working class in the industrial market economies. This in turn stemmed from a combination of the *embourgeoisement* of many manual workers as their living standards had risen during the boom, and the impact of changing technology in steadily reducing the proportion of manual or 'blue-collar' workers in the labour force and correspondingly boosting that of 'white-collar' (clerical and professional) workers. The result was that the industrial proletariat – on which Marxists had for generations pinned their hopes of revolution – had almost ceased to exist as a significant political reality.[2]

Just as decisive a blow for the traditional left was the evident economic deterioration of the Soviet Communist empire from the early 1970s, even though this was initially masked by the surge in Western lending to Soviet bloc countries. As the cracks grew ever more conspicuous in the 1980s, culminating in the total collapse of the Soviet economy and empire by the end of the decade, any residual belief among the left in Western countries that it might be considered in any sense an alternative model to capitalism was inevitably swept away. In truth, most parties and supporters of the left in Western Europe had long since rejected 'Stalinism' as politically unacceptable, without perhaps even being aware of the full enormity of its failings as an economic system. The most telling sign that it was losing credibility even with its most loyal adherents in the West was the emergence of what became known as Eurocommunism in the late 1970s. This amounted to a formal rejection of the Soviet model, in favour of something more akin to social democracy, by most of the Communist parties of Western Europe, notably by the Italian Communist Party (the largest of all of them) under the leadership of Enrico Berlinguer.

Yet even though most of the left in OECD countries had been highly critical of the Soviet system for many years – and had at times appeared more vigorous than the right in demanding greater democratisation in the Soviet bloc – they could not prevent its collapse acting as a major political reverse for themselves. For the conspicuous and simultaneous failure of both Keynesian mixed-economy capitalism in the West and Marxism-Leninism in the East was easily presented by their opponents as a mortal blow to the whole idea of the efficacy of state intervention in the economy. Thus by the time the Berlin Wall came down in 1989 it was quite plausible to claim that there was a new political consensus throughout the Western world in favour of liberal market ideas and the 'minimalist state'.

Rebound of the Right

It is possible, but facile, to portray the impact of these same events on the right of the political spectrum as simply the mirror image of their effect on the left. Undoubtedly the events of the 1970s and 1980s in both East and West represented a propaganda gift to those ideologues – of whom the Austrian economist Friedrich von Hayek was perhaps the most eminent – who had always regarded the departure from *laissez-faire* principles as unacceptable and unsustainable. There were indeed some who sought to suggest that the collapse of Communism signified the definitive triumph of the free-market capitalist model of society and, even more fatuously, 'the end of history'.[3] Yet it would be quite false to suggest that all supporters of the political right, particularly among the leaders of the corporate sector, had simply been yearning for such an opportunity to overthrow the Keynesian post-war consensus in favour of more traditional orthodoxy.

Indeed most of big business – which is, of course, as natural an ally of the political right as organised labour is of the left – had been just as comfortable with the mixed-economy model of the post-war era as had the trade unions and non-Marxist parties of the left. Such an attitude is scarcely remarkable, moreover, given the great benefits derived by the private corporate sector from sustained rapid growth and the comforting propensity of governments to finance infrastructure (social as well as physical), to intervene in support of private investment, and to provide markets for private-sector output. Thus as long as the model continued to deliver a stable economic environment permitting both sustained expansion and adequate profitability, while at the same time leaving companies largely free to control their assets, there were few complaints from organised capital.

Hence, as on the left, many political parties of the right continued, throughout the 1970s and beyond, to foster the belief that sustained

growth could be revived and full employment restored, thus avoiding the need for radical revision of the mixed-economy model. Indeed despite the persistent adverse trends in the subsequent period
– with steadily declining growth, chronic fiscal deficits and the disappearance of any hope that full employment (as conventionally
understood) can ever again be a reality – there has been continuing
reluctance on the part of many leading politicians of the right to
accept the implications of this. This has been most conspicuous in
continental Europe, where Christian Democratic parties (notably that
of Germany, for so long the dominant force in that country) and
the French Gaullists still feel politically unable to abandon their
national consensus favouring the 'social market'.

Elsewhere, particularly in the Anglo-Saxon countries, there was a
relatively rapid movement towards rejection of the post-war consensus and in favour of a revival of *laissez faire*. Yet, as revealed in our
earlier analysis, even under the avowedly radical right-wing regimes
that held power throughout the 1980s and beyond in the United
States and Britain it was found politically impossible to revert to
full-blooded financial orthodoxy. Rather, it was for long considered
more expedient to pretend that deregulation and cutting income tax
rates (especially those affecting the wealthy) would themselves
amount to a sufficient cure for the persistent economic malaise.

By a convenient irony, the inevitable collapse of the short-lived
boom resulting from this liberalisation craze in the industrial market
economies coincided with the final fall of Communism in the Soviet
bloc at the end of the 1980s, thus providing a smokescreen for what
was in reality a serious reverse for the 'new right' prospectus. But if
the Communist débâcle excluded the possibility of the left putting
more radical proposals on the agenda – going beyond traditional
Keynesian interventionism – the bursting of the *laissez-faire* economic
bubble finally obliged the right to begin grasping the logic of their
own orthodox rhetoric. For it exposed the delusion – essentially a
hangover of the Keynesian era – that there was some formula of
economic management which could deliver renewed growth, and
thus compelled governments to consider more drastic approaches to
the mounting crisis of public deficit and debt.

It went without saying that any such measures could not be
allowed to threaten the profitability of the private sector and thereby
undermine the inflated market value of securities, since the inevitable
consequence – a massive crash of global financial markets – remained

the most intolerable outcome of all. Instead, as we have seen, the recurrence of recession from 1990 meant that further large subventions from taxpayers were needed to bolster failing financial institutions, particularly in the United States, as well as to sustain production and investment by other private-sector enterprises.

At the same time any reversal of the personal tax cuts made in the 1980s would have been both unacceptable to the core constituency of the right and damaging to the credibility of governments which had but lately been insisting on the importance of cutting taxes to stimulate enterprise. The most telling political argument against such a move, however, was and is that in the new global economy, where money is free to move across national frontiers, any significant increase in direct taxes – affecting either corporations or highly paid individuals – will now tend to result in a flight of capital and entrepreneurs to other countries.

It has thus been perceived that there is no alternative to a further attack on public spending if deficits and debt are to be curbed. Yet given the extent of cuts already imposed, there has been limited room for manoeuvre in this area as well. In fact, it has become clear that any serious reductions in public spending commitments must above all involve a major curtailment of the welfare state (the biggest and most rapidly growing area of public spending) – as well as a progressive withdrawal of the state from the provision of other public services and infrastructure.

Baldly presented in these terms, however, such an alternative is no more politically acceptable than that of reversing the tax cuts. Consequently an effort has had to be made to put it in a less negative light. The arguments being used to sell it to a sceptical public, in Britain and elsewhere, have typically been that

- The welfare state is becoming unaffordable because of the dwindling proportion of the population in employment relative to that of pensioners and unemployed. On this view the problem is defined in terms of the rising 'dependency ratio' – on the basis that the ever growing welfare burden is being borne primarily if not solely by those still in employment (an argument which ignores the reality that the costs of social welfare are in almost all countries already funded by revenues other than the social insurance contributions of those in employment, and that in any case there is no inherent reason why they should not be).

- Reliance on the welfare state detracts from individual liberty and consequently citizens will feel liberated by being allowed to make private provision for their health care, education, pensions and unemployment. It is even being argued that private provision of pensions may be more cost-effective for the individual than state pensions, although experience has already shown this to be untrue.[4] (In fact, aside from the question of cost-effectiveness, it is obvious that a high proportion of the population could not afford the extra costs, which would be equivalent to a huge rise in personal taxation if such provision were made compulsory.)

At the same time the privatisation of public services and the introduction of private capital into the financing of public infrastructure is presented as a benefit to users as well as taxpayers because of the presumed greater efficiency of the private sector in constructing or operating such facilities. This despite the very real problems encountered in Britain (the pioneer of this approach among OECD countries) and elsewhere in finding compromises between governments' need to obtain value for money for the taxpayer and investors' need for a market rate of return on their investment (see Chapter 8).

Forced Unanimity

The obvious flimsiness, indeed absurdity, of many of these and other arguments put forward in support of abandoning the central tenets of the post-war socio-economic order in the industrialised capitalist world is a clear indication of the panic and confusion now gripping the ruling establishment in the face of an objective prognosis which is increasingly grim. Even more striking is the lack of coherent political opposition to what amounts to an attempt to put the clock back, in terms of social progress, by half a century or more. Likewise the failure of any audible voice on the left to articulate a reasoned alternative strategy is truly remarkable, even making due allowance for the propaganda setbacks – mentioned above – which the movement has suffered since the mid-1970s.

Perhaps the most shocking demonstration of how far leftist dissent has effectively been stifled in the 1990s was the adoption by the supposedly socialist Labour Party in Britain of a 'welfare to work' strategy as the centrepiece of its successful election campaign in

1997. The essence of this initiative is to use the money raised by the party's only significant tax-raising proposal – a one-off levy on the excess profits of privatised utilities – to supplement the wages of unemployed people to be given jobs in the private sector. Although presented as a measure to help the jobless acquire sufficient work experience to enhance their long-term employability, the promised inclusion of a coercive element in the programme – so that un-employed individuals rejecting offers of work under it would be denied any social-security benefit – indicates a far more reactionary purpose behind it. Moreover, because there is no way of preventing employers from substituting new employees subsidised under the scheme for existing (unsubsidised) staff, the effect seems more likely to be one of marginalising even more of the workforce than to enhance the prospects of the unemployed or reduce the 'depend-ency culture'. Hence the policy, which is partly modelled on schemes in certain US states, looks more like an attempt to curb the long-term cost of social welfare by deterrence while ensuring that the residual welfare budget is deployed to give maximum possible sup-port to the profits of the private sector. As such, despite being presented to the public as part of the 'modernisation' of the British welfare system, it bears an uncanny resemblance to the notorious 'Speenhamland system'[5] adopted in parts of England from the 1790s under the old Poor Law – requiring the destitute to work as farm labourers in return for the relief they received from the parish – and if implemented seems likely to be just as pernicious in its social and economic effects.[6] Notwithstanding these portents, leading trade-union officials have allowed themselves to be co-opted into advising on implementation of the programme.

Resistance to these tendencies is arguably stronger elsewhere – notably in France, where sustained industrial unrest in late 1995 forced the rightist government of President Chirac to abandon or postpone some of its more drastic 'reforms'. Yet such opposition is scarcely being articulated in any OECD country by any of the mainstream political parties and hence offers no effective counter-weight to the *laissez-faire* juggernaut.

It is impossible to offer a documented explanation for this lack of meaningful opposition to the overwhelming tide of reaction. However, one is bound to assume that it is connected with the vital significance of the issues at stake for the ruling vested interests and the fact that they feel almost any means are justified by the end of maintaining the existing economic order intact. In what still pass for democratic societies, such means must clearly include, first and foremost, a ruthless propaganda campaign in which the truth is systematically distorted and heterodox analysis or opinion is marginalised, if not actively suppressed. Of the numerous examples of such distortion cited in the present work, perhaps none is more chilling than the continuing insistence of Western officialdom that 'shock therapy' is the appropriate remedy for the appalling economic problems of the former Soviet bloc – in defiance of all the objective evidence that it is making the situation even worse (thus contributing directly to loss of life), not to mention the experience of all existing market economies. Yet the effectiveness with which the overwhelming majority of Western aid administrators, consultants, journalists and academics have been co-opted to defend it as the only way forward to the creation of a viable market economy (often parroting the same manifestly bogus arguments) would suggest that an indoctrination effort worthy of the old Soviet Communist Party itself is at work.

An important role in fostering this new consensus has clearly been played by the powerful mass media, which are inevitably in thrall to the same dominant interest groups. This is not to suggest that there is no argument in the press or broadcast media on issues of economic and social policy. Yet for a long time the debate has been conducted within a very limited ideological spectrum, so that typically the impression is created that the choice is essentially between two broad economic models (the Neo-Classical and Keynesian), even though each has a proven record of failure. Increasingly conscious of the sterility of this inhibited discourse, the political establishment can seemingly find no better alternative idea than the essentially meaningless concept of the 'stakeholder economy' (see Chapter 11). In contrast, despite the clearly unmanageable scale of the economic problems now engulfing the world, it is still possible to dismiss any suggestion that the capitalist system might after all need to be fundamentally reshaped, if it is to survive at all, as an example of old-fashioned Marxist thinking unworthy of serious consideration.

In this vacuous debate the economics 'profession' has been conspicuous by the inadequacy of its response. Its failure to come up with more rational solutions to the chronic weaknesses of the economic system is seemingly ascribable to two linked causes:

(1) Its material dependence on institutions which have an in-built tendency to support the status quo. Thus a high proportion of the most able economists are employed by major financial institutions, which typically pay them high salaries. Yet in Britain and the United States particularly they are the 'experts' most commonly called on by the broadcast media to comment on the economic situation, the prospects for the financial markets, and the policy changes which may be needed to correct any perceived adverse trends. Very often, moreover, their views are implicitly presented as entirely objective without any suggestion that there might be a sustainable contrary opinion – despite the fact that a moment's reflection would suggest that they have a powerful motivation for saying nothing contrary to the vested interests of their masters. It is true that the other main category of economists who pronounce through the media – the academics – are in principle less institutionally bound to reflect establishment views, and indeed have in the past been a significant source of dissent. However, it has been noticeable in recent years that very few have shown any sign of departing significantly from one or other of the approved orthodoxies – Keynesian or free market. Given the growing financial strictures placed on universities (particularly in Britain) because of the state fiscal squeeze, and their consequently greater dependence on private-sector funding, it is plausible to suppose that this may have affected their intellectual independence and capacity for more radical analysis.

(2) The limitations of conventional theory. Despite a long-standing critique and recognition of the oversimplification inherent in much of traditional economic theory, it is still common to find uncritical acceptance of models and policies based on remarkably crude assumptions as to the uniformity and constancy of human behaviour (whether individual or corporate). There could be no better example of this than the notion – which underpins the theories of the supply-side school – that reducing marginal tax rates results in higher investment and output, notwithstanding the copious empirical evidence that it is just as likely to have the opposite effect. This traditional tendency to present bigotry as science is increasingly compounded by the chronic propensity of the discipline either to discount any factors (such as human life or the environment and other important 'externalities') which cannot be readily quantified, or else to give them arbitrary values which cannot sensibly be based on purely economic criteria.

Another powerful influence constraining free discussion of economic problems is the very practical consideration of the need to maintain confidence in the financial markets. Any suggestion that a radical switch in government policies might be contemplated – involving, for example, large increases in corporate taxation or tighter control of capital movements across frontiers – would be liable to provoke a substantial sell-off of financial securities and a corresponding drop in their market value. This in turn would tend to undermine the balance sheets of the more overextended institutions, thus raising a 'systemic' threat to the entire financial system. Likewise, even a hint that any national government was contemplating taking such measures in isolation from the rest of the world would engender an immediate and damaging run on its currency – to the extent that this was not pre-empted by the rapid introduction of exchange controls. Thus by its very nature a *laissez-faire* capitalist economic structure precludes free and objective debate on how to solve its own problems.

It would be wrong to suggest that there is a totally effective conspiracy of silence over the deep-seated economic problems facing the world. Yet it is noticeable that the work even of those commentators who have recognised and drawn attention to some of the dangerous and revolutionary trends now affecting the world economy is permeated by a studied fatalism. Thus those who have pointed out the risks of financial collapse or the potentially devastating impact of the information-technology revolution on the demand for both capital and labour tend to imply both that such adverse developments are inevitable and that it will only be possible to neutralise them, if at all, through the strenuous efforts of individuals to come to terms with them. Above all the notion that state power – whether at national level or through multilateral collective action – could be mobilised to combat the trend to a global power vacuum is vigorously, and almost unanimously, discounted.[7]

Popular Red Herrings

At the same time political commentators, and even economic ones, seek to distract attention from issues of substance by trying to explain economic decline in non-economic terms. In particular there has in recent years been a plethora of rather synthetic soul-searching over the supposed decline of the Western industrialised countries in relation to the allegedly more dynamic economies of East Asia. The implication is that the latter reflect a more robust culture of single-minded dedication to national collective goals – often glibly identi-fied with Confucianism – in contrast to the rather self-indulgent individualism of the West. Yet, aside from demonstrating an extra-ordinary ambivalence about the much vaunted economic benefits of the *laissez-faire* ideology based on the pursuit of enrichment by indi-viduals, such analyses betray a total detachment from reality. For an objective reading of the recent economic history of East Asia would be forced to recognise that (a) Japan, the original success story of the region on which all the 'Tiger' economies (South Korea, Taiwan and the rest) are essentially modelled, has fallen into chronic financial crisis and stagnation since the late 1980s, such that by the mid-1990s it was growing even more slowly than the USA or the EU; and (b) much of the growth of the Tiger economies has been dependent on capital and technology supplied by Western as well as Japanese investors and corporations, mostly drawn to these less developed economies by the availability of cheap labour.

Indeed the game of international comparisons is a favourite device of politicians and commentators in all countries who are either unwilling or unable to confront the more fundamental problems. Politicians are, of course, occupationally prone to point to particular indicators of their country's economy (always with the crudest selectiveness) to try to demonstrate that it is better or worse than that of other countries, depending on whether they are in or out of power. More generally, however, the advantage of this style of analysis is that it helps to sustain the delusion that there is somewhere a model form of market economy which is working much better than that at home and hence that a few quite minor reforms – such as giving autonomy to the central bank or doubling expenditure on vocational training – will suffice to produce economic success. Typical of this syndrome is the long-standing British obsession with the country's relative decline vis-à-vis not only Japan but other European countries such as Germany, France and Italy, all of which have overtaken it in terms of national income per head since 1950. Yet those who seek to draw conclusions from this in terms of how Britain could or should seek to emulate the performance of these countries steadfastly refuse to recognise that all of the latter are themselves now suffering from much the same economic problems as Britain, and in some respects may be even worse placed.[8]

Strategies of Desperation

In such an unreal ideological climate, mainstream political debate is becoming ever more confused and empty. Thus in the United States, politicians get elected by hysterically demanding a sharp reduction in the role of government – and hence the level of taxation – only to insist once returned to office on maintaining or expanding Federal programmes vital to their constituencies (of which the big-business interests that have funded their campaigns are naturally the most important).[9] In other OECD countries, notably Britain, majorities of the 'haves' have been put together by applying quite crude electoral bribery (underpriced shares in privatised enterprises and heavily subsidised home ownership), while the 'have nots' have been increasingly marginalised – an approach evidently being continued, as noted above, by the 'socialist' government elected in 1997. Elsewhere in Europe, while residual faith in the importance of state intervention is still proclaimed, there is no more realism than in the USA as to how to deal with the state budgetary crisis, nor recognition that participation in a deregulated global economy is bound to make the task even harder.

In the late 1990s, however, there appears to be a dawning awareness that the chronic and interrelated problems of relatively slow growth (punctuated by increasingly frequent recessions), continually rising public debt burdens and mounting structural unemployment have become so intractable that only drastic measures can avert financial and economic chaos. For the dominant capitalist interest group this must imply the steady, or even rapid, dismantling of the welfare state – despite the obvious impossibility of reconciling this with the promise of greater prosperity or social stability. It is a measure of the severity of the crisis that such a politically risky strategy – perhaps provoking the ultimate revolt of the middle class – is now being contemplated.

Indeed such is the unattractiveness of this option that political leaders still find it easier to turn up the volume of lies told to the public rather than confront it with the truth. Thus at the time of writing it is being officially claimed in both Britain and the United States that the economy is growing rapidly and opening a new era of sustainable prosperity – even as these claims of success are belied by still intractable budget deficits and a public debt burden mounting to ever more precarious levels. All the while the threat of a massive crash in the market values of securities grows, the only question being when the financial illusionists will run out of ways of manipulating them.

Yet on top of the mounting costs of artificially supporting the value of capital, the need to respond to the economic and social devastation spreading across the non-Western world is bound in any event to render it less and less feasible to hold down public spending in the OECD countries if widespread political upheavals and civil disorder across the globe are to be avoided. War and destruction, it is true, may be regarded by the military–industrial complex as a welcome market opportunity, and may also be viewed by some as a convenient way of eliminating excess population. But even if it is imaginable that such a cynical strategy could be consistently pursued by the Western ruling establishment, it must be doubted whether the 'benefits' could long outweigh the damage caused by long-term global instability to the overall economic and investment climate.

An Ideological Impasse

As signs of overwhelming economic and social breakdown accumulate around the globe, it seems ever more extraordinary that no section of the body politic in the major industrialised countries is able to question any fundamental assumptions of the existing order, nor to propose any solutions which do not amount to going back down the blind alley of past failures.

In this respect the political climate seems strangely to resemble that of the declining phase of the Soviet Union. There in the twilight years of President Brezhnev the single ruling party became increasingly paralysed by its inability to halt, let alone reverse, its slide to disaster without calling in question the fundamental principles of its own monolithic ideology. This paralysis was, of course, reinforced by the totalitarian nature of the regime, under which not only was any public discussion of radical alternatives precluded but officials found it was in their interest to conceal the harsh realities of the situation from their superiors. The result was that no change was possible until the system had virtually collapsed from within – although even then the Gorbachev administration faced a bitter struggle with entrenched vested interests in forcing the Communist Party and the *apparat* to start thinking the unthinkable.

Another historical parallel that irresistibly springs to mind is that of the French *ancien régime* before the revolution of 1789. For a familiar interpretation of that upheaval is that the one factor above all which rendered it unavoidable was the obdurate refusal of the aristocracy to give up the financial privileges which largely exempted them from taxation, even though – like their present-day counterparts, the private corporate sector – they alone possessed the resources that could save the state from long-threatened financial ruin.

In the supposedly pluralist democracies of the modern industrialised West one might have expected a greater capacity to come to terms with unavoidable change. In view of what is at stake – in terms of the retention of enormous concentrations of economic power in very few hands – it is scarcely remarkable that the 'power elite' should shrink from confronting the agonising dilemma that now faces it. Yet the fact that it has thus far been possible to prevent any significant discussion of radical alternatives, such as the situation clearly demands, may indicate that Western public opinion is as much deluded about the strength of its democracy as it is about the efficacy of free-market capitalism.

The failure hitherto of such radical alternatives to emerge can be attributed, as suggested above, to a combination of the historic weakness and fragmentation of the traditional opposition on the left and a quite Orwellian level of manipulation, misinformation and self-deception by the ruling establishment itself. If the parallels with the fall of Soviet Communism or the French *ancien régime* hold, however, it must be doubted whether determination to maintain the status quo will survive the financial disaster which now seems inevitable. Yet the tragic prospect arises that, as is happening in many parts of the fallen Soviet empire (and did likewise in revolutionary France), the denouement may be so chaotic that the chances of reasoned democratic debate of alternatives will wither in the face of irrational political extremism.

Notes

1. See A. Crosland, *The Future of Socialism*, Jonathan Cape, London 1956.
2. See A. Gorz, *Farewell to the Working Class: An Essay in Post-industrial Socialism*, Pluto Press, London 1982.
3. F. Fukuyama, *The End of History and the Last Man*, Hamish Hamilton, London 1992.

4. Notably in the case of pensioners of Mirror Group Newspapers in Britain, who suffered severe losses as a result of theft by the Group's controlling shareholder, Robert Maxwell, before his mysterious death in 1991. Less sensationally but still more significantly, a report by Britain's Office of Fair Trading in 1997 exposed the poor value for money provided by private personal pensions as compared with the State Earnings Related Pension Scheme (SERPS). Meanwhile, as noted in Chapter 8, company occupational schemes in the United States are only considered acceptable as long as they remain underwritten by the federal government – an obligation which has cost the taxpayer over $1 billion a year (on average) in bail-outs since the early 1980s.

5. So called after the parish in Berkshire where it was first applied in 1795.

6. See E.P. Thompson, *The Making of the English Working Class*, Penguin, Harmondsworth 1968, pp. 247–9.

7. See W. Rees-Mogg and J.D. Robertson, *The Great Reckoning*, Sidgwick & Jackson, London, 1991; P. Drucker, *Post-Capitalist Society*, HarperCollins, New York 1993.

8. See W. Hutton, *The State We're In*, Jonathan Cape, London 1995.

9. No better illustration of this tendency could be found than the performance of the Republican-controlled Congress (supposedly dominated by the rabidly anti-interventionist forces of the radical right) in formulating proposals in 1997 purporting to lead to a balanced budget in 2002 – which would be the first since 1969 – while yet enacting tax breaks aimed at several specific industries that were quite blatantly a pay-off for campaign contributions. See 'Death, Taxes – and Corporate Welfare?', *Business Week*, 14 July 1997.

14

Essential Features of a Sustainable World Order

Despite the strong grounds for pessimism just outlined, we are duty-bound to try to envisage what more rational models of economic organisation might evolve in a less repressed political environment. Yet precisely because of the present climate of stunted debate in the industrialised West (and indeed throughout the world) it is hard to make a reasoned assessment of the prospects. Before making the attempt it is perhaps appropriate to summarise the main strands of the preceding analysis of how the world system has reached its present impasse – if only to remind ourselves of the central constraints to continuing with the status quo.

The legacy of Keynesian failure   By the end of World War II it was universally accepted by governments in the industrialised West that capitalist economic structures would only be tolerable in future if subject to extensive stabilising intervention by the state, including provision of comprehensive welfare programmes to eliminate mass deprivation. The subsequent introduction of the 'mixed economy' model of capitalism ushered in the most prolonged period of rapid growth in the world economy since the Industrial Revolution. Consequent overconfidence in its efficacy led to widespread failure to grasp the significance of the downturn after 1973, so that continued attempts to manage demand in the 1970s produced only inflation and a steep rise in public debt.

Neo-orthodoxy and liberalisation – a twin disaster   The purported resort to more traditional financial orthodoxy from around 1980 was largely a sham. This reflected the inescapable dependency of the private sector on state support and the political impossibility of making significant cuts in the welfare budget as unemployment and social deprivation rose. The consequent inability to make significant public spending cuts meant that 'supply-side' strategies of tax cutting (the main plank of US policy in the 1980s) simply produced bigger state deficits and debt. Simultaneous financial deregulation – intended to 'unleash the forces of enterprise' – helped to generate a brief, largely speculative, world boom from 1985. The subsequent renewed recession was only prevented from turning into a major financial catastrophe by the timely application of taxpayers' money to prop up financial markets and institutions. The overhang of debt resulting from the bursting of this bubble none the less inhibited recovery in the 1990s (notably in Japan), resulting in even slower growth than in the 1980s.

The chronic surplus of capital   A combination of intensifying competition and technological change has caused a decline in the growth of fixed investment since the 1960s even greater than that of output overall. The result has been a chronic and intensifying shortage of outlets for the reinvestment of the growing volume of capital generated by corporate profits. Instead of allowing this to be reflected in a fall in asset values, the authorities have instigated or connived at various stratagems to maintain them artificially, including:

- lower corporate taxation;
- state bail-outs or de facto nationalisation of failing financial institutions;
- privatisation of state-owned companies and other assets – to help absorb some of the surplus;
- subsidisation and stimulation of increased investment in securities;
- use of creative accounting or financial 'engineering' techniques (such as share buy-backs) to enable companies to manipulate their own share prices.

The impact of technology   The recent pattern of technological innovation (particularly in the field of information technology) points to a progressive move towards types of economic activity which are both less capital-intensive and less labour-intensive, but more 'knowledge-intensive' in both manufacturing and service sectors, with increasing emphasis on 'software' and high-grade 'human capital' rather than on large-scale fixed investment. This implies not only a continuing progressive decline in the demand for labour but the disappearance of the key factor leading to the triumph of capitalism in the nineteenth century, when the technological innovations that fuelled the Industrial Revolution demanded large concentrations of capital which could only be raised under a capitalist economic structure. Ultimately this means capital will be shown to be as largely redundant as labour has in a sense already become.

Emasculation of the state The combination of slowing economic growth, deregulation, tax cutting and the diversion of a greater proportion of public resources to propping up the value of capital has left governments increasingly unable to cope with many of their traditional responsibilities, let alone deal with the mounting problems threatening global stability. Above all they cannot begin to address the economic and social chaos now overwhelming the former Soviet empire and most of the Third World. Unable to offer anything like the vast amounts of aid funding needed by both the latter, they are instead maintaining the pretence that radical free-market policies will actually enable them to escape from their collective destitution – notwithstanding all the evidence of economic history that this can never be the route to development.

The erosion of legality As a result of (a) the weakening of state power, (b) the continuing reliance of private corporations on state support, and (c) global economic and financial deregulation, the opportunities and incentives for fraud, corruption, tax evasion and criminal infiltration of big business, if not of government itself, have vastly increased. The resulting climate of lawlessness is such that the legitimacy of the whole economic and political system is increasingly being called in question.

Fading prospects of growth recovery Although it is impossible to forecast long-term growth trends with any certainty, history suggests a sustained revival of growth rates such as those achieved in the 1950s and 1960s is highly unlikely. Without it, however, there is ultimately no prospect of averting a catastrophic fall in capital asset values or restoring the state to solvency.

It follows from such a negative prognosis that there is really no choice but to consider a radically different approach – based on the imperative need to neutralise the demands of the profits system – if a more durable economic environment is to be attained.

An End to Growth-Dependency

The truth must at last be faced that there is no realistic hope of expanding demand (and hence aggregate global output) fast enough to

- absorb the ever-accumulating capital surpluses generated by the private sector;
- contain, let alone reduce, the rising burden of public-sector deficits and debt under the existing pattern of income distribution and taxation;
- permit a significant reduction, let alone a closing of, the huge gap in average living standards as between the rich 15 per cent and the poor 85 per cent of the world's population.

Since supply-side factors – notably environmental constraints – may in any case require restriction of the expansion of certain sectors of the economy, traditional policies of seeking indiscriminately to maximise GDP will have to be jettisoned, especially in the case of the high-income industrialised countries. This does not mean that governments will necessarily have to aim for zero growth rates; still less that the level of economic activity will cease to be a matter of concern to them. What it does imply, however, is that it must no longer be considered acceptable to hold out the prospect of higher growth as grounds for not addressing directly the imbalance of income distribution both within and between nations.

A New Collectivism

It is self-evident that free-market, profit-maximising capitalism is incompatible with a low-growth or no-growth economy, since to survive it requires the possibility of perpetual accumulation of profits and expansion of shareholders' funds. From this it must follow that the untrammelled pursuit of profit maximisation by corporations can no longer be accepted as their primary objective, at least as long as they enjoy the privilege of state protection or subsidy.

Once it is accepted that the maximisation of profit can no longer be the main basis for allocating resources, other criteria must be established. Since one of these is bound to be the need to reduce the share of value-added going to company shareholders, it follows that

- Mechanisms for limiting the return on capital achieved or retained by major private sector companies must be established. In the light of the experience of regulating privatised utilities in Britain and elsewhere, this should entail public influence not merely over pricing but over investment strategy as well.

- Private investors will tend to find the rates of return deemed compatible with financial stability too low to compensate them for the risk of loss. This means the state will either need to guarantee them against loss or take over the ownership of enterprises itself – or, where possible, break them up into small enough units to enable them to operate independently of external shareholders (that is, as private companies).

- Enterprises whose finances are ultimately underwritten by the taxpayer will have to be publicly accountable and subject to public approval of their policies, whether at local, national or international level. Pre-eminently this must apply to financial institutions, bearing in mind the already recognised principle (noted in Chapter 5) that the stability of the financial system is a public good.

- The value added which will no longer be needed to provide a high return on overvalued capital will be applied instead mainly to a combination of (a) reducing public-sector deficits and debt, (b) reduced prices to consumers, (c) adequate and equitable wage levels for the employed, and (d) improved social benefits and services, including a guaranteed minimum income for the non-employed.

- Any compensation to existing private owners for the necessary transfer of assets to collective ownership must be based on values far below existing market levels – both because the fiscal resources will not be available to pay more and because the objective must in any case be to reduce the huge overhang of surplus capital which is destabilising markets. Priority will need to be given to ensuring the livelihood of pensioners and other small savers most affected by the resulting devaluation of securities.

Since profit maximisation is to be severely downgraded, if not completely eliminated, as the basis for allocating economic resources, it is obvious that alternative indicators of performance will need to be formulated. While these may perhaps include a requirement to achieve a minimum rate of return on capital – except in the case of essential services such as health care – they will also need to incorporate other considerations (such as social and environmental priorities) far more explicitly.

Since such criteria would almost by definition tend to lay less emphasis on market competitiveness, other spurs to cost-effectiveness – such as measurable performance targets linked to incentives – would need to be defined and their application subjected to transparent scrutiny and audit. Failure to do so would be bound to result in the kind of bureaucratic inefficiency, corruption and waste that have been characteristic not only of the Soviet Union but of other state-dominated economies which are nominally more democratic.

Explicit recognition of the limited scope for growth would also have profound implications for income distribution, especially given the projected continuing rise in the global surplus of labour. For whether this imbalance was resolved by some form of work rationing or simply through the social benefits system, the unacceptability of allocating labour through a purely competitive market mechanism would also require – at the very least – some limitation of the disparities in reward between the highest and the lowest paid. A move towards less unequal incomes would also be implied by the substantial elimination of risk, the high level of which is often used (in most cases quite falsely) as the justification for large rewards to senior executives.

A New Democracy

Any criteria used as alternatives to the supposedly impersonal one of profit maximisation would need to be derived from conscious political choices. Critics of such an approach traditionally argue that it puts in the hands of politicians and bureaucrats decisions which should properly be those of consumers, mediated by the marketplace. Even if by now the myth of 'consumer sovereignty' under capitalism has been exploded, it must be conceded that such critics have an important point. For it must be the presumption under a democracy that the purpose of any economic system is, broadly speaking, to provide the mass of people with what they want – or, ideally, what they would want if they had full knowledge of the choices open to them. Handing responsibility for deciding this to bureaucrats or politicians is never likely to provide durably satisfying results. Mechanisms will therefore need to be devised to enable the wishes of citizens to be reflected in the determination of priorities in resource allocation. In the case of most consumer goods and services, market forces would continue largely to determine the pattern of consumption and supply. Where certain enterprises or industries were not sufficiently profitable to retain the support of their owners, they would in principle be required to restructure or else be humanely phased out in line with normal market criteria – although in such cases the opportunity for new investors (including public-sector agencies or local collectives) to acquire the assets would normally need to be assured.

In cases of 'market failure' – such as, for example, the imperfect reflection of the relative costs and benefits of public transport vis-à-vis private cars in their monetary costs to the user, particularly in relation to public health and the environment – decisions would have to be made on the basis of a far more open democratic debate than generally occurs under present norms. It would be pointless here to speculate on the precise institutional forms which might emerge to fulfil this requirement. What can be set out, however, are some general principles regarding the conduct of both the democratic institutions of government (national or local) and commercial corporations (whether in the private or public sector).

Enhancement of the democratic process   The right to vote in periodic elections in which (a) the party manifestoes have normally been drawn up without any wide consultation, and in any case are frequently very similar to each other, and (b) commercial interests are often allowed to dictate the agenda by virtue of their contributions to party funds (secret or not), can no longer be accepted as a meaningful expression of the popular will. Hence it will be essential to

- increase the frequency and diversify the forms of consultation of the electorate (including greater use of referenda);
- combine maximum decentralisation of collective decision-making with greater international integration;
- strictly enforce tight and equitable limits on political funding;
- subject all public officials (elected or appointed) to transparent but fair scrutiny of both their political and personal integrity, with the possibility of rapid removal of defaulters from office.

Transparency Full public access to all information relating to key economic policy or investment decisions must be assured. This would apply to all decisions both by public-sector corporations and by private-sector corporations where there was any state support, equity participation or statutory regulation involved.

Corporate governance The protection of limited liability would only be extended to corporations subject to the supervision of a state-appointed regulator – as presently in the case of privately owned public utilities in the USA and Britain. (This restriction, it should be emphasised, is not proposed solely out of a concern to enhance corporate accountability and reduce the scope for fraud. It also reflects a recognition of the fact that, because of the permanently diminished demand for capital resulting from the technological transformation of the last twenty years – discussed in Chapter 7 – it is no longer necessary, nor indeed desirable, to provide the same incentives to equity investment as were appropriate in the nineteenth century).

Media openness Effective limits on control of the press and broadcast media by individuals or corporations should be assured, with guaranteed access for minority opinion.

The theme of all such reforms of the democratic process would be the enhancing of *accountability*. Those who object that such a high degree of democracy is without precedent or practicality need to be reminded that democracy is in any case still in its infancy as a world phenomenon. At the beginning of the twentieth century virtually no country enjoyed universal suffrage, and most European countries did not give women the right to vote until the end of World War II. Seen in the perspective of the long span of Western political evolution, therefore, such changes should be viewed simply as logical steps in pursuit of the democratic ideal to which all pay lip-service.

Moreover, the need to enhance democratic accountability is implicit in much of the critique (muted though it often is) of contemporary political and economic institutions expressed in all parts of the world. Indeed the lack of more outspoken criticism is clearly itself a symptom of the often brutal repression of free speech in most countries, including many in the Third World which are treated as respected members of the 'free world', even as their governments object to complaints at their systematic abuse of human rights as an unwarranted neo-imperialist attempt to impose 'Western values' on them. Yet the failure of such authoritarian (and often blatantly corrupt) regimes to silence the fierce resistance to them – particularly among the young – in countries such as South Korea, Indonesia and even China is a clear demonstration (if one were needed) that the desire for democracy and respect for human rights are universal values.

In the Western industrialised world one sign of incipient concern to promote greater accountability is the emerging emphasis on the need to ensure that rights are balanced by responsibilities, an idea notably espoused by the leader of the British Labour Party, Tony Blair (elected prime minister in 1997). Ironically, this notion is perhaps better understood in East Asian and other Third World countries where society remains more based on quasi-feudal relationships – precluding the indiscriminate pursuit of profit maximisation – than in the West.

More generally, it is hard to see how the legitimacy of state authority, whose weakening we have identified as a consequence of chronic economic failure in the world as a whole, can be restored without compelling state institutions to be more responsive to the interests and concerns of the general public. Likewise it would seem obvious that only by greatly strengthening the democratic process will it be possible to create structures of accountability effective enough to make the mass of people prefer them to the anarchy of the 'free' market. Hence to persist with the kind of institutions which today present public officials everywhere (whether elected or not) with ready opportunities and incentives for corruption and abuse of power is bound to lead to the rapid discrediting of any new model of economic collectivism. Of course it is precisely because they recognise this truth that those with the loudest voices – who also see themselves as having most to gain from continued anarchy – will tirelessly decry the possibility of democratic reform while yet continuing to proclaim the virtues of democracy.

A New Globalism

Clearly it must be expected that the transition to anything resembling the model of economic organisation outlined above would take decades rather than years and would occur at different speeds in different countries and regions. It follows that during such a transition period the free movement of capital between those economic areas moving rapidly to adopt a more restrictive approach to private profit and those more resistant to such change will not be admissible. The logic of this view is now in fact implicitly being conceded even by such pillars of the existing world order as the OECD and the European Union. Both these organisations have in early 1997 voiced complaints about the damaging economic impact of tax competition in reducing state revenues and thus contributing to governments' inability to stem the rise in public deficits except by cutting their spending below what are increasingly seen as minimum tolerable levels (although, needless to say, neither body can propose any solution to the problem as long as they remain wedded to the ideology of global liberalisation without harmonisation of tax regimes).

At the same time, given the explicit recognition that demand growth will tend to be limited in relation to global capacity, trade flows will have to be increasingly managed so as to minimise market disruption (consistent with the maintenance of reasonable standards of efficiency – to be assured by processes of transparent regulation, as proposed above for limited liability companies). This in turn implies the need to restrict growth in the supply of specific tradable goods and services, either globally or at least within given trading blocs. In such an economic environment of limited global scope for growth it would also follow that

• Official policy should tend to discriminate in favour of the most disadvantaged areas (particularly in the former Soviet bloc and the Third World) in promoting increased output and employment, so as to enhance the capacity of all countries or regions for relative economic autonomy within a more integrated global or regional framework.

• The pattern of employment and income in all countries should be structured so as to provide much greater equality of both opportunity and outcome. In any case, given the likely much reduced emphasis on competition and risk, the justification for big disparities in reward would disappear.

In view of the clear and growing danger to international stability posed by the marginalisation of most Third World and ex-Communist states, the need to find ways of bringing them into the global economic mainstream has never been more pressing. Since the traditional approach of transferring resources from rich to poor countries through bilateral or multilateral aid agencies – whether or not linked to conditions involving economic policy 'reform' – has so demonstrably failed to lift the Third World out of poverty, it is necessary to recast the whole relationship between the developed and developing worlds.

This would mean encouraging developing countries to become part of an increasingly integrated global economic structure in which the harmonisation of enforceable rules under a régime of democratic accountability would replace the present pattern of lawlessness and corruption. It would entail recognising that

- Independence is a total illusion for the vast majority of LDCs, in that they neither actually nor potentially possess a large enough economic base to support the infrastructure – governmental, physical or social – consistent with a quality of life at the minimum level acceptable in a modern state.

- The developed nations – which are themselves having to confront the prospect of diminished national sovereignty in a more interdependent world – must collectively undertake to assure a substantial and more or less permanent flow of resources from the rich to the poor regions of the world in order both to sustain administration of minimum adequacy and to make possible sufficient economic development to reverse the present downward spiral.

Such a model would effectively require LDCs (as well as the industrialised countries) to give up their notional independent sovereignty in return for progressive integration into a functioning world community based on representative institutions. At first sight this proposition may strike many in both the developing and developed worlds as outrageous neo-imperialism, if not simply utopian. Yet, as revealed in our earlier consideration of the donor community's efforts to contain the deepening crisis in Africa, moves in this direction are already afoot – as witness the de facto acceptance by donors of the need for them to help fund the current budgets of several bankrupt African states. Moreover, within the broader international community it should be seen as no more abnormal than the current use of the European Union's regional and social funds to compensate for income disparities between member states and regions of the Union.

Such recognition by the international donor community, however grudging, of its responsibility for ensuring that minimal public services are maintained in those parts of the Third World where they would otherwise have collapsed altogether is highly significant. It must be presumed to stem from a recognition that failure to provide such support can only lead to further instances of the complete breakdown of civil order – similar to that experienced in Somalia and elsewhere. Given that the costs of such disorder are being felt in the form of civil wars and humanitarian disasters – which the international community will have to address (at great expense) through United Nations peacekeeping missions and support for refugees – it would hardly be surprising if some in the international community were beginning to see more direct intervention in the administration of these countries as ultimately a less costly way of addressing such problems.

It is true that the donor agencies involved continue to insist that such direct intervention by them is not to be seen as a permanent phenomenon, but rather as a stop-gap response to a crisis which can be expected to be overcome in the relatively short term, paving the way for the recipient countries to resume full financial responsibility for these services.[1] Yet, bearing in mind the macroeconomic prognosis facing most of the Third World, this looks as great a piece of wishful thinking as proved to be the case with the confident forecasts in the 1980s that the LDCs would be able to repay their debts.

Furthermore, the tendency to more direct involvement by donors in the actual administration of bankrupt LDCs evidently reflects a recognition that the attempt to influence their performance through the mechanism of policy conditionality attached to 'structural adjustment' programmes has signally failed. For the latter approach boils down to a permanent threat to impose economic sanctions (i.e. the withdrawal of aid) in the event of governments' failing to adhere to the conditionality – in circumstances where it is often difficult to determine whether such failure is due to the obduracy and/or incompetence of the particular government concerned or else to the fact that the conditions were either unrealistic from the start or simply invalidated by unforeseeable events. Yet it is undoubtedly recognised by the more intelligent members of the donor community that, as in the case of most such economic sanctions, their application is an extremely blunt instrument which (as noted earlier) tends to harm the impoverished mass of the population more than the ruling elite, thereby perhaps creating even greater social and political instability. In short, the separation of power and responsibility is ultimately not a viable basis for government – and is even less so today than it was when practised, under the name of 'indirect rule', by the British and other colonial regimes.

Yet if, as seems likely, the donor agencies are drawn into a long-term involvement in the running of such bankrupt countries, this will obviously raise serious issues of accountability and democratic legitimacy. If charges of neo-imperialism are to be avoided, a constitutional framework will need to be devised which ensures that those who are assuming responsibility for administration are legally answerable to the citizens of the countries affected as well as to the wider international community.

If such a model is to be both effective and politically acceptable in the donor as well as the recipient states, it must be based on the same principles of accountability as we have insisted must be enshrined in the revitalised democratic structures of the industrialised world. Otherwise it would inevitably be seen either as an attempt to revive outmoded imperialist relationships and/or a continuation of the kind of corrupt patron–client association – in which major donor institutions (themselves subject to only the remotest form of democratic accountability) make deals with blatantly unrepresentative Third World governments – which has proved so unworkable ever since decolonisation. It would nevertheless clearly need to be based on a conscious rejection of the ancient shibboleths of non-interference in the internal affairs of 'sovereign' countries and non-discrimination in trade, thus challenging the sanctity of the nation-state as enshrined in the United Nations Charter and most existing international treaties.[2]

Hence, in place of the traditional and highly wasteful pattern of development aid, resources should be made available on a long-term basis only to those states which are willing to embark on the path to integration with the developed world. Countries which chose to stay out of the integrated structure would also be entitled to support for their development as well as to trade with the core bloc of countries – provided they also adhered to basic standards of democracy, accountability and human rights – but on a less privileged basis than the 'integrators'. Those states which refused to comply with such basic standards could expect to receive little more than humanitarian aid and being subject to a trade embargo (although the pretence would need to be abandoned that the fate of tyrannies is a matter of indifference to the world community and that any action to promote their overthrow is inappropriate).

It is important to recognise that for such a system to retain lasting political acceptability there could be no exceptions. Thus even countries such as Saudi Arabia, with its important reserves of petroleum, and China, with its potentially huge market for imports from OECD countries, would need to be subjected to the same principles. In fact, an important benefit of the less profit- and growth-oriented economic order outlined above would be that it would be much harder to argue, as at present, that democracies are required by their own economic interests to deal with such un-savoury regimes.

In order to gain acceptance of such a vision it will, of course, be necessary to resist the inevitable pressures to retreat from global cooperation behind national protectionist barriers under the illusion that this will permit states to solve their own problems of over-capacity and a shrinking tax base on the basis of isolationism and autarky. For if we have learnt only one lesson from the inter-war period it is surely that such a resort to economic nationalism is a certain recipe for global conflict. On the other hand, it would be unrealistic to expect rapid moves to create a comprehensive structure of global economic cooperation based on common goals of stabilisation. Indeed it is presently difficult to envisage a plausible chain of developments likely to shift the world in this direction, especially when most of the political initiatives to have occurred in the world in the 1980s and 1990s have been of a nationalist, sectarian, even quasi-fascist character.

That political charlatans – such as the leaders of the National Front in France, the resurgent neo-fascist National Alliance in Italy, most of the political leaders to emerge from the ruins of the ex-Communist states, and religious extremists all over the Islamic world – should seek to exploit economic and social decline by appealing to bigotry and racism is all too unremarkable. What is more alarm-ing is the lack of any vision from mainstream political circles in the industrialised world of a model of international economic relations other than that of the anarchic, deregulated global market – a model which, as already demonstrated, is perfectly designed to fan the flames of xenophobia. The lack of leadership in this area is particu-larly striking in the case of the United States, whose leaders – perhaps affected by delusions of grandeur now that the country finds itself the only 'superpower' – refuse to countenance any form of world order of which the USA does not remain the ultimate arbiter, and which cannot therefore be readily manipulated in the interests of the US corporate sector.

Amid this generally dispiriting scene the most hopeful prospect is arguably provided by the European Union. Notwithstanding its manifest divisions and weaknesses, the original vision of a group of countries coming ever closer together on the basis of their common espousal of democratic values remains intact forty years after its founding. Likewise there is no diminution in the desire of non-member states to join, not only among European former members of the Soviet bloc but also among non-European states of the Mediterranean area such as Turkey and Morocco. This apparent underlying strength of purpose appears to reflect Europe's history in the twentieth century, when more than any other continent it has experienced the appalling consequences of unbridled nationalism and the denial of democracy and human rights. This may help to explain its steadfastness in requiring Greece, Spain and Portugal to put dictatorship and militarism fully behind them before they could be admitted as member states and in continuing to impose the same condition in the way of Turkey's accession to the Union. In this respect it clearly has an advantage as the basis for expanding global economic cooperation over the fledgling North American Free Trade Association, where the United States and Canada have been prepared to accept a much more superficial commitment to democracy on the part of Mexico as qualifying it for membership.

There is thus reason to believe that the European Union has the potential to evolve into the nucleus of a new global economic model such as that sketched out above – or at least that it can provide a pointer to the kind of international economic and political organisation most likely to prove viable in future. For this to happen it would, of course, need to proclaim itself more than a mere European regional grouping and to be as inclusive as possible, open to all countries willing to accept the democratic ground rules. Its ultimate capacity to do this should be enhanced by its strong historic ties with every other part of the world. Obviously, however, it is easy to see obstacles to the smooth emergence of such a new model. For instance, it can hardly be imagined that integration based on democratic structures could occur very rapidly if it was required to absorb poor countries of the size of India or Bangladesh on the basis that the deeply impoverished majority of their citizens would immediately be able to outvote the far richer but less numerous population of Western Europe on the allocation of resources within the Union as a whole.

It would be idle, however, to try and anticipate here all the problems that would confront any such newly evolving structures of international organisation, economic or political, let alone to envisage the solutions to them. Our purpose is simply to highlight the need to pursue such a broad goal with the minimum of dogmatism, in the knowledge that only through a willingness to experiment with such new forms of international association, transcending the nineteenth-century model of the nation-state, can we hope to address the crippling problems of global economic imbalance and the related rise in civil disorder.

An Inescapable Choice

It needs perhaps to be reiterated that the indications given in this final chapter of the possible future shape of economic society in a more sustainable world order is intended to be as much predictive as prescriptive. To suggest otherwise would be contrary to the author's (somewhat banal) conviction that human history is essentially an evolutionary process and that attempts to replace one system instantaneously with a quite different one will always fail. This view is also based on the historical reality that, as pointed out in Chapter 1, essentially opposed economic systems such as feudalism and capitalism have coexisted to varying degrees over the centuries – and indeed continue to do so.

It remains true, however, that the overwhelming evidence of this book shows that profit-maximising capitalism has, by the last third of the twentieth century, outlived its usefulness as a vehicle for human progress. Despite this, it will come as no surprise to find that any suggestion that we can or should seek to evolve a more viable economic order in its place will be dismissed as inherently utopian. For, as already emphasised many times, in contemporary Western society, as in any other throughout history, 'the ideas of the ruling class are the ruling ideas',[3] and therefore any suggestion that the status quo will need to undergo fundamental adjustment is bound to be portrayed as eccentric.

Precisely for this reason the possibility of any initiatives for radical change occurring only arises where the status quo is becoming manifestly untenable – which, as this work has sought to demonstrate, is now unquestionably the case. Indeed, as governments of the right struggle vainly to reconcile the needs of the profits system with the demands of the welfare state – by seeking to phase out the latter and revive a nineteenth-century world where the rising numbers of destitute people will once again be treated as paupers and vagrants – it is the ruling elite themselves who may be most plausibly charged with lack of realism.

A spirited attempt is being made by the apostles of *laissez faire* to present a move back to self-reliance as both liberating and enriching (morally as well as materially) for the mass of the population. Yet no amount of sophistry or brainwashing can disguise the fact that any such attempt to undo the social gains made in the industrialised West over the last hundred years would go completely against the grain of history. Moreover, even if a majority could be persuaded to endorse this reactionary vision, it would fail to resolve the deepening economic crisis whose only possible denouement, without some radical alteration of course, will be a financial holocaust on such a scale as to bring comprehensive ruin even to the most convinced supporters of the status quo.

Such a disaster could undo all the considerable gains so painfully made by Western civilisation in the five centuries since the Renaissance and usher in a new Dark Age such as that foreseen by Winston Churchill as the likely consequence of a Nazi victory in 1940. For those who would avert the realisation of this nightmare the moment of truth has surely come.

Notes

1. M. Foster, *Financing Structural Adjustment Via the Budget*, Overseas Development Administration, London 1996.

2. As the international community has effectively already begun to do in relation to the former Yugoslavia.

3. Karl Marx, *The German Ideology*.

Index

Other Zed Titles on Globalization

Globalization has become the new buzzword of the late 1990s. Despite the very different meanings attached to the term, and even more divergent evaluations of its likely impacts, it is clear nevertheless that we are in an accelerated process of transition to a new period in world history. Zed Books' titles on globalization pay special attention to what it means for the South, for women, for workers and for other vulnerable elements.

Nassau Adams, *Worlds Apart: The North–South Divide and the International System*

Samir Amin, *Capitalism in the Age of Globalization: The Management of Contemporary Society*

Asoka Bandarage, *Women, Population and Global Crisis: A Political-Economic Analysis*

Michel Chossudovsky, *The Globalization of Poverty: Impacts of IMF and World Bank Reforms*

Bhagirath Lal Das, *An Introduction to the WTO Agreements*

Bhagirath Lal Das, *The WTO Agreements: Deficiencies, Imbalances and Required Changes*

Diplab Dasgupta: *Structural Adjustment, Global Trade and the New Political Economy of Development*

Björn Hettne et al., *International Political Economy: Understanding Global Disorder*

Terence K. Hopkins, Immanuel Wallerstein et al., *The Age of Transition: Trajectory of the World-System, 1945–2025*

Hans-Peter Martin and Harald Schumann, *The Global Trap: Globalization and the Assault on Prosperity and Democracy*

Lydia Potts, *The World Labour Market: A History of Migration*

Harry Shutt, *The Trouble with Capitalism: An Enquiry into the Causes of Global Economic Failure*

Henk Thomas (ed.), *Globalization and Third World Trade Unions*

For full details of this list and Zed's other subject and general catalogues, please write to: The Marketing Department, Zed Books, 7 Cynthia Street, London N1 9JF, UK; or email Sales@zedbooks.demon.co.uk

Visit our website at: http://www.zedbooks.demon.co.uk